D0070756

The Impulse
to
Philosophise

ROYAL INSTITUTE OF PHILOSOPHY SUPPLEMENT: 33

EDITED BY

A. Phillips Griffiths

RECEIVED

NOV 5 1992

OHIO STATE UNIVERSITY
LIMA CAMPUS LIBRARY

CAMBRIDGE
UNIVERSITY PRESS

Published by the Press Syndicate of the University of Cambridge
The Pitt Building, Trumpington Street, Cambridge, CB2 1RP
40 West 20th Street, New York, NY 10011-4211, USA
10 Stamford Road, Oakleigh, Victoria 3166, Australia

© The Royal Institute of Philosophy and the contributors 1992

*A catalogue record for this book is available
from the British Library*

ISBN 0 521 43981 7 (paperback)

Library of Congress Cataloguing in Publication Data applied for

NOV 5 1992

Origination by Michael Heath Ltd, Reigate, Surrey
Printed in Great Britain by the University Press, Cambridge

Contents

Proem

'I made the discovery that I had grown up a natural Kantian, beginning with the antinomies of time and space and going on to the unconceptualizability of things as they are in themselves independently of our experience' (p. 178). Bryan Magee's impressive—and fascinating—case for this claim is made in his autobiographical article in this volume. I heard him hint at some of this many years ago in an interview on the BBC's 'Man of Action' programme; the memory of which, together with a more recent encounter with Colin Radford's *The Examined Life* ('Philosophy is not confined . . . to the professional activities of philosophers but pervades human life.' (p. 1)), led to the implicit question in the title of this series of lectures given at the Royal Institute of Philosophy in 1991–2.

Is there a *natural* impulse to philosophise? Having a basis in our normal constitution? 'A wisdom given by nature; not educated by study'? Not artificially made or constructed? John White offers some serious doubts about supposed examples in the case of children. Tennyson is said to have spent hours as a small child sitting by the wainscot intoning 'Evermore . . . Evermore . . .'. Was this natural poetry, and was he already a poet? Or might this better be compared to the murmurings of innumerable bees? 'The cuckoos, two, would sing in rhyme, as once they did. . .'; '. . . or seemed to do', Hardy goes on. Why the doubt? Isn't the dawn chorus as surely music as an *objet trouvé* is an *objet d'art*?

What counts as an impulse to philosophise obviously depends on what counts as philosophising: including the Yoruba fragments will give *one* sort of answer. The prior question is to the fore in many of the contributions to this volume. Many are less autobiographical than those of Bryan Magee or Michael Tanner. Some of us feel a reticence in this regard, not sharing the rarely valuable tendency to self-exposure of St. Augustine and Rousseau. One fears that one's woodnotes would not be forgiven solely for their wild nativity.

But perhaps to parade in even less than sackcloth and ashes can be allowed as a penance; and it will bring out one doubt I have, of the connection between those woodnotes and the sounds of my professional scrannel-pipe. My education was—is—almost entirely based on the pages of the splendid ten volumes of Arthur Mee's *Children's Encyclopaedia*, which contained articles—whole courses—on nearly everything: history, literature, astronomy, palaeontology, the Bible, art, biology, all of which I constatly absorbed: except one section, called 'Wonder', by which I suppose was meant philosophy. I found it quite boring. It wasn't *about* anything. So at fourteen I was completely innocent of the subject, when it became obvious to me with a risible clarity that we could only think what we could think, and anything beyond that was beyond thinking. Nothing could be thought to be that was not in thought. This did not lead me into solipsism: what seemed to me absurd was that there could be thought to be anything not in thought, not that there could be thoughts other than my thoughts. I was not concerned about how I could know whether there were other thoughts than mine. My views were not engendered by any epistemological problems (or, as far as I remember, by any problems at all). If they could be dignified by such epithets, they were not epistemological but metaphysical and ontological. If anything, I was a dogmatic, and not at all a problematic, idealist. The nearest I ever came to what might seem an epistemological remark was 'You can only *know* what something is by *being* it'. Unfortunately I was given to repeating that and other odd remarks, engendering in my school fellows not only derision but irritation, exacerbated by the fact that I couldn't keep quiet about it while my laughter at the sheer simple obviousness of it all seemed to be mockery of their common sense. This was doubly uncomfortable: first, because at my school the way of dealing with a foolish nuisance was to hold him by hands and feet and bounce him up and down on the asphalt playground; second, because while I had no doubt whatever that I was absolutely right, I didn't like being universally thought to be not only wrong, but a tiresome ass: a view reinforced by my teachers who regarded my obsessions as just another excuse for my determined avoidance of school work, showing an arrogance ill befitting one just promoted from the bottom of the fourth form to the fifth remove. But I borrowed from a friend, who had a collection of Sir John Lubbock's 'Hundred Books', a copy of G. H. Lewes's *Biographical History of Philosophy*. I was amazed to discover that I was not the only human being to have a vision of the ultimate nature of reality. Schopenhauer, Kant as I had misunderstood him, and above all Berkeley as I had understood him had seen what I had seen and had had their ideas written about in books. What they were doing was philosophising, so what I was doing was philosophising; and I was invited by the newly opened doors into their, and other philosophers', other rooms. At a price, however: while not led into this by problems, problems inevitably arose from it. Until then, unlike Berkeley I had regarded common sense as simply false, able to make no better than irrelevant empirical objections, such as kicking stones, to my *a priori* thesis. Now I encountered more ingenious objections. Sure that they could be overcome, I became determined to pursue philosophy, left school at sixteen because there wasn't any there, and scraping through matriculation examinations, at seventeen enrolled in my local University (conscription for eighteen year olds had so limited their student numbers that they were willing to accept almost anybody); not so much to learn the truth as to learn how I might better defend it. I was impervious to Mr J. M. Thorburn's attempts to convince me from the standpoint of Heidegger that my absolute refusal to countenance the relevance of anything empirical was wrong-headed. Eventually I got to Oxford, and what happened after that is unremarkable. One don is supposed to have written in a reference 'he came up enthusiastic about metaphysics, but by the time he went down he was just one of the boys'. Vision was shaded by the prison-house of argument. I am no longer convinced; though the withered shoot of that juvenile idea is still buried there somewhere under all the debris of subsequent horticulture.

That is one way of telling the jejune story, leaving out what might be a significant half of it. My sudden illumination happened when I was given time and loneliness in which to think (if not to ratiocinate, to meditate). We were distressingly poor because my father was too ill to work, bedridden and nursed by my mother. My brother contracted scarlet fever, but was allowed to remain at home in isolation, because my mother was a qualified fever nurse. Over the months, nursing them began to affect my mother's health so that she became thin and frail. I was convinced that my father was dying (rightly), and that so was my brother (wrongly, he will be glad to hear), and I feared for my mother. Because of my brother's contagious illness, I was isolated from school and schoolfellows. I spent months bicycling alone around the Vale of Glamorgan looking at gothic churches and cromlechs, but on the empty wartime country roads I thought about *what there is*. A rather unpleasant situation, but hardly uniquely so, and some are more resilient than others. Admittedly, though bombs were dropping on Landaff Cathedral and nearer by, I don't remember it as a time of great unhappiness; if anything, rather the contrary: almost as an idyll, compared to what happened later; while my thoughts themselves seemed to engender an almost mystical joy. But I may have repressed my feelings then, and in any case one may now be prone to idealise the past (*that* is why Hardy said 'or *seemed* to do'). It would be plausible to surmise that a boy would try to escape from his grim circumstances by denying their external reality, especially if his fantasy could take the form of a superior wisdom to set against his being the class dunce. There is no limit to the wiles of the unconscious; nor to their arbitrariness. It might alternatively have engendered a religious obsession in someone who in consequence would become an academic theologian (but not in me, who already had religion, more than compatible with my and Berkeley's vision). As if, to escape a constable, Dick Whittington had hopped on the nearest 'bus, which happened to be going to London.

But such explanations of *why* it was, even if true, may be positively misleading as to *what* it was, in the way that Freudian explanations of Berkeley's immaterialism in terms of infant potting seem utterly irrelevant to the significance of his philosophy. Perhaps the consideration of such cases merely add colour but not substance to the implicit *conceptual* question, of whether there is a 'natural' impulse to philosophise, in the sense in which there cannot be a 'natural' impulse to marry; or one more peculiar and specific to philately, which is intelligible only in terms of a particular and artificial social institution, than the instincts we share with jackdaws.

A. Phillips Griffiths

The Examined Life Re-examined

COLIN RADFORD

In Part One of *The Examined Life* (Radford, 1989) I recalled certain episodes from my childhood and youth in which, as I came to realize later, I had been exercised by a philosophical problem. By so doing I hoped not only to convey to non-professionals what philosophy is—or is like—but to show them that they too were philosophers, i.e., had been exercised by philosophical questions. In Part Two I gave some examples of how such problems may be treated by a professional, in articles.

In one, for example, I tried to show that just as our being frightened by films and fictional characters in them is irrational, so is our being moved by and for fictional characters in films, plays, and novels. This tendency to irrationality is of course present in almost all of us, and is not only innocent but enhances our enjoyment of such works and the attention we pay them; so we should not regret it. But we should not—*therefore*, perhaps—deny that that is what it is. (None the less philosophers continue to do so.)

I did not essay a definition of philosophy or attempt to give any general account of the connected matter, namely what prompts it, relying on the examples to speak for themselves. But if I had to do so, I would say that they show that when we do philosophy we are engaged in reflective, critical thought. We are puzzled—or merely intrigued—by some matter, and trying to understand and sort it out involves not further observation or information, or calculation, or mere remembering, but intellectual scrutiny, critical reflection, aided very often by imagination.

Thus defined, philosophy is not confined to the domestic scenes portrayed in my book or to the professional activities of philosophers but pervades human life. The astronomer wondering if he could test his assumption that natural laws hold constant throughout space; the lawyers pondering how to decide at what age persons should be held to be legally responsible for their actions; the historian worrying at the thought that some of his explanations commit him to counter-factual claims which his narrative cannot prove; the couple whose comfortable views about the objectivity of morality are shaken by the discovery that they do indeed agree about *everything* except whether it is right for the woman to have an abortion; the politician struck by the perhaps

1

unwelcome thought that if poverty is not a cause of law-breaking (because many poor persons do not break the law) then drunkenness is not a cause of driving accidents; what is the relevant difference between these cases? All are engaged in philosophical thought. But so of course is the professional philosopher, say Thomas Kuhn, when he strives to describe and examine the epistemological and ontological implications of how scientists proceed and how scientific thinking changes. Philosophy need not involve confusion, puzzle solving or anguish.

Unless these anodyne remarks about philosophy and what prompts it are comprehensively wrong, it follows that one engaged in philosophy may critically examine not only his own thoughts—including his earlier philosophical ones—and those of others, but the sometimes unreflective, unexamined thoughts, beliefs and ways of behaving thus 'informed' that are institutionalized in not only his but other cultures. And these thoughts about the unexamined life can sometimes have practical consequences for how he and others do and should think and act.

To offer a further illustration: in the Judaeo-Christian tradition and in some others, individuals are—or were—exhorted, required, commanded to have faith in God, to believe in Him, i.e., to believe without proof or evidence that He exists, and to think and behave accordingly. Those few who revealed that they lacked faith were pitied or even reviled, threatened, punished, and told that they would be punished in the afterlife by the God in whom they lacked faith. They have even been put to death. No wonder if, perhaps, many remained silent, behaved as if they believed and even wished that they did.[1] But to those with the slightest capacity to be puzzled, and the inclination and in this case the courage to try to sort out these problems by further thinking, there are myriad problems here. For example, why should God require faith of us when He could offer compelling evidence for His existence? Why will He not do so?

In any case, how can one be required to have faith? Faith is not subject to the will: it is not something we do or, therefore, fail to do. It is something we have or lack. And supposing it is something we could acquire, as we can acquire Latin or a more muscular body, and suppose there *are* ways of acquiring faith—in some cases behaving as if one believed seems to generate the faith of which in other cases it is the expression—why should those who try and fail be blamed and punished; and why should any of us try to acquire it?

To say that, among much else, we shall be punished if we do not do so, is, among much else, to beg the question. And Pascal's wager could

---

[1] Perhaps the loss of faith since medieval times is in part illusory?

at most only give us reasons for wishing that we believed or could believe. What we then lack are good reasons for having faith.

As I perhaps failed to realize when these thoughts occurred to me when I was an altar boy, this last statement is oxymoronic. For if faith can be justified, i.e., shown to be warranted, reasonable etc., it is otiose, unnecessary; indeed it becomes impossible (I cannot continue to have faith that you will come when I see you coming). None the less, if it cannot, why should we have it? Why should one hold certain beliefs if there could be proof of or evidence for them, and there is none? And, taking the matter a step further, why should one believe if, under further scrutiny, these beliefs can be seen to be unclear, incoherent perhaps, or morally offensive?[2]

How offended one would be—as some of us have been—to be told by a priest that the whole beauty and essence of belief is that it is offensive to reason. How much further astonished and offended one would be if someone who himself lacked such faith and was a philosopher, defended this whole way of thinking and acting against the criticisms of his fellow philosophers (and who derided as vulgar, confused, even dishonest, perhaps, those who sought to show that belief was reasonable, and condemned as superstitious those who lost their faith as a result of some misfortune which, had God existed, He would or should have prevented) (cf. Wittgenstein, 1966, 56–59).

It is this which gives my anodyne generalizations about philosophy their interest. They have been denied, almost in their entirety, by the foremost philosopher of his age, Ludwig Wittgenstein.

Wittgenstein defended the enormous variety of unreflective, human attitudes, beliefs, ways of talking and acting against what he saw as the reductive, confused accounts and misplaced criticisms given of them by philosophers, and robbed philosophy of any possibility of criticizing anything but its own confusions. In this paper I want to defend what can and has been achieved by reflective, imaginative thought—the examined life.

Wittgenstein never had very much to say about why we engage in philosophy, except that the superficial appearance of language invites the confusions of philosophers. But he always maintained that philosophical remarks—for example, the reflections produced by

---

[2] Of course, we may admire some who have faith and do so for the qualities they have that are connected with their faith, peace, calm, integrity, strength, conviction, detachment, etc. We may envy them, we may find distasteful the shallowness, shrillness, self-regard of some of those who revel in their disbelief. But, again, although such things may give us reasons for wanting to believe, they do not give us reasons for believing those beliefs are true.

mathematicians about the nature of mathematics—are nonsense. The only proper task of philosophy (which in his Tractarian period did not itself avoid talking nonsense) is to show that and why this is so and thus to put an end to it. In the *Tractatus* this involved showing that philosophical remarks are not 'scientific', by which he meant empirical, for they will not translate into truth-functions of 'atomic' propositions in which all the constituent symbols are 'names' the meanings of which are the 'simples' which they stand for. In his verificationist period he held (of course) that the meanings of remarks are determined not by their syntax and the meanings of their words but by what tells for or against their being held to be true. Despite their superficially substantive appearances, philosophical remarks, which are not and not intended as tautologies, have no method of verification—if they did they would not be philosophical—and so are meaningless. He had abandoned the earlier static, substantive account of meaning for a dynamic one.

This is taken further in his last period where the philosophical task is now simply to 'assemble reminders' (Wittgenstein, 1953, 127) about what and how words actually mean, and how language is actually used. For he now held that the view that words mean by standing for things is not just a philosophical illusion but is also the source of many, if not all, philosophical confusion and nonsense. And although the verification of a statement makes some contribution to the meaning of those remarks that are assertions, it is not all that we mean by 'meaning' (ibid., 353). In any case, not everything we say is an assertion—that is another philosophical illusion which produces confusions.

Thus, the prefatory remark 'Ah—that reminds me!' is not an assertion since we do not treat it as such, and if—or when—we did we should be faced by an unanswerable and therefore unreal Humean question, 'Did it indeed remind me?' The superficial grammar of the remark combined with the assumption that words mean by standing for things produces this philosophical misunderstanding and sceptical problems about our knowledge of the workings of the mind. As to whether we actually do remember something on a particular occasion, i.e., when this is a real question, we will still go wrong if we construe 'remember', 'remembering', 'memory', etc., as meaning by standing for something. For the question of whether the individual has remembered is settled not by establishing the existence of some mental or brain state or process, but roughly, by establishing if what he claims to remember actually took place and he is able to give some account of it without looking at notes or repeating what someone is telling him, i.e. unaided. These, as Wittgenstein would say, are the 'criteria' for whether someone has remembered. (Brain or mental states or processes may be causally necessary for his remembering, though that is an hypothesis.

And it is not his remembering.) We can now see why Wittgenstein pleaded with philosophers, 'Don't think, but look!' (ibid., 66).

These remarks seem to me to be wonderfully illuminating about the source, and nature of many philosophical speculations, and of how to respond to them. But do they show that *all* philosophical problems, even about remembering, are theoretically inspired, unreal misunderstandings (unreal because they have no practical consequences for how the philosopher thinks and acts)? Do they show that philosophy can only assemble reminders about the way words are used and how language works (ibid., 127) and must abandon its critical pretensions? How could they do so? We are being offered not just a partial account of philosophy, but what without argument, claims to be a comprehensive one which thus seeks to transform, constrain and—in a very powerful sense—reduce philosophy.

Suppose, for example, in retrospect, I *am* puzzled why the smell of polish on the table top, which my face approached as I bent to pick up some coins, reminded me that I must get to the shops: and I may then go on to wonder if it indeed did so. How can I tell? Answers to the first question seem possible in principle and might be offered at more than one level (brain processes, psychological associations) but they presuppose what they explain; and how can I be sure about that? Our best method (which can itself raise philosophical problems), viz. the controlled experiment, is not available here—perhaps not even in principle. And in this particular case it is difficult to imagine how we might set about trying to—if not resolve to—throw some light on what is an admittedly 'idle' question in that nothing of any practical sort is likely to turn on it. But if that meant it was confused and nonsensical then so would be all those questions raised by historians about why certain, non-repeatable historical events took place, especially when the matter is elusive and, very probably, their disagreements fierce. And could the fact that a conviction or civil judgment may turn on similar questions when debated by lawyers give them an intellectual respectability, a coherence, sense, etc. they would otherwise lack?

Wittgenstein does show however that the meaning of a word cannot be any sort of *thing*. Philosophy does make progress and this, I think, is the clearest and most important example of its doing so. His argument comes down to the simple but profound and conclusive observation that there is no thing acquaintance with which could have the same consequence as being acquainted with a word's meaning. He then applies this aperçu to philosophical problem after problem, with devastating effect. Without perhaps ever having read Book III, 'Of Words', of Locke's *Essay* (Locke, 1979),[3] he helps us to see that it is Locke's

[3] He would have done so by 1938 (cf. Redpath, 1990, 70).

unquestioned assumption that words *do* mean—*must* mean— by stand-ing for 'ideas' which brings Locke's whole account to grief. Moore makes it concerning 'good' in his *Principia Ethica* (Moore, 1903). Once our eyes have been opened we can see it everywhere, even in much post-Wittgenstein, professional philosophising.[4]

Of course we immediately want to ask, 'But what then *is* the meaning of a word?', and does not our question cry out for a substantive answer, i.e., an answer in terms of a *thing*? So Wittgenstein advises us not to ask this question but others which are less likely to mislead us, e.g., 'In what circumstances should we say that someone knew the meaning of a word?' And here the answer will be in terms of his or her understanding remarks in which it is used, his being able to use it himself, his being able to tell if someone else knows its meaning, i.e. how it is used, his being able to teach it to another, explain it, etc.

Again we are tempted to ask 'But what does someone know, what must he know, if he knows how to use it? Surely he must know something which informs and guides his correct use?' and we shall think in terms of, perhaps, a mental picture—Locke's view—or possi-bly something like a formula or an equation. But, according to Wittgen-stein, this is simply to substitute a more rarefied thing for a less rarefied thing. We know the meaning of a word if we know how to use it, *and we know how to use it if we use it as others do who know how to use it!*

I have now reached the central problem, the paradox, of this paper. I once thought that Wittgenstein's view of philosophy derived, to use one of his memorable phrases from a 'one-sided diet' of examples (Witt-geinstein, 1953, 593), and I do still want to say that he is guilty of essentialism, and a sort of conservatism, quietism, and indeed obscurantism. But now it is clear to me that I can only sustain these criticisms, and what I think of as an unexceptionable and, indeed, an ungainsayable account of philosophy, if I can drive a wedge between that part of Wittgenstein's remarks about meaning which *are* ungain-sayable, viz. that the meaning of a word is not a thing, and what seems to be an irresistible consequence of that viz. that we can give no account of meaning except in terms of praxis, i.e. of what people say and how they act and react. But unless this can be done, 'what people say' and

[4] Anyone still doubtful of the correctness of Wittgenstein's view should remind him or herself that we can refer to one and the same thing using phrases which differ in meaning. The only way to escape this argument is to postulate an analysis of meaning which devolves on words or phrases which, if they refer to the same thing, physical, mental, or whatever, have the same meaning as any other word or phrase which does so. This takes us back to Wittgenstein's 'names' and 'simples'. And this theory will not work because the simples have to be 'colourless', i.e., devoid of any features, and the 'names' (therefore) devoid of meaning.

how they act will indeed transcend the possibility of coherent, cogent philosophical criticism, and what remains, i.e. substantive matters, are not decidable by mere thought. So philosophy will have nothing to do but correct its own confusions.

As Wittgenstein remarks (ibid., 242, and see also 241), 'If language is to be a means of communication there must be agreement not only in definitions but also (queer as this may sound) in judgements.' He adds, 'This seems to abolish logic, but does not do so.' Certainly without some agreement in judgments there could be no disagreement. There would indeed be no public language, and language is a public phenomenon, and 'agreement' in definitions would be spurious. The question is: at what point or level or in regard to what must there be agreement? For although in any disagreement, any challenging of what someone has said, thought and done there must be something in common between the disputants, it does not follow that that itself might not be in turn subject to scrutiny. (Wittgenstein struggles with this thought in his somewhat confused and unconvincing discussion of 'hinge propositions' in *On Certainty*.)

How to proceed? Wittgenstein is reported (Wittgenstein, 1975a, 183) as saying—of an invented word 'boo', taught merely by saying 'this is boo' without any guidance as to what was being said—'you would all automatically follow certain rules'. He goes on 'it sounds as if your learning how to use it were different from your knowing its meaning but the point is that we all make the SAME use of it. To know its meaning is to use it in the same way as other people do.'

Wittgenstein is right in saying that human beings do tend to react in similar ways (and to an as yet unconceptualized reality when they have not yet learned to talk), and if they did not there would be no language; and no doubt his class members would have learned to say 'boo' in the same situations and in this way follow 'the same rule for its use'. If 'boo' turned out to be an adjective like 'blue', or a noun like 'square' (which is what Wittgenstein seems to have had in mind), 'using it in the same way' would mean applying it to the same cases, and Wittgenstein is right in implying that until there is, and unless there remains, a common reaction, a general agreement or consensus about which things are boo, there cannot be disagreement even in a relatively few particular cases. None the less *once this happens*, i.e. once there is genuine disagreement, the meaning of 'boo' cannot be equated with its use *qua* application (for if it were, those who disagreed about its application would really be differing about its meaning and so talking at cross purposes).

But does the identification of meaning, use, with received application have any plausibility at all when we are considering not 'boo' or 'blue' or 'table' and 'chair' but more richly theoretical notions? I will try to show that it does not, that understanding remarks involving these words, and being able to use them, embraces such a wide, open-ended range of things that we can (and do) 'know how to use' such words and yet radically disagree with each other about their application. In which case Wittgenstein's aperçu that the meaning of a word is not a thing, that it is 'less confusing' to think in terms of knowing how to use it, understanding remarks in which it is used, etc., will not have the consequences for philosophy that seemed unacceptable and yet unavoidable. Examples may help to make these matters clearer.

In about 1485 the Catholic Church accepted as part of its doctrine that there were witches. Witches could be identified as such by the presence of certain physical stigmata, such as supernumerary teats, and also by certain strange behaviour. 'Ducking' was also used, and under torture at least some thus identified would confess to being witches. They were confessing, of course, not to having supernumerary teats or being able to float, etc., but to having had sexual commerce with the Devil and having given up their immortal soul to the Devil in exchange for these mysterious, maleficent powers. Whatever this means, if it means anything at all, this is what 'witch' means and what persons know when they understand talk about witches. But of course this definition of 'witch' could not be used as a test for someone's being a witch; it was having supernumerary teats and so on that were supposed to indicate that a person was a witch. That was precisely the theological doctrine that the Church espoused and imposed for nearly three hundred years.

But was it right in doing so? The Church's doctrine has the form of an inference based on an hypothesis and it would not matter how generally, naturally, automatically, unquestioningly that inference was made, it would still be an inference. And, fortunately, there were always some who saw that it was an inference, that there was no warrant for this inference, perhaps that what was inferred was not merely unverifiable but incoherent, but which meant that victims of the inference were adjudged wicked, damned and properly to be burnt.

So in the case of at least some words, knowing the meaning/use of a word is not to be identified, even in part, with knowing the circumstances in which those who know its meaning apply it and doing the same. It is not just that a person might disagree against the multitude as to whether some poor wretch had a supernumerary teat, he or she could also mean by 'witch' what the others mean and disagree that supernumerary teats or anything else are indicative or at any rate that there is any good reason for thinking so. Indeed (s)he might think not only that there were no witches, or at least that this could not be shown, but that this whole business of 'finding' witches and killing them was wicked nonsense.

The critics of witch-hunting, some of whom were philosophers, understood what the orthodox meant by 'witch' and some understood that the term was nonsensical and therefore any tests for being a witch could not be so.

So knowing the definition of a word or phrase, knowing what is meant by it, knowing how it is used, knowing what is accepted as sufficient grounds for its application do not even preclude that the word or phrase is meaningless, where this is a critical, 'philosophical', rational epithet. Most of us who speak English know very well what 'travelling backwards in time' means and can enjoy stories like *The Time Machine*, plays like *An Inspector Calls*, films like *Back to the Future*, in which this is represented as happening. But it is precisely because—or, to be cautious, if—some of us can see that the notion is incoherent that we deem it nonsensical.

With regard to many, though certainly not all, philosophical doubts, it may seem that they could not arise if and when the tests for a word's correct application exhaust what is asserted in applying it. (Whether those conditions *are* satisfied, how we know this, if we know this, may in turn be subjected to philosophical scrutiny, though once again in order for there to be dispute this must be underpinned by agreement, which in turn etc., etc.) Perhaps there are such words and perhaps Wittgenstein intended his 'boo' as an example of such a word. A promising real example might be 'Wednesday'. For although Wednesday, historians claim, was thus named in honour of the Norse god Woden, the sole criterion for today's being Wednesday is that yesterday was Tuesday, and so on. And that is all that we are saying if we say that today is indeed Wednesday. (How and when did this system of nomenclature start? Perhaps no-one knows, neither is it necessary that anyone should in order to know the days of the week and which day this is.) So to doubt if, if yesterday was Tuesday, today is Wednesday would not be a sign of intelligible and perhaps fruitful doubt for what could be its point, i.e., what could the person be trying to call into question, and why? It could be a sign of madness, though this apparent doubt would be more likely to indicate a failure of memory, which need not amount to dementia and therefore madness, or, most probably, an imperfect grasp of English. Yet this is not to rule out that the earth may not gradually slow in its diurnal rotation or that, as has actually happened, our calendar might lag behind the way the world goes and we might go straight from one particular Tuesday to a Thursday.

It may also seem that to have doubted, when the old standard metre bar in Paris operated as the standard of metrical length, that something agreed to be the same length as the standard bar was a metre in length would be nonsense. It would be to doubt if the metre bar was as long as itself. Both that 'tautology' and the putative doubt that it was a metre long Wittgenstein did indeed regard as nonsense (Wittgenstein, 1953, 50). Yet here he is too quick. Suppose one morning the metre bar looked appreciably shorter than it had the night before? Then even if it had looked as if it had not been tampered with, or that there had not been a dramatic fall in the temperature within its case, if other metre measures were laid against it and it was shorter than these, we should be presented with a choice; and doubtless we should opt for the view that somehow some joker had managed to interfere with the bar, or, even more mysteriously, it had shrunk. (We should scarcely opt for the view that everything but the metre bar had expanded.)

This example shows that even in regard to the role of standard objects, which Wittgenstein said are 'part of the language' (ibid.), and which are used to provide an object in comparison with which others are said to be one metre long, middle C, cobalt blue, etc., very general facts of nature are presupposed, and presupposed as holding constant. In fact Wittgenstein pointed this out to us. But what this means is that even in regard to words where the tests for their application apparently exhaust what is said in applying them, and these tests are met, a doubt can creep in. It need not even be overtly 'philosophical'. It may arise, as it did in regard to Einstein's theories about space and time, in science.

Consider weight: something weighs one standard unit of weight, for example a kilogramme, if it weighs as much as the standard unit. We establish this by weighing it on accurate scales. We construct these in the following way: take another lump of whatever and add to or take from it until whichever pan it is placed in it is precisely balanced by our standard weight. So it would seem that to say of a lump of something that it weighs x standard units of weight is just to say that it would balance against that weight of standard units in an accurate scales. But of course we could perform this test on the moon but both what we weighed and the standard units that we used to weigh it both weigh considerably less on the moon.

Scientists anticipated and have explained this by distinguishing between mass and weight. But someone ignorant of this distinction would notice that he or she felt less heavy on the moon and that this was not just a 'subjective' impression because he could jump far higher there than on earth. And yet of course he would also notice that he was not less fat on the moon; going there was not a slimming cure! Something remained the same.

But mass and weight do not always maintain an invariant relationship even on earth. And before scientists had made the distinction between them clear to us we can imagine an athletic, philosophically-minded individual saying, 'When I jump into the air I suddenly *seem* to weigh nothing—no, I *do* weigh nothing at the high point of my jump and when I am falling to earth. Of course, when I actually land I seem to—no, I *do*—weigh very much more!' No doubt his earthbound contemporaries would have said that he was talking nonsense.

What I think these examples show is that even in relation to concepts whose application is determined by certain procedures, these 'criteria' for their application do not exhaust their meaning and so doubts that something is x even though the doubter agrees that it has satisfied the tests for something's being x may be not just coherent but perceptive and fertile.[5]

It might be said that these questions and their corresponding doubts and confusions, are not philosophical—and so nonsensical, on Wittgenstein's view—but scientific. But they can occur before we have any way of resolving them, and doing so may well involve giving up the received criteria for the application of a term the application of which term seemed to involve no more than saying that those criteria were satisfied. Ancient speculations about the shape of the earth or the nature of the heavenly bodies might be said to be have been contingently and temporarily 'philosophical' and ceased to be once adequate ways were devised for testing them. There is truth in that, but this is to overlook the point that devising these new techniques meant only *that*, together with the abandoning of old ones, which were inconclusive or misleading. Wittgenstein would say that if these different tests were, or were treated as 'criterial', then the concepts, e.g., of the earth's shape have changed, the topic of speculation has, as it were, been changed. This seems to me a paradoxical and yet shallow view. I would add here, no

[5] At this point no philosopher's thoughts could but turn to colour. For surely our talk about colours, our colour vocabulary, is entirely free of theory? Things are, for example, blue if and only if they are the same colour (hue) as the unclouded sky. And something is the same colour as the unclouded sky if those with normal colour vision would say that it looked the same colour as the unclouded sky (in daylight, i.e., outdoors when the sky is unclouded).

But aside from the fact that something's being blue is here elucidated in terms of the more complex notion of something's looking blue, and that natural and man-made disasters could force us to rely on our memories or standard objects other than the unclouded sky, suppose for example there were to emerge persons with supernormal colour vision, i.e., a group of persons who could make all the colour discriminations which normal persons can make and more. What should we say then if they said that the unclouded sky was no more the colour of delphiniums than were delphiniums all the same colour?

But this is an unnecessary extravagance, for anyone acquainted with the history of philosophy and therefore the history of science knows that what we refer to when we talk about the sky is not unproblematic and that scientists have doubted if anything *in rerum natura* is coloured. This is not to say that in some ways such talk is not confused but that does not mean that it is not also illuminating, not just about us and our confusions but us and our relation to the world we inhabit.

doubt cryptically, that grammar is *not* always autonomous. (But see below.)

Let us return to witches. For Wittgenstein, or his defenders, might say that of course he is not committed to the existence of witches and would not have regarded doubts about their existence, even those expressed in the seventeenth century as philosophical and nonsensical. That a term has meaning does not *eo ipsi* mean that it has application. That is a Tractarian view which he rejected. Grammar is autonomous. For definitions have no existential import and our concepts are not imposed on us by an unconceptualized reality. Knowing what a word *x* means, means knowing how to use it, but that does not mean that one knows that there are *x*'s, only what something is if it is an *x*. Only when that conceptual, conventional, linguistic, grammatical matter is in place—grammar tells you what (sort of thing) a thing is—can we investigate and debate the extra-linguistic matters of discovering 'symptoms'. And such substantive matters as these cannot be settled by reflective thought. Hence there is no task left for philosophy to perform except to correct its own confusions.—There is nothing left for philosophy to *say*. For Wittgenstein is not committed to identifying even part of the use of a word and hence its meaning with empirical knowledge about symptoms.

But this defence does not succeed, even as an account of the later Wittgenstein's views. It ignores what we have noticed he says in the *Investigations* both about the role of standard objects and samples and the need for there to be agreement not just in definitions but judgments. More importantly, it uncritically accepts the distinction between what it perceives to be purely verbal matters, definitions, criteria, and substantive, extra-linguistic matters, 'symptoms', which I have tried to show simplifies and distorts the way in which at least *much* of language works.

It could be said that Wittgenstein himself appreciated this last point as early as his Tractarian period. And although, to quote a much-quoted passage he wrote in 1933, in the *Blue Book* (Wittgenstein, 1958, 25), 'I call "symptom" a phenomenon of which experience has taught us that it coincided in some way or other, with the phenomenon which is our defining criterion', he immediately adds that 'In practice, if you were asked which phenomenon is the defining criterion and which is a symptom you would in most cases be unable to answer except by making an arbitrary decision *ad hoc* . . . in general we do not use language according to strict rules . . . We are unable clearly to circumscribe the concepts we use: not because we do not know their real definition but because there is no real "definition" to them' (ibid.). He also says that 'this need not be a deplorable lack of clarity'.

Of course this passage could not show that Wittgenstein did not continue to think, very often inappropriately, of natural languages working in terms of this distinction. There are indeed many passages in the *Investigations*, e.g., his notorious remarks about dreams, which show that he did. And *unless* he did, we can give no account of his view of philosophy. Wittgenstein's apologists could then defend him only by saying that really his concern was only with problems arising from confusions inspired by and about language, especially those in which we confuse symptoms with criteria or think that there are nothing but symptoms (cf. Wittgenstein, 1953, 354: 'The fluctuations in grammar between criteria and symptoms makes it look as if there were nothing but symptoms.' See also ibid., 314: 'The mistake is to take a conceptual investigation—in the realm of grammar—for an empirical one'; and ibid., 383: 'We are not analysing a phenomenon but a concept.').

At this juncture it is instructive to return to the passage quoted above where he also writes '*We*, in our discussions on the other hand, constantly compare language with a calculus proceeding according to strict rules'. In the next-but-one paragraph he writes (1958, 25–26) 'When we talk of language as a symbolism used in an exact calculus, that which is in our mind can be found in the sciences and in mathematics. Our ordinary use of language conforms to this standard of exactness only in rare cases. Why then do we in philosophising constantly compare our use of words with one following exact rules? The answer is that the puzzles which we try to remove always spring from just this attitude to language.'

If Wittgenstein were right about this, it would follow that if he is confused it is because he wrongly thinks of some part of language as a calculus working according to 'strict rules', i.e., in terms of symptoms and criteria (or if he assumes that where it does not it is unclear—or both). And that he generally does so is, of course, part of my criticism.

Now embedded in the passages from which I have been quoting Wittgenstein also writes (ibid., 25) 'Doctors will use names of diseases without ever deciding which phenomena are to be taken as criteria and which as symptoms; and this need not be a deplorable lack of clarity.' Presumably then this part of science does not conform to the standards of exactness which can be found elsewhere in the sciences. No doubt it can be found in the sciences, but now I want to consider a part of science which does not proceed in terms of symptoms and criteria and *for that very reason* (i.e., not because we assume that it does) presents us with problems which are philosophical but not linguistically inspired confusions.

I borrow my example from an outstanding article by Chihara and Fodor (1965).[6] It concerns the relation between the bands of fog that

---

[6] Page references are to Pitcher (1968).

can be produced in a Wilson cloud-chamber and the paths through the chamber of high-speed charged particles, ions. Current scientific thinking interprets, construes, understands, explains these bands of fog as being condensation trails caused by the passage of the particles through the supersaturated steam filling the chamber.[7] But this is a substantive hypothesis about the trails, viz. that they reveal the movement and indeed confirm the existence of the ions; that they do so is not a conventional, definitional, grammatical matter. That is to say the trails are not Wittgensteinian 'criteria' for or 'criterial' of the presence and movement of these particles. They are, rather—and given accepting a lot of background theory, machinery, observations and predictions—indicators and very good indicators of the existence and various features of the ions. (By 'very good' I mean both convincing of their existence and revealing of their charge, weight, speed, etc.)

Are the trails then not what Wittgenstein calls symptoms of the presence and movement of particles? But to say this is to say that 'experience'—presumably here observations of some sort—have shown us that the occurrence of the trails 'coincides' or correlates with another phenomenon which is a (or the) criterion for the presence, movement etc. of fast-moving, highly charged ions. But there is no such phenomenon; and given the nature of ions, i.e. how we define 'ion', the vapour trails are probably the best indicators we could have of the existence of particular particles, their movements, etc.

So to wonder if vapour trails do indicate the presence of ions, and indeed if there really are such things as ions is not to be guilty of linguistically inspired confusion. Such a doubt may run counter to scientific orthodoxy, it may be gratuitous, silly, uninformed, but it may also be brave, imaginative and, in retrospect, be seen as inspired; but it always makes sense. Appreciation of this philosophical point may lead to—or be inferred from—scientists and philosophers of science wondering whether in such areas of inquiry we can ever do better than strive to find the best explanation of the phenomena which interest and exercise us. Perhaps here truth or knowledge of the truth must forever elude us? And, in seeking good explanations, why do we prefer economical and wide-ranging, unifying theories, deemed 'beautiful' by scientists? Are such preferences merely aesthetic, or does beauty go with truth—or, in these matters and others, is it that beauty *is* truth, as Keats said, or the most and best that we can aspire to?

Science abounds with philosophical problems which are integral to it and which only rarely and even then only in part have their source in

---

[7] The example is from Chihara and Fodor (1968), but they cannot be held responsible for my understanding and presentation of it. The original discussion can be found in Pitcher, 409–410.

linguistically inspired confusions. Problems in conceiving how there could be a vacuum might have been inspired in part by thinking that a meaningful word must stand for something, and a vacuum is a nothing and so a nonsense. But the greater problem surely was trying to understand how anything could pass through a vacuum. It was believed that something called the aether must exist in order to do this job, and though it seemed to receive its quietus at the turn of this century, it is ironic that Einstein's physics quickly re-filled the void.

But do we find such patterns of explanation in the non-scientific, 'ordinary' parts and aspects of our lives, thoughts, actions, language? Wittgenstein's thoughts on this matter seem to me undeveloped, unclear and inconsistent, but he was, I think, always committed to the view that logically and genetically the central part of our lives and language is untheoretical, i.e., natural, common, unreflective and to be accepted, for without it neither language nor explanation, theory, philosophic confusion or its treatment could exist.

While I find this species of transcendental argument compelling, it does not I think follow that even our most natural 'attitudes' are not theoretical in the following sense, that they commit us to beliefs, claims, explanations which we can coherently examine and question. Does an external world exist? Even to ask the question seems mad, gratuitous and, if not incoherent, then unanswerable and hence idle. Yet is it an illusion that not only philosophers and philosophically minded individuals, and students who encounter it as they begin their studies by reading Descartes, understand it as soon as they encounter it? Of course, we must remind ourselves that in a way which fails to guarantee coherence we 'understand' talk about witches, travel in time, the survival of death, swapping bodies, etc. But what are our grounds for saying that an external world exists? Surely it is our experiences, but could not these be produced by something other than the external world, and in such a way that we could never realize or establish this?

Perhaps Wittgenstein's reaction to such philosophical scepticism would be to say, as he says in reply to those sceptics who ask if how what has happened in the past could not ('should' not?) convince him that something would happen in the future, 'if *these* are not grounds, then what are grounds?' and goes on to say '. . . here grounds are not propositions which logically imply what is believed' (Wittgenstein, 1953, 481).

I do not disagree. My own rather pedestrian view is that human beings are 'programmed', 'hard-wired' to believe that there is an external world and that creatures resembling them are rather like themselves, and that individuals who do not react and think in this way are mad and at a great disadvantage (so they will get selected out). Of course, this pedestrian view presupposes that there is indeed an external world, etc., but it does not claim that there are logically compelling reasons for believing it true.

But this is just to say that the phenomena which are our grounds for this belief or 'attitude' are neither criteria nor indeed symptoms of that in which we believe. They are indicators. So how can Wittgenstein reject questions about what they indicate as nonsensical confusions?

These remarks must be almost shocking to many who appreciate Wittgenstein's stature as a philosopher and who believe, rightly, that they have learned so much from him. But is not it disturbing, over-rigid—indeed unWittgensteinian—to assume that we can draw a sharp division between the theoretical parts of our lives and language and the pre-theoretical unchallengeable parts? In any case, have we not already noted that some parts of the most theoretical scientific enquiries are predicated on substantive assumptions which can be coherently questioned but logically cannot be tested?

The suggestion that we cannot always and everywhere distinguish between theoretical and 'ordinary', non-theoretical descriptions, or explanations of 'phenomena' also conceals by indulging, embracing and so accepting further false dichotomies.

It has long been observed that pregnancy follows intercourse by menstrual women (only the Trobrianders have been reputed as failing to observe this) and is indicated by the cessation of periods, followed by swollen breasts, areola, etc. These are indeed diagnostic symptoms, called 'signs' by doctors, of early pregnancy. But of course there are false pregnancies, and other conditions which initially 'present' as pregnancies, and many women lose a 'child', i.e. what is now called a foetus or even an embryo and did so at a point in their pregnancies and at a time in the history of the human race when the distinction between pregnancy and the rest were *intelligible* in a crude way but could not actually be *made* until the pregnancy, if that is what it was, was far advanced.

But before the development of science in the last ten or twenty years, was there a *criterion* for early pregnancy? There was not, but that was a contingent matter. Of course we now have biochemical tests which, though not wholly reliable, are very good tests for whether a woman is pregnant, and though doctors are reluctant to use more direct tests to establish if a woman is pregnant if it puts the future of the embryo or foetus—or the mother—at risk, they have them. They can X-ray the womb and see (or is it 'see') the growing foetus, or they can use echo-sound to reveal 'gestational sacs' at an even earlier stage, or, if they were entirely indifferent to the outcome, or wished to procure her abortion, they could introduce an endoscope to see if they could see the embedded embryo or zygote.

Are these 'phenomena' that doctors can observe 'criteria' for being pregnant or mere symptoms? Well, biochemical 'symptoms' are often better and safer tests for pregnancy than more directly observational tests and I do not know; but this resembles my ignorance of the colour of Hamlet's eyes or what he had for breakfast on the day he saw his father's ghost. What this strongly suggests is that whether we have criteria for the occurrence of some pretty 'untheoretical' thing or fact can be a function of our state of scientific knowledge.

Secondly; as pregnancy develops, the symptoms of pregnancy, properly called, i.e., the sickness, etc., develop into what doctors call 'signs'. But in late pregnancy, are the visible movements in the woman's womb, the shapes revealed by palpitation, the foetal heartbeat, merely signs or symptoms or are they criteria of pregnancy? When, where, how, do signs become criteria?

Finally; the foetal heartbeat is indeed a criterion of pregnancy. But is what the anxious physician hears through his trumpet a foetal heartbeat? Could it not be the putative mother's pulse or the pounding of blood in his own ears? With a late pregnancy, time will resolve these doubts, and we should not—except pejoratively—call them philosophic. But where time does not, and where it could not do so, are our doubts, questions, uncertainties, and attempts to resolve them, all sterile confusions?

We who are examining this small part of medical science are engaged in philosophical enquiry. And although it is true that it was motivated by the desire to clear up the confusions of another philosopher, it need not have been. Our interest could have been quite disinterested, pure, gratuitous. Moreover, some medical researcher working on 'flu, AIDS, post-puerperal infection (though Semelweiss knew virtually nothing about what we call infection), 'Yellow Jack' as yellow fever was called, smallpox—might not (s)he thus be engaged in, be driven to philosophical thought? Suppose in some case he were to say to himself, or his colleagues, 'Look. As far as we can establish, this condition has no cause. But what am I saying? There is no *lesion*. Could there be no cause?! How? Ah—could there be no *physical* cause?' And then having opted for and having had some success with treating certain cases of, say, blindness, as hysterical, suppose he finds himself asking 'Does the fear somehow inhibit part of the functioning of the visual system and if so how? At any rate, in that case there is some physical basis for the condition. Or does it not, in which case surely these people can see? So either they are lying, or, if they are not, they are not aware of what they see? Oh God I'm in a mess'. Perhaps that may lead to a new way of thinking about the condition, which gets empirical confirmation, and which resolves—perhaps by bypassing—the earlier confusions. *But these confusions were fertile, helpful, perhaps even necessary for the emerging of the later theory.*

Philosophical thought *suffuses* our reflective thought. We can sometimes tell them apart, but we cannot always tear them apart and if we try to do so we are left with something unrecognizable and dead. How could the philosopher who talked so illuminatingly of family resemblances and said that mathematics was a motley have characterized, caricatured philosophy as he did?

Learning to understand remarks involving a word such as, say, 'influenza', and thus being able to make them oneself, being able to teach others—all of which, according to Wittgenstein, are constitutive of learning the meanings of words—involves learning a whole range of things.—Imagine trying to teach this word to someone ignorant of Western medicine.—And a person's grasp may be incomplete. Laymen and tyros do not fully understand what they are told when experts talk to them, even though they are addressed in their native language. So 'semantic' matters cannot always be separated off from everything else we learn in learning to understand a language, a discipline, an activity (say dancing).

Quine perhaps first made this point but as is so often the case with philosophers, including Wittgenstein, he transformed, elevated an illuminating observation, the making of which demanded imagination, into a quite general and distorting thesis which produced, as with Wittgenstein, a great mass of largely unproductive controversy.

We can now see why Wittgensteinian exegetists have been unable to produce a satisfactory account of what Wittgenstein meant by the 'use' of a word and also why Wittgenstein liked to talk about chess to show how language works and what philosophy can intelligibly do. But when Freud apparently astounded a late nineteenth-century convention of 'mad-doctors' by saying that men suffered from hysteria, was he proposing a new definition of hysteria—and what could be the grounds for that, if definitions are purely conventional, 'grammatical'? And what would it have availed his opponents if they had responded by saying as perhaps some of them did, 'That is nonsense, for "hysteria" means "apparently functional disorders, especially paralysis, caused by pathological movements of the womb"'? To borrow a happy phrase from Austin, and despite its etymology, it is the symptoms of hysteria which have turned out to be wearing the semantic trousers. What was crucially important about Freud's claim was how these symptoms were produced. If purists or conservatives had insisted he used another term he could have done so but it would have been more difficult for him to show just what he was claiming, *viz.* that a belief hallowed since the time of the ancient Greeks was quite mistaken.

Or when Wat Tyler raised a rebellion against the poll tax introduced by Richard II should we say that he was defending the established concept of justice in such matters against a radically new one, or that he was wishing to preserve the meaning of the phrase 'just taxation', or rather that he thought Richard's tax was unjust? Or to take a very different example, the implications of which are somewhat different, when purists say, as they do, 'Folk music played on electric instruments isn't folk music', are they making a semantic point?

Or again, and this realization is accompanied by a wonderful feeling of intellectual release and opening of the eyes, it is simply no good reminding those who are exercised about freedom of the will of the circumstances in which we say that someone acted freely. This is what puzzles them and we can now see why that need not be confusion. This language game is indeed played but, for example, the diagnosis of a soldier tried and convicted of stealing fruit juices while on the front line in the Desert War in North Africa as suffering from diabetes over-turned the verdict of a drumhead court martial. Might we not discover more and more determinants of human behaviour which are sufficient for that behaviour and are not within our control? Could not this happen, and indeed as it does, does not our concept of the active self more and more closely approximate to the colourless, featureless, extensionless simple of the *Tractatus*? (Is not this precisely what is happening in professional sport, for example cycling, where the selection of physiologically suitable athletes, training programmes, diet, and the monitoring of the cyclists' heartbeat, etc., in the course of the race merely make explicit what was true all along?) And would uncaused decisions or actions save the notion?

Curiously, Wittgenstein apparently agreed that it was conceivable that we might make such discoveries and, he says, 'we would change our terminology—and say, "He's as much compelled as if a policeman shoved him". We would give up this distinction then; and if we did I would be very sorry!' (Wittgenstein, 1975a, 242). It is not entirely clear if Wittgenstein would have been sorry if all human behaviour was mechanistic, or if this were discovered, or if its discovery led to our abandoning free will as an illusion. Neither is it clear why he would regret any of these. None the less it seems that on this occasion Wittgenstein quite casually abandoned everything central to his philosophy.

But I want to conclude this paper, which is at once a critical examination of Wittgenstein's view of philosophy and a defence of the examined life, with a few cursory observations about proof, and mathematical and logical necessity. According to Descartes, who will not distinguish between what we should call logical and natural necessity, necessity devolves on God's choice. According to Wittgenstein, non-natural necessities devolve on ethnography, human practices (cf. Wittgenstein, 1980, 38; 1975a, 249).

Is it a logical truth, is it logically necessary, is it a tautology, that Wednesday is the day after Tuesday or that there are seven days in a week? We who speak English call the day after Tuesday, Wednesday, but we could call it something else. We could decimalize the week. Indeed, I believe the French revolutionaries succeeded in doing that briefly. Here it is very tempting to say with Wittgenstein: we have these conventions, these rules, which are more or less convenient and which come to no more than how we talk, think, act ('It's Wednesday, oh, so it's Phil. Soc. at 4, and so I am going to give my dry run for the Institute lecture, etc'). We have no grounds for these practices, no reason for saying that Wednesday is the successor of Tuesday, except that is what we say in English. But Wittgenstein seeks to give what he sees as the same demystifying but in fact highly 'philosophical', counter-intuitive, and paradoxical account of all logical and mathematical necessity. He writes (1975a, 183–184) '. . . the truths of logic are determined by a consensus of opinions. Is this what I am saying? No. There is no *opinion* at all; it is not a question of *opinion*. They are determined by a consensus of *action*: a consensus of doing the same thing, reacting in the same way.'

But does this not mean that if a fallacy such as perhaps the Monte Carlo fallacy is generally believed to be, treated as, valid it is valid? (A difficulty here is that this fallacy *is* regarded as valid by all but a very few!) And if sufficient think that this does not follow, does it *follow* that it does not?

Wittgenstein is right in pointing out to us that, for example, we have to learn what a week is, what the word 'week' means, that there are seven days in a week, i.e. we have to learn to understand remarks involving the word 'week' and to make them ourselves, in learning English. And we should not learn English if we did not react to those informal lessons as others do. Similarly we learn, probably a bit later, what a 'fortnight' is, what this word means. But we do not have to further learn, especially not as a further *rule*, or convention, or practice in English to say or agree that a fortnight is longer than a week. Wittgenstein denies this: he, as it were, treats every 'remark' as idiomatic. But before trying—perhaps again—to explain why he does so, I must look at the kinds of example that Wittgenstein tended to concentrate on here, simple arithmetic, i.e. counting, addition, subtraction, etc.

We simply absorb or learn by rote the first nine/ten or so words which in English represent the beginning of the natural number series. We learn to write these numerals down. We learn that we get to the next number in the series by adding one, and the mechanical rule for developing the series, i.e. how each successive number is represented. We also learn to say when there are only two cherries left, but there are four apples in the dish, three peas in the pod, and so on. But does the bus conductor have to be *taught* or to learn as *a further rule* that, say, there are forty-five passengers packed on the lower deck? Does he not rather see, notice the fact that there are a lot of people downstairs and then counts them to establish their precise number? And if there is a rule which states that there cannot be more than thirty-two passengers on the lower deck, it follows 'mathematically' that thirteen must get off. But it is a legal rule which requires them to do so. And the only 'decisions' (cf. Wittgenstein, 1953, 186) which have to be made here, which are neither legal nor mathematical, are which passengers if any are to get off.

Following the rule for constructing the natural number series we go, of course, from 1000 to 1001, 1002, etc. Wittgenstein suggests (1953, 185) that it might be natural for some to go on 1002, 1004, etc., and he insists it would be no good saying such things as 'You haven't understood, or you've made a mistake. Anyway, you're not going on in the same way. That's wrong' if despite our best efforts their puzzled and extremely puzzling *reaction* continues to be 'No, we're going on in the same way.'

Now if one *assumes* that this is what happens then of course nothing we can say or do will be effective, but I think what Wittgenstein wants to say is that it would be meaningless, not just pointless, for us to insist that we are right and they are wrong, that they are not going on in the same way (Of course, he does say that they act differently from us but perhaps parochialism cannot be avoided in presenting such a case.)

Why does Wittgenstein say this? Because, once again, if meaning is use, if meaning cannot guide use, if the formulation of a rule can always be interpreted in different ways, following the rule and hence the rule itself collapses into what people do, find natural to do, when, for example, obeying the injunction to add one. Logical necessity collapses into consensus of 'reaction'. The unrestricted application of the necessarily ill-defined doctrine that meaning is use, i.e., its fresh application to every remark—which Wittgenstein of course denied was a doctrine—here wreaks its most dramatic, puzzling and unacceptable consequences.

But now I might be asked: what explanation would you give of logical truth, necessity, inference? But *this* is philosopher's nonsense, for in trying to explain it I should have to invoke, deploy, presuppose and you would have to understand what it is for one proposition to follow of necessity from another. If you try to explain it in terms of anything else you reduce it—and fail to preserve its necessity. And there really is *nothing* to explain. All one can do, ironically, is to adopt the Wittgensteinian procedure of offering what one hopes will be perspicuous examples so that our philosophical puzzlement is dissipated.

So: given the meaning of the numeral '50', i.e. the rules for its construction, and the same for '60' and the use of '>' to symbolize 'is greater than' we do not need a further rule to justify 60>50 for 60 comes after 50 in the natural number series and that is what '>' means here. If we did we should be involved in an infinite regress. (Wittgenstein seems to have learnt much from Lewis Carroll but unfortunately not this point.)[8] That 60>50 does not depend on some further practice. If we denied that 60>50, either we should have contradicted ourselves or we should have changed the rules for the use of '50', '60' and '>'. If we ask why this is so, what is the source and nature of this necessity, no further answer is possible or necessary.[9]

Lastly, I must very briefly mention Anthony Kenny's attempt (1982) to offer a more positive account of Wittgenstein's views about philosophy. However, he writes (ibid., 9) 'Wittgenstein insists that philosophy is only philosophical problems . . . and their removal.' How then can he claim that (on his account) it follows from Wittgenstein's views that '"philosophy", like so many other words, is a family-likeness concept' (ibid.)? And in attempting to answer Ryle's question 'What has a fly lost who never got into the fly-bottle?' (cf. Wittgenstein, 1953, 309) he writes, 'if you have done philosophy in the right way . . . you have gone through a discipline which enables you to resist certain temptations' (ibid., 14). This is the temptation to philosophy as original sin (cf. ibid., 15). My whole burden is that not all philosophy is of this sort and to purport that it is confuses us and diminishes it.

As with F. R. Leavis (who resembled him in his concern with the particular, the intensity of his scrutiny, and his authority and seriousness) so with Wittgenstein. It is so hard not to swallow him whole—or spit him out entirely; and I have tried to show why in terms of the philosophy rather than the man. Critical reflective and imaginative

[8] Cf. my "What Wittgenstein failed to learn from Lewis Carroll", 15th International Wittgenstein Symposium, August 1992.

[9] Watson made virtually the same point (cf. Wittgenstein,, 1975a, 100). Wittgenstein's reply was to obfuscate. He says 'I might say that the multiplication of 136×51 makes me adopt a new rule. I proceed from certain rules, and I get a new rule: that $136 \times 51 = 6936$.' But what is this new rule, i.e., to what does it apply, and how does he 'get' it? On p. 58 (ibid.) he says 'The only criterion for his multiplying 113 by 44 in a way analogous to the [earlier] examples is his doing it in the way in which all of us, who have been trained in a certain way, would do it. If we find that he cannot be trained to do it in the same way, we give him up as hopeless and say he is a lunatic.' Well, if that did happen why would he call him a *lunatic*?

thought shows that his view of the nature of philosophy does not follow from his major philosophical insight. And assembling reminders about the actual history of philosophy, and its achievements shows that it is wrong.

I conclude then that the philosopher's treatment of a question is not and should not always be like the treatment of an illness, it does not always amount to putting into order what we already know, and it does not leave everything—not even language itself—as it was. The examined life is indeed worth living.

Trouble with Leprechauns

MARTIN HOLLIS

The impulse to philosophy is often provided by leprechauns, mischievous little sprites who lurk at the end of fine chains of reasoning and make trouble. They delight in absurdity and paradox, and are especially happy to help ambitious thinkers dig their own graves. Philosophers spend much of their lives trying to put a stop to leprechauns or fencing them out with the aid of reason. But in truth the relationship is symbiotic. If a realm of thought can be made fully coherent, there is no work for philosophers to do in it. Science is the obvious case but the remark applies, paradoxically, to philosophy itself. A philosopher who solved all the problems of philosophy would be about as popular as a huntsman who shot the fox or a theologian who proved the existence of God. Luckily there is no serious risk. At least on the view of philosophy to be taken here, there will always be leprechauns to keep us busy.[1]

The view is that philosophy flourishes on the border between closed and open questions. By a closed question I mean one where the method of answering is not in doubt. Science cannot as yet fully identify or isolate the AIDS virus and cannot immunize against it. But, provided that no revolution in medical techniques is required, ignorance does not stop questions about it being closed. On the other hand there is some reason to suggest that AIDS research needs to include psychological and sociological understanding and what counts as a revolution in technique is unclear. In that case method is in doubt and, since there is no established way of integrating physical, mental and social enquiry, there is still an open question here. How open it is is a matter of degree. In 1839 the House of Commons responded to an outbreak of cholera in the East End of London by decreeing a day of prayer and fasting. If similar calls to repentance over AIDS had any merit, it would be a very open question whether control of AIDS was within the grasp of science

[1] That is no doubt why a philosopher has been included in the project on the Foundations of Rational Choice Theory at the University of East Anglia funded by the Economic and Social Research Council (award R 000 23 2269). The theme at the core of this lecture is part of the project and I would like to thank Robin Cubitt, Shaun Hargreaves Heap, Judith Mehta, Chris Starmer and Robert Sugden for many fertile discussions of it. I am also grateful to A. Phillips Griffiths for his comments on an earlier draft.

at all. Much philosophy is to do with the scope of science and its relation to any other modes of rational thought. Since reason is itself a topic for reason, there are always open questions, where attempts to specify a method of answering seems doomed to circularity. This is good news for leprechauns and also, in the end, for philosophers too.

Some leprechauns thrive in the shadows of ignorance. Early Victorian concern to improve health by improving hygiene was plagued by a belief that many diseases were spread by miasma. This led progressive cities to flush their sewage into the river, which killed not only the smell but also people living downstream. It was also one reason why childbirth was transferred from the foetid homes of the poor to light and airy hospitals, for the sake of lowering infant mortality. As a result many more babies died. (That was because doctors, still wearing the blood-stained, germ-ridden clothes donned for surgery, were a far greater threat to life than home-based midwives.) It is easy to spot the hand of leprechauns in these examples. It is visible in the paradoxical quality of the mischief, when progress turns out to make things worse. But these are only minor mischiefs, since medicine had by then advanced far enough and previously open questions about disease were already closed. Better techniques soon discovered the truth about germs and stopped the mischief.

Other leprechauns love the light of reason. Their playground is among the sunlit constructions of clear, systematic thought, where they use the system itself to produce ridiculous conclusions. Their aim is to force closed questions open again, by showing the closure to have been premature. They are to be taken seriously, because the more ridiculous the conclusions are, the more enlightening the mischief becomes. But they are not to be trusted, since they take as much pleasure in fooling us with spurious paradoxes as in disconcerting us with genuine ones. To illustrate this theme I shall next introduce a thoroughly ridiculous result, which threatens to subvert a thoroughly reasonable-seeming philosophy of action. Then I shall reflect more widely on the role of paradox in the current debate between modern and post-modern philosophy.

It may be as well to say now that I shall not try to prove in detail that the paradox in the philosophy of action is genuine. That would require a more intricate discussion than there is space for. But it is at least disconcerting and, genuine or not, it usefully illustrates the borderland between open and closed questions. In general I take the progress of reason to consist in closing questions, first by showing in principle how their subject can be conceived so as to fit the canon of rational enquiry and then definitively by supplying assumptions which ground all further theories. The philosophies of action proposed by Thomas Hobbes in the seventeenth century and David Hume in the eighteenth both set about making human beings a subject for science. It is widely held that they succeeded, or at least broke the back of the problem. Although I cannot pretend to refute this belief in a few minutes, I hope that it will still be instructive to watch leprechauns at work on it.

Closing the question

Why do people act as they do? That sounds an unprofitable question. Offhand, people act for all sorts of reasons or for none. All kinds of ideas and urges prompt their conscious motives or lurk beneath them. Kings and clowns, poets and jockeys, warriors and bankers, saints and cannibals seem too various to contemplate together. Yet many attempts have been made to bring all actions under a single scheme of explanation. Those most typical of modern philosophy have been aimed at advancing a science of mind, hoping to apply the scientific revolution to human affairs. Hobbes and Hume are crucially important authors of much current thinking along these lines, since they pioneered an approach which relies on dissecting human nature in the name of a universal theory of action.

'Reason is the pace, increase of science the way, and the benefit of mankind the end', Hobbes wrote in *Leviathan*, published in 1651 to demonstrate how commonwealths can be made and maintained. *Leviathan* opens with several chapters on human nature, which display men as thoroughly mechanical creatures driven by a desire for 'felicity'. Although we have many passions (chapter VI) and various causes of quarrel (chapter XIII), we are all insatiable in our search for felicity and hence in the pursuit of power after power which endeth only in death. 'Reason' is both part of the human condition, in the sense that we cannot escape a human nature which is rationally geared to the demands of self-preservation, and the means to such felicity as we can attain. Here lie the origins of the rational egoism which continues to inspire much social science, especially in economics.

David Hume is often presented as a sceptic and he is certainly a powerful critic of the pretensions which Reason acquired in the seventeenth century. But he is no sceptic about the prospects of a science of mind and action, as the introduction to *A Treatise of Human Nature* (1739) makes plain. This aim is prominent too in *An Enquiry Concerning Human Understanding* (1748), where we learn that 'there is a great uniformity among the actions of men in all nations and ages, and that human nature remains still the same, in its principles and operations. The same motives produce the same actions. The same events follow from the same causes' (Section VIII.1). Human nature is then credited with seven motives. 'Ambition, avarice, self-love, vanity, friendship, generosity, public spirit: these passions, mixed in various degrees, and distributed through society, have been from the beginning of the world and still are the source of all actions and enterprises, which have ever been observed among mankind.' Although it is hard to see quite how Hume picked out this bundle of four self-regarding motives and three outgoing ones, he clearly means what he says, when he adds, 'Mankind are so much the same in all places and times that history has nothing to teach us in this regard.'

Behind this empirical-sounding thesis lies an entirely general theory of action, which it is hard to resist. Action is the product of two elements, passion and reason, or, in current terms, desire and belief. The agent seeks to satisfy his passions; reason advises him how best to do it. This is why human nature is everywhere the same in its principles and operations. All actions have a common structure, as displayed whenever clowns pull faces, poets write verses, bankers make money or saints give it away. Differences are due to variety in the mixture of the basic passions but, whatever the mixture, it works in the same uniform way.

Hobbes and Hume share the view that human beings are basically rational. Hobbes builds reason more deeply into human nature by making it partly constitutive of a need for self-preservation which can be satisfied only if we are able to calculate our best means to felicity. Hume firmly subordinates reason to passion, most explicitly in the *Treatise* where 'reason alone can never be a motive to any action of the will . . . Reason is and ought only to be the slave of the passions and can never pretend to any other office than to serve and obey them' (Book II, Part III, section 3). It is Hume who is the origin of the familiar doctrine that to act rationally is to do whatever is instrumental in furthering one's desires or satisfying one's preferences, no matter what those desires or preferences are.

This doctrine is built deep into standard theories of rational choice and hence into the standard theory of social interactions as 'games' between rational agents. It is, I shall argue, a major source of some wicked paradoxes which make the theories a leprechauns' playground. Reason is not an utterly humble slave of the passions for these purposes. It insists that a rational agent's preferences be consistent. Relatedly and more tendentiously, it demands that consistent preferences be commensurable, so that a rational agent can always compare the likely consequences of any two courses of action. This demand is standardly expressed by introducing the notion of utility as a universal comparator, so that a rational agent never lacks the apparatus for choosing between apples and pears, or between guns and butter, or between liberty and death. He can be indifferent between a fourth apple, a fifth pear and a contribution to the war effort. He can also be uncertain what to do, when the possible consequences of his action involve risks hard to assess. But in principle everything can be traded against everything in the balance of expected utilities.[2]

To put it more formally, a rational agent has complete and consistent preferences over the possible consequences of each action open to him; he has rational beliefs on all relevant matters; he has an internal computer able to perform all needed calculations of expected utility. He always performs an action which maximizes his expected utility, or, where no single action has this character, never chooses action x if there is an action y whose expected utility is greater. Since this formula is silent about sources of utility, reason is still only the slave of the passions. Since it is entirely general, it is no surprise that mankind are so much the same in all places and times that history has nothing to teach us in this regard.

The expected utility of an action is the utility of its various possible consequences discounted for the likelihood of their not occurring. The basic idea is that of a wager: whether it is rational to buy a £1 ticket in a raffle for a prize worth £100 depends on how many tickets are sold. Although the theory of probability is full of problems, the basic idea is enough to work with, while we are considering an agent making rational choices in a world where probabilities can be estimated consistently. Call such probability-guided choices 'parametric', in the sense that the probabilities of the various outcomes form a set of given parameters within which the agent is to calculate the rational choice. Social life involves plenty of parametric choices. But it also involves 'strategic' choices, where the expected utility of Adam's action depends on what Eve chooses and her rational choice depends on what she expects him to choose. Strategic choice is the subject of the theory of games, which turns out to be paradoxical to its very core.

The theory of games explores what happens when rational agents interact. It does so by abstracting to an ideal-type world where the agents have 'common knowledge' of everything relevant to the game including the fact that all players are rational. The simplest case is where two players, Adam and Eve, each choose separately between two actions, x and y, and there are thus four possible outcomes, xx, xy, yx

---

[2] Professor Phillips Griffiths has kindly drawn my attention to this pithy comment on Holbach's version of the doctrine by Marx in *The German Ideology*. 'Holbach represents every activity of individuals in their reciprocal intercourse, e.g. speech, love, etc., as a relation of utility and exploitation. These relations are thus not allowed to have their own significance but are depicted as the expression and representation of a third relation which underlies them, *utility* or *exploitation*. These individual relations no longer have value on their own account, as personal activity, but only as a disguise for a real third purpose and relationship, which is called the relation of utility.'

Martin Hollis

and *yy*. Each knows how the other ranks the outcomes, and chooses in the knowledge that the other is using this information too. The simplest game is one of co-ordination, where Adam and Eve both prefer an outcome resulting from similar choices, for instance where both choose to keep left (or right) when their cars pass on the highway, and thus avoid a collision which neither wants. This game is often held to be fundamental for social life and for understanding it at large, as well as for many particular features of it, especially language. It seems that nothing could be simpler to analyse than co-ordination among rational agents. But that is an illusion.

Certainly we need to co-ordinate. Even if there is no uniquely right way to use words or to conduct social life in general, we must often all do it in the same way. Schematically, the situation is often as in *game 1*, where either way of co-ordinating will suit both parties nicely and neither way is better than the other. (The four boxes represent the four possible outcomes and the pairs of numbers give the players' utilities, with Adam's first in each case. Thus (1, 1) indicates that both prefer (left, left) to (left, right) etc.) Here reason has no advice to give, at least for a single play of the game, since Adam has no preference independent of Eve's choice, nor she of his. If they succeed in co-ordinating, it will be by luck. Social life, one might say, starts here, with a small problem, readily overcome by the emergence of a convention.

Adam

		Left	Right
Eve	Left	1, 1	0, 0
	Right	0, 0	1, 1

Game 1

Game 1 seems to capture an everyday situation where people meet as strangers, for instance as motorists on the highway who do not know each other. Yet it cannot capture it in full, since motorists do not collide on average half the time. That is unpuzzling because there is a convention that (in Britain) drivers keep to the left. Once the convention is in place, everyone knows that everyone knows it and is therefore no longer indifferent between left and right. Left has become 'prominent' or 'salient', to use the game-theoretic terms. That presumably gives Adam and Eve a reason to choose left, or so one is inclined to assume. It would take a very tiresome leprechaun to see any problem about that.

The same can be said about another simple and fundamental co-ordination game, where both players actively prefer one of the successful outcomes to the other. In *game 2* the pay-off for (left, left) is

(2, 2), as against (1, 1) for (right, right). Presumably there cannot be any mystery about why a rational agent chooses left, when (left, left) is the uniquely preferred outcome for both.

		Adam Left	Right
Eve	Left	2, 2	0, 0
	Right	0, 0	1, 1

Game 2

Reopening the question

Can there not? There would indeed be no mystery, if the effect of the convention or higher pay-off were to give either player a *parametrically* rational choice. For instance if the rules of the highway decreed that any driver found on the right of the road would be beheaded, and this was a worse fate than being involved in a collision, there would be no problem in *game 1*. Similarly in game 2, if Adam and Eve each took an independent pleasure in staying close to the left curb, there might again be no problem. But that utility numbers in both games would need revising, if choices are to be made unconditionally rational in this way. As the diagrams stand, the numbers make it clear that choices are *strategic* in the sense that whether Adam is rational to choose left depends on whether he rationally expects Eve to choose left, and *vice versa*. It is crucial to stress this, since it is the point of entry for the leprechauns. So I hope to be forgiven for spelling it out. Adam's rational choice is left, if he rationally expects Eve to choose left, and right if he rationally expects her to choose right. Eve's rational choice is left, if she rationally expects Adam to choose left, and right if she rationally expects him to choose right. This is true both for *game 1*, with or without a Keep Left convention, and for *game 2*, despite the higher utility of 2 for each player. No one has an independent or unconditional reason to choose left (or, for that matter, right).

Very well, the leprechauns ask innocently, and how exactly does reason steer Adam and Eve leftwards in these two games? Disconcertingly I can find no answer to this childlike question, at any rate none within the scope of the game theory scheme sketched so far.[3] In *game 1*

[3] David Lewis *Convention: A Philosophical Study* (1969) is central to more recent discussion. Margaret Gilbert (1989) argues that, on Lewis's account, rational agents 'act blindly' when co-ordinating, because reason cannot guide them. Robert Sugden (1991) endorses doubts about the scope of strategic reasoning and suggests that rational agents must rely on simple induction.

the players are indifferent between (left, left) and (right, right) and a Keep Left convention does not make them less indifferent. In *game 2* Adam prefers (left, left) but only because it yields higher utility for him, and Eve prefers (left, left) because it yields higher utility for her. Neither prefers (left) unconditionally and neither prefers (left, left) because it yields higher total utility. Although it seems obvious that, even so, Reason has enough to work with, I am afraid that it is not obvious at all.

Does the emergence of a Keep Left convention not make it more probable that the other driver will keep left? Strangely, while rational choices remain strategic, the answer seems to be no. Standard notions of probability are all parametric, in that they refer to tendencies in an independent environment like nature. Pruning the roses makes it likelier that they will flower well because, on one account, pruned roses are usually more prolific than unpruned. But for Adam and Eve, each choosing strategically, the convention makes it likelier that each will keep left only if it has somehow thereby already become likelier that the other will. It does not raise Adam's probability independently, if he is a rational agent estimating Eve's likely reasoning as a rational agent, and *vice versa*. Eve cannot rationally decide to keep left, until she is confident that Adam will; and she realizes that he cannot be counted on until she has rationally decided. Disconcertingly, the existence of a Keep Left convention seems to make not the slightest difference.

Conceding this to the leprechauns for the moment, we might try to wrest *game 2* from them, on the grounds that Reason is being too servile. The point that Adam prefers (left, left) in *game 2* only because he prefers its pay-off to himself (and similarly for Eve) may suggest that Reason should tell him not to be so self-centred. In some accounts it is made of sterner stuff. In Adam Smith's *Theory of Moral Sentiments* (1759) it bids each of us heed the impartial spectator in our breast. In Kant's *Critique of Practical Reason* (1785) it directs us to make the moral choice arrived at by asking what it would be right for everyone in Adam's place to do. But this attractive thought is no help while, in Hume's words, 'reason alone cannot be a motive to any action of the will'. The obstacle is very fundamental indeed. Reverting to Hume's list of seven motives, we might suppose that self-love has covertly driven out public spirit and that, if Adam were only to be public spirited, the fact that Eve also prefers (left, left) would be decisive. Hume himself is fond of saying that 'reason and reflection' can overcome the short-sightedness which results from self-love. He says it, for example, when explaining why even a 'selfish knave' will subscribe to artificial principles of justice, although apparently able to do better for himself by flouting them discreetly. (Hume, 1748b.) Can reason and reflection not persuade even a Humean that 'left' is the rational choice in *game 2*?

The answer is definitely no. Standard rational choice theory has no regard to sources of utility. Its analysis of motivation is neutral between passions, in whatever proportions they may be mixed. For pure public spirit and pure self love alike it says only that a rational agent seeks to maximize expected utility. The sole difference which friendship, generosity or public spirit could make is to raise the utility for Adam of doing what raises Eve's utility. That would make no difference whatever in *game 2*. Adam already gets more utility from (left, left) than from any other outcome. To raise the utility numbers in the top left box makes no sense if the numbers are merely graphic representations of ordinal rankings and makes no difference if they are cardinal. The puzzle is unaffected.

It is worth pausing to stress how bizarre this apparent result is. Those who came to this lecture by car will have driven along the left hand side of the road without qualm or accident, secure in the knowledge that everyone benefits from the convention and no one has reason to depart from it. Yet we seem to have learnt that safe driving depends on blind faith. Reason seems to say only 'Keep left, if others will keep left; keep right, if others will keep right; but do not suppose that the highway code gives sufficient reason to do one rather than the other.' If this is truly what it says, then the standard theory of rational choice is simply unable to account for social interaction, even where there are no conflicts of interest among the interacting parties. Travel on the highway is a tiny thread in a social fabric of co-ordination which includes most of our basic social institutions, starting with language. If the apparent result holds, it is catastrophic. Reason could no longer even advise us to call the next spade a spade, since that is a rational way to continue to talk if and only if other people will also call it a spade. It could not recommend the striking of mutually advantageous bargains, while it is rational to do one's part if and only if others will do theirs. It could not recommend the use of money, if the value of money as a medium of exchange depends on everyone's rationally accepting it. In short, unless reason can direct Adam and Eve each to play left in *game 2*, it has bizarrely little to say about rational action at all.

Where exactly are the leprechauns hiding? Let us return now to the point about the fully strategic character of the choices which Adam and Eve are trying to make. Revert to *game 1*, where each is indifferent between left and right, provided that both make the same choice. The introduction of a Keep Left convention made no difference because we insisted that Adam and Eve had no reason to follow it prior to and independently of what each rationally expected the other to do. Perhaps that was a mistake. Perhaps conventions work by changing the parameters within which choices are made. In other words, perhaps the emergence of a Keep Left convention does make it more likely that each motorist will keep left without requiring a detour through expectations about what other motorists are likely to do.

That would be plausible enough if conventions worked as programming devices which introduced reliable tendencies into human behaviour. Indeed, from some points of view, this is just what they do. A child who learns to call a spade a spade gets into the habit of doing so and stops having to think whether to call it a spade or a fork. Drivers in the habit of keeping left have learnt to by-pass the reflection that alternative conventions would work as well. By emphasizing the obvious importance of habit in keeping social life on the road, perhaps we can reintroduce the independent source of probabilities which I said earlier must wait on a solution to the co-ordination puzzle. If the puzzle is insoluble without them, it looks a good move to inject them from the start. Adam would then have a simple inductive reason to expect Eve to be, like other trained drivers, in the unthinking habit of keeping left. Since this is the same non-strategic sort of reason which he has for pulling in for more petrol when the petrol gauge nears empty, we are back in the innocent realm of parametric choice. As Hume might remark, 'Custom, then, is the great guide of human life', since 'nothing is more useful for writers, even on moral, political or physical subjects, [than] to distinguish between reason and experience', and to realize that 'all inferences from experience, therefore, are effects of custom, not of reasoning' (1748a, Section V, part 1).

Notice, however, that Hume holds custom to be as crucial in parametric choice as in strategic choice. This is the result of his notorious scepticism about induction, which leads him to deny that reason can ever have the final word. Consequently his science of mind is ultimately an enquiry into the customary working of mind and it relies, presumably, on the customary practice of science. This strikes me as a deeply paradoxical view of his own enterprise, and one which we may wish to avoid. In that case we shall need to insist that inferences from experience can be effects of reasoning and that custom itself can embody reasoning. At any rate, this seems to me a more attractive way to think about conventions and how they operate in solving co-ordination problems. The Keep Left convention does not cause drivers to keep left mindlessly or to presume that other drivers are tootling mindlessly along, as is plain when something disturbs the rhythm of the highway. Why pretend that it is as if our fellows were automata, when we know that they are not? The answer just proposed is that the attempt to justify fully strategic choices lands in a regress, which needs breaking with a non-strategic element like habit. But, if that means agreeing with Hume that even parametrically rational choices are 'effects of custom, not of reasoning', the price seems to me too high; and, if reasoning is allowed, then it is surely involved in following the Keep Left convention.

But Hume is not being quirky. His scepticism about complete rationalizations is all of a piece with his conviction that 'reason alone cannot be a motive to any action of the will.' In *game 1* Adam and Eve are indifferent between the two solutions to their co-ordination problem. Neither has a passion or preference which inclines them to one rather than the other. A Keep Left convention does not affect this and so can operate only by raising probabilities, and, it turns out, in a way which owes nothing to reason. Commonsense may still find this absurd. But the symmetry of the setting and the interlocking of expectations see to it that reason can give no such assurance, unless it can motivate rational agents in some fresh way.

The obstacle remains, however, that rational choice theory has a firmly mechanical model of mind. Rational actors are propelled by expected utilities. The utility numbers in *games 1* and *2* serve both as data for purposes of calculation and as ineluctable sources of motivation. This dual function can be awkward even for parametric choice by a single agent. Buridan's ass, poised between two equidistant bales of equally succulent hay, has a mechanically insoluble problem in my view. The obvious solution is for the ass to pick at random. But this simple manoeuvre requires that the poor beast be able to reflect on the limitations of the basic decision procedure and thus circumvent its own indifference. For Adam and Eve the manoeuvre needed is more complex. The ass has only to act on the advice which it would receive from an impartial spectator. Adam and Eve must *each* act on the advice which *both* would receive. That seems to me impossible, unless impartial reflection alone can serve as a motive to the will.

To draw this conclusion is not, of course, to prove that a coherent alternative philosophy of action is possible, and still less to provide one. It is only to locate the immediate source of mischief. Hume attempted to close a profound question about the essential character of action by laying the basis of a science of mind. He thus inspired the kind of 'economic' thinking about action in which human agents are rational maximizers of expected utility, identified with their preferences and equipped with internal computers. This approach yields the fashionable theory of games as a logical consequence. By making mischief in the most elementary and important game, the leprechauns are causing trouble at source, in the underlying philosophy of mind. If they cannot be stopped, the original question about the character of action is reopened.

Martin Hollis

Does the riddle exist?

The paradox means that rational utility maximizers cannot even co-ordinate, although ordinary humans do it all the time. Is it genuine and how deep does it go? The challenge is to explain why it is rational for Adam and Even to make the obvious choices in *game 2* and how the emergence of a salient or focal point, for example, the Keep Left convention, furnishes them with the obvious motivating reasons in *game 1*. Since my purpose is only to illustrate the role of paradox in philosophy, I shall not try to analyse further the fierce and intricate debates now raging over this and other apparent paradoxes in rational choice theory. Since initial reaction by those new to the argument is likely to be that nothing could be simpler, however, let me risk admitting that I think the paradox genuine. Although it took me a long time to overcome my incredulity, I am convinced that the leprechauns have a point. In games of strategic choice, Adam's calculation of expected utility waits upon Eve's and hers upon his. The fact that both prefer (left, left) in *game 2* is curiously ineffective, and I do not see how salients or focal points can be a source of reasons in *game 1*. Something is amiss.

Since none of this tends to paralyse the traffic on the road outside, the next reaction is to presume that we have found a technical flaw needing a technical fix. Much sophisticated work is going on with this aim and, if it succeeds, the paradox will have been shown to be of merely local interest. But, as a philosopher with great respect for Hume, I doubt whether the trouble is solely technical. To escape their impasse Adam and Eve need to distance themselves from the information contained in the pay-off tables and from the standard connection between expected utilities and actions. A philosophy of action where reason alone cannot be a motive to any action of the will disallows any such distancing. Hume is too good a philosopher to leave scope for replacing parts of his theory of action without affecting other parts. I doubt whether fixers can succeed without being drawn deep into the philosophy of mind.

That raises wider questions about the analysis of practical reason but it does not yet show the paradox to be fully genuine. If an alternative, coherent account of practical reason were on offer, that would put a stop to the leprechauns. Admirers of Kant will be quick to suggest a promising source. In Kantian ethics a moral agent is moved by duty, as distinct from inclination. The imperatives of duty are categorical, applying to anyone and everyone in a similar situation, regardless of their desires, passions or preferences. In coming to recognize that something is one's duty one thereby acquires a reason to do it. Such reasons motivate a rational moral agent. This implies a moral psychology, wider than a psychology of ethical decision, in which reason alone can be a motive to the will. Kant's analysis of practical reason is on general offer to Adam and Eve. As they head towards each other along the highway, each recognizes that there is a reason for both to keep left, each thereby acquires the reason and each is thus motivated to act on it.

A Kantian moral psychology may or may not do the trick. But, if it were to emerge victorious from struggles in the philosophy of mind and were to resolve the co-ordination puzzle, the question would have been reopened only to be closed again. Fully genuine paradoxes prevent closure of every sort and it is a mark of modern philosophy, or what it is fashionable to call 'the Enlightenment project', to deny that there are any. There are open questions at various stages of the progress of reason, in that reason has yet to devise a method for seeking rational answers to them. Paradoxes draw attention to these gaps or expose premature attempts to close them. For example, Zeno's paradoxes of motion were a serious obstacle for many centuries but, at least according to many histories of mathematics, Cantor finally disposed of them by closing the questions which they raised. But no genuine question is open in principle, whatever the state of progress in practice. As the *Tractatus* puts it, 'the riddle does not exist'.

Few thinkers have been so bold. Even Descartes held that there are mysteries beyond the reach of reason. Even Kant found an antinomy in the contrast between the rational reconstruction of agency and its causal explanation. Hume too left leprechauns playing havoc with his science of mind, as he confessed gracefully in the appendix to the *Treatise*. On the other hand few thinkers have blamed even the deepest paradoxes on the paradoxical nature of the world, in the spirit of that favourite among graffiti: 'do no adjust your set; there is a fault in reality.' Perhaps the idea that historical processes have a dialectic comes close, when it is couched in a language of internal contradictions among historical forces. But even here the claim, supposing it to be intelligible, seems optional, since there is always the alternative of locating the dialectical contradictions in thought rather than in a reality external to thought.

The thesis that 'the riddle does not exist' implies both that the world itself is a cosmos, a coherent set of facts or series of states, and that we can represent it coherently in thought and language. The current dispute between moderns and post-moderns is mainly about the latter claim. It is tempting to describe the dispute as one between Enlightenment thinkers, like Descartes and Kant, who hold that thought can indeed represent reality without distortion, and recent anti-Enlightenment thinkers, who deny us any standpoint for making the root distinction between thought and reality. But this drawing of the battle lines seems to me mischievous in the extreme. It results in a stark and destructive dilemma. Either there is no problem left once we have stopped raising a dust and then complaining that we cannot see, or all claims to knowledge are relative to a discourse with no external criteria of meaning and truth.

I do not fancy either horn myself. The first has certainly been tried, notably by logical empiricists and positivists who took it as their sole task to clear the rubbish which lies in the way to empirical science. It has also been tried, less obviously, by linguistic philosophers, whose vacuum cleaners sucked the philosophical dust off the surface not only of science but of ordinary language and who wanted nothing further to do with questions of appearance and reality. This way of taking the linguistic turn did expose ambitious empiricists as secret metaphysicians, pretending to stand outside language and experience when claiming to describe the anatomy of reason. But the vacuum cleaners left a vacuum in the theory of knowledge, ready-made for relativism. This is the other horn and its advocates are plentiful.

The thesis that 'the riddle does not exist' is an open invitation to leprechauns, who have given it a hard time from the start. Their tactic has been to enrol in the philosophical search after truth as malignant demons or sceptics with two services to offer. One service is to detect absurdities in previous or rival systems of thought by pushing them to the limit, thus proving that an open question has been prematurely closed. The other service is then to let themselves be refuted by their employer, thus proving that the new system indeed closes the question. They are, of course, happy to perform the first service and have not the least intention of performing the second. When ordinary language philosophy banned them from Middle Earth, the lazy ones took a grateful nap, while the energetic emigrated to America and went to work on pragmatism.

To escape between the horns of the dilemma, we might start by recalling that Descartes and Kant both recognized that there is an old question about appearance and reality which defies easy answer. There is some ground for holding that Descartes tried to deal with it by making the knowing mind self-effacing in moments of unclouded intuition. But intellectual intuition in the Cartesian system involves a recognition of perspective. It is the limiting case of the mind allowing for its own standpoint in knowing how things objectively are. In Kant the mind is denied all possible acquaintance with things as they are (*Dinge an sich*), since it cannot avoid imposing categories and concepts in every act of judgement. Yet the idea of objective judgement is retained by insisting that there is a uniquely coherent conceptual scheme which reason can identify. If his analysis holds, then the Enlightenment project is not destroyed by our inability to climb out of our own heads, so to speak, in order to discern the reality of the external world.

So I do not despair of a modern philosophy which shows us how rational thought can represent the order in the world and how we can intervene effectively by rational action. But the project is undeniably prone to paradoxes. Those of rational action are especially startling because they give trouble both for theoretical reason in its attempt to represent the social world and for practical reason in its attempt to recommend interventions. None is more startling than a paradox which threatens to make nonsense of the game-theoretic analysis of the simplest interaction. Adam and Eve, trying to pass peaceably on the highway, therefore threaten us with a central antinomy. The thesis is that every choice by a fully rational agent can be inferred by applying expected utility theory, except where the agent is justifiably indifferent between courses of action. The antithesis is that a fully rational agent can sometimes have a uniquely rational choice which cannot be so inferred. The synthesis is elusive.

The thesis should apply readily to co-ordination games. Any reason which Adam has for keeping left is self-reinforcing, because, being known to Eve, it inclines her to keep left, thus strengthening Adam's warrant. But the antithesis has no trouble in proving that the same goes for any reason which Adam has for keeping right. The argument is rigorous and its conclusion absurd. Those who accept it must either limit the damage by snipping game theory off from the theory of action or console themselves with Hume's view that all our reasonings on matters of fact rest in the end on custom. Those who reject it must either repair the damage by technical amendments to game theory or dispute the philosophy of mind which Hume intended to ground a science of custom in action. I pin my own hopes on a theory of practical reason where reason alone can be a motive to the will. But this road too is prone to paradox, notably Kant's third antinomy of pure reason where freedom and causality conflict, and those who take it must expect to be ambushed by leprechauns somewhere along the way. Meanwhile, there is a more immediate problem for anyone who means to return home by car. With a lot of rational agents about, keeping left may be no safer than keeping right. Drive carefully!

On Why Philosophers Redefine their Subject

STUART BROWN

My title is intended to recall a well-known aphorism about philosophy, which runs something like this:

> When a clergyman loses his faith he abandons his calling. When a philosopher loses *his* he redefines his subject.

There is probably a correct version of this aphorism somewhere and an author to whose intentions what follows will do less than justice. I want to pick it up much as a composer might pick up a dimly remembered melody and I am going to develop it and produce my own variation on it. My topic is not centrally about loss of faith as generally understood, though it is centrally about the changing definitions of philosophy. My concern is with at least some of the reasons people have for doing philosophy and, in particular, about how their motives for doing philosophy connect with what philosophers think their subject is. My hope is that some light is thrown on this question by considering cases where people have changed their conception of philosophy—where, in other words, they have redefined their subject.

If I had to guess a rough date for the source of the aphorism with which I began, I would pick on late nineteenth or early twentieth century as the most likely. Much before then the problem of clergymen losing their faith would not be commonplace. On the other hand, the aphorism cannot be too recent since nowadays its point is somewhat blurred. At least to many nowadays it may no longer be obvious that a clergyman who loses his faith cannot just redefine his calling. The originator of the aphorism was taking it for granted that Christianity is something fixed and non-negotiable, so to speak, and that the calling of the clergy is derivatively so. It is just this that it is being claimed is not true of philosophy—which (by contrast) is represented as lacking a stable identity. Disillusioned philosophers can, unlike disillusioned clergymen, it is being suggested, redefine what it is they are supposed to be doing.

I take the aphorism to be blasé about clergymen but as earnest—indeed as saying a true word in jest—about the nature of philosophy. I take it to imply that there are motives for doing philosophy which are internal to one or other of its possible identities. When there no longer seems any point in pursuing philosophy in one way, the subject can be reconceived so that there is a point in doing it once more, only a different one.

I look later in this paper at how two philosophers—Russell and Wittgenstein—have redefined their subject. I thus consider three different conceptions of philosophy, including the conception of philosophy Russell was concerned to reject. My intention is to illustrate how, and suggest that philosophy is a large family of pursuits, variously though not all closely related to one another. There is, I want to suggest, a correspondingly large variety of motives people may have for engaging in philosophy.

But first some further preliminary remarks are called for to amplify what I am saying and to connect it with what might be claimed for other subjects than philosophy.

I

In the first place, I should say something about what is popularly understood as 'philosophy'. Outside the academic world, many have been impelled to do philosophy in the expectation that it will enable them to cope with the vicissitudes of human life. That has been part of the almost perennial appeal of Stoicism right down into our own century. And if an academic philosopher from the First World is unlikely to be motivated in doing philosophy nowadays by the desire to achieve an indifference to misfortune, this perception of philosophy is none the less deeply embedded in the language and in popular views of the subject. Taking a 'philosophical' attitude means remaining calm under adverse circumstances one cannot control.

That view of philosophy is sufficiently embedded in Western culture and in the English language that it naturally arouses expectations of the subject that professional philosophers nowadays would make no claim to fulfil. In this kind of way lay people who become students in publicly funded classes find philosophy is not what they were expecting. If they persist with their study of the subject it may be because, though their original motive is frustrated, they acquire a new one. They may thus come to accept a different definition of the subject from what was implicit in their earlier expectations. This process might be produced by an explanation by the teacher of why philosophy cannot do for them what they had originally hoped. In this way they might be led to a new conception of the subject through disillusionment with the conception they had before. But they may alternatively be offered no explanation and quietly drop their earlier views and expectations. In neither case do they redefine the subject themselves. They accept the redefinition someone else has offered them.

On Why Philosophers Redefine their Subject

From this it is apparent that the aphorism I quoted at the beginning does not apply to new students of the subject but to established practitioners. Indeed it is apparent that it can only apply to rather exceptional practitioners. Redefining one's subject does, after all, require very considerable sophistication. In so far as the aphorism is true at all, it is a truth about philosophers who are able and original enough to give their subject a new direction. Only a good philosopher could articulate a new definition of the subject and it is characteristic perhaps only of great philosophers that they are able to get their redefinitions sufficiently established to make their work a landmark in the history of the subject.

What I am saying of philosophy is, I suspect, true of the humanities in general, including some of the subjects classed as 'social sciences'. The identities of subjects in the humanities appear to go through phases of relative stability when orthodox views of their aims prevail. But it seems impossible to put their identities entirely beyond controversy. This seems to have to do with shifts in the reasons for doing the subject that are licensed by how the subject is conceived. In this respect I regard as fruitful the suggestion of some philosophers of the Frankfurt School that the identity of psychology or sociology becomes different when there is a different 'cognitive interest' in pursuing them.[1] The Frankfurt School were concerned to identify the limitations of a human science too closely modelled on the natural sciences. But the notion of a 'cognitive interest' could usefully be developed in relation to other subjects, like philosophy, where the motive for pursuing it was not to achieve control over our environment.

Of the more familiar humanities one could allude to the transformation of the subject known as Literature from literacy criticism with its 'humanistic' aims to cultural theory with its very different aims and identity. Again the History of Art used to be, at the hands of writers like Berenson, aimed at enhancing one's appreciation of great works of art. The amateur who said 'I don't know much about art but I know what I like' might have been encouraged with the thought that, if he learnt more about the subject, this would increase the range of works he could enjoy. It was part of the point of the subject as then conceived to cater for the higher pleasures of looking at paintings. But this aim has been repudiated by the professionals for some time. The first Professor of the History of Art at the Open University, Aaron Sharf, was fond of baffling his colleagues in other subjects by saying 'I know all about art but I don't know what I like.' I think the large number of students who take to this relatively new subject with enthusiasm secretly enjoy looking at paintings. But, academically at any rate, the History of Art is no

[1] See Apel (1979, 1980) and Habermas (1971).

more directed to producing that enjoyment than Military History is intended to make people enjoy fighting.

But, though periodic shifts of identity may be one of the distinguishing features of the humanities generally, it is something to which philosophy is particularly prone. Other subjects seem never to have more than two or three rival identities in contention at any given time. The choice in philosophy is much greater. Philosophy in most of its forms, moreover, equips its practitioners better to reflect on the nature of their discipline and, in some ways, even the nature of other disciplines, than a routine training in most other subjects. Dubiously perhaps, only philosophers claim to advance by announcing their methodologies first and promising results for later. More obviously to their credit, philosophers have historically played a leading part in the shaping of other disciplines, especially in psychology and the social sciences. In doing so they may in some cases have thought they were innovating within, say, moral philosophy, when we would say, from the standpoint of modern subject identities, they were actually contributing to the development of another subject. It may be that some of what we think of as branches and types of philosophy will become institutionalized as separate subjects.

As with other subjects, there are all sorts of motives for pursuing philosophy that are extraneous to the subject itself. It helps some towards a degree, others to make a living and still others to keep their minds active. But the existence of such motives gives little or no clue as to the nature of the subject. There are, on the other hand, motives for doing philosophy that do take us to the heart of the subject—those that are internal to how the subject is conceived. To take a fairly obvious example, in the tradition of analytical philosophy the desire to achieve clarity and indeed a particular kind of clarity is a motive licensed by that conception of the subject.

This point has a general consequence of some importance—namely that we do not necessarily need to have special access to biographical information in order to know what impelled a writer to do philosophy. We do not need to discover secret diaries of Spinoza, for example, to interpret his motives for doing philosophy. An interpretation of Spinoza's *Ethics* should already contain an answer. The answer will perhaps link the search for a right understanding of the world with a right attitude to it and a right conception of how human life should be lived. Spinoza did not invent this identity for philosophy but drew it from cultural resources available to him such as the Stoic tradition. His greatness as a philosopher rests perhaps on the fact that he re-established such an identity as possible for philosophy in a Modern (post-Cartesian) context. A mature understanding of philosophy can, I think, only be achieved by those who have visited such landmarks in the history of the subject as Spinoza's *Ethics* and entered into the conception of philosophy such works embody. No doubt they will conclude that we cannot achieve the kind of God's-eye-view of the world to which Spinoza aspired and perhaps they will think, in any case, that they would not be able to derive a right attitude to life from it. But, if we cannot achieve what Spinoza sought to achieve, it is worth our understanding why not—why philosophy, if we are to pursue it, must be different from what Spinoza took it to be.

I will make this point stronger by suggesting that we do not really understand what philosophy is unless and until we have come to terms with how it has been conceived in the past. For philosophy would not be what it now is apart from that past. We need to have worked through its past identities and perhaps even relive the disillusionment with what philosophy has been in the past to understand why philosophy cannot now be like that for us. But the past is not just a repository of errors. It is also a source of alternatives in philosophy that is one factor in the process of disillusionment and redefinition that, I am suggesting, is endemic to the subject. The process need have no end except, of course, that civilization will not go on for ever.

These are large claims to make and I make them at least partly to stir philosophers who assume that philosophy has finally arrived at its true identity from their dogmatic slumbers. It has been one of the assumptions of analytical philosophy, though earlier philosophers have been guilty of it too, that the true identity of the subject has at last been discovered in our own century. If this is true, the history of philosophy is a repository of error and confusion, a source of useful exercises for students but not in itself a valuable pursuit for real philosophers. If what I am saying here is right, on the contrary, the history of philosophy will be part of its essence, since it is in the nature of philosophy for its identity to change. Countering one dogma with another would in itself help to promote a suspense of judgment and thus an open mind on the subject in question. But I hope I can do better and offer some examples that illustrate the shifting identity of philosophy and at least provide some inductive support for the expectation that this identity will continue to change in the future.

II

Although I have failed to identify the author of the aphorism with which I began, my short list of possibles included Bertrand Russell. Whether or not he is the author, it seems to me that Russell most exactly fits the description of a philosopher who loses his faith and responds by redefining his subject. In other cases it is not strictly the loss of faith in the same sense as that in which it would be understood if applied to the clergy. In other cases it is more a matter of disillusionment with philosophy as one has understood it. This might be understood as analogous to a loss of religious faith. It might, for example, lead to a drop in commitment to the subject. But it need not relate to religion at all and in other cases I look at, such as Wittgenstein, it does not.

In Russell's case, however, the loss of religious faith and the philosophical disillusionment went hand in hand. For his acceptance of Idealism for a period in the 1890s helped him to cling on to a residual religious belief. He then accepted the conception of philosophy, as did others, which aroused the expectation that it would provide its practitioners with some of the benefits of religion. When he ceased to find Idealism credible he also gave up what religious belief he had left. Thus his loss of religious faith is internally connected to his quest for a new conception of philosophy. He rejected the religious impulse to philosophy entirely and, as I bring out, his redefinitions of philosophy are in large measure driven by his sense of the proper reasons for doing it.

Absolute Idealism was still the prevailing philosophy in the Cambridge of Russell's undergraduate days. Amongst the personal influences on him were McTaggart, Stout and Joachim, though he was also affected by his reading of others, such as Bradley. His own account stresses the comfort his acceptance of Idealism gave him:

> In this philosophy I found comfort for a time. . . . There was a curious pleasure in making oneself believe that time and space are unreal, that matter is an illusion, and that the world really consists of nothing but mind . . . (Clark, 1975, 45).

Comforting though he found such philosophical beliefs and the residually religious belief they helped to support, Russell was unable to retain his conviction in either. He reverted to Agnosticism. The hypothesis of an almighty First Cause seemed to him still to be a possible explanation of the Universe. But he no longer felt competent to assign any degree of probability to it. He evidently found this very distressing, complaining of the 'great pain' caused by his 'loss of certainty':

> To feel that the universe may be hurrying blindly towards all that is bad, that humanity may one day cease its progressive development and may continually lose all its fine qualities, that evolution has no necessarily progressive principle prompting it; these are thoughts which render life almost intolerable. (Russell, 1983, vol. i, 108.)

Russell's search for certainty continued to be a major factor in his philosophy. But later, as I bring out below, he came to hold more exacting views about the kind of certainty it was proper to look for in philosophy. For a while, however, he was eager to find any support for a comforting, optimistic, view of the universe and the part played in it by human life. This is the context in which we should understand that apparently comic episode when Russell came to see, or thought he had come to see, that one of the traditional arguments for the existence of God was, after all, valid:

> I remember the precise moment, one day in 1894, as I was walking along Trinity Lane, when I saw in a flash (or thought I saw) that the ontological argument is valid. I had gone out to buy a tin of tobacco: on my way back, I suddenly threw it up in the air, and exclaimed as I caught it: 'Great God in boots! the ontological argument is valid.' (Russell, 1963, 10)

By the end of 1897 Russell had come to the view that it was improper to seek the kind of assurance and comfort that Idealist philosophy had previously seemed to offer. Moore had wanted him to write a paper for the select Cambridge discussion society known as the Apostles. The suggested topic was heredity. But Russell was not able to write on that topic at such short notice. Instead he wrote a paper on a subject which had been pre-occupying him more. This was a radical criticism of Idealism. The central point he wished to make against Idealism in this paper was that, as he put it, 'for all purposes which are not purely intellectual, the world of Appearance is the real world' (Russell, 1983, vol. i, 105). To mark his protest against the Idealist division between the world of appearance and the real world he called his paper 'Seems, Madam? Nay, It Is'. He told Moore he was particularly concerned to oppose 'McTaggart's notion of getting religion out of Philosophy' and it is clear from the paper itself that he meant by this that philosophy should not be a source of comfort.

The paper began with these words:

> Philosophy, in the days when it was fat and prosperous, claimed to perform for its votaries, a variety of the most important services. It offered them comfort in adversity, explanation in intellectual difficulty, and guidance in moral perplexity . . . But those happy days are past . . . (Russell, 1983, vol. i, 106)

Russell suggested that people by that time looked to Science rather than to Philosophy for the resolution of their intellectual difficulties. Apart from 'a few exceptional questions' Philosophy no longer made claims in this area and the claims it did make were 'regarded by most people as a remnant of the dark ages'. As for moral perplexity, he pointed to the fact that the leading philosophers of the time—McTaggart and Bradley—had abandoned the traditional claims of philosophy to offer guidance of the kind sought. This left 'the power of comfort and consolation' which was 'still supposed by McTaggart to belong to philosophy'.

Russell linked this supposed power of philosophy to comfort and console with the thought, encouraged by Idealism, that the impulse to Philosophy might be similar to the impulse to religion, as though Philosophy should aim to achieve something like the beatific vision. He quotes Bradley as evidence of the desire of the Idealists to get religion out of Philosophy:

> Some in one way, some in another, we seem to touch and have communion with what is beyond the visible world. In various manners we find something higher, which both supports and humbles, both chastens and supports us. And, with certain persons, the intellectual effort to understand the Universe is a principal way of thus experiencing the Deity . . . And this appears to be another reason for some persons pursuing the study of ultimate truth. (Russell, 1983, vol. i, 110)

Russell was no longer, by this stage, much inclined to believe that ultimate truth lay in the direction sought by Bradley. He even doubted whether it would be desirable if it did. Fact and value were, at all events, quite distinct. The emotional value of an experience was something quite separate from the degree of truth that attaches to it. As to truth he thought that there was such a wide gulf fixed between Appearance and Reality that we had no reason to believe that some experiences were closer than others 'to the perfect experience of Reality'.

The conclusion of Russell's paper was that engaging in metaphysics in order to derive comfort and consolation was the source of 'a good deal of fallacious reasoning and intellectual dishonesty' (Russell, 1983 vol. i, 111). He had by now repudiated his own earlier impulse to philosophy, what he described as hoping to find 'religious satisfaction' in it. Instead he proposed that the only proper motive for doing metaphysics was the same as that which justifies the practice of science, namely, intellectual curiosity.

Some years later, in a lecture 'On Scientific Method in Philosophy', Russell returned to a simlar theme. He divided philosophers into those whose motives for doing philosophy were primarily religious and ethical and those whose motives were primarily scientific. In the first category he placed Plato, Spinoza and Hegel, and in the second he placed Leibniz, Locke, and Hume. In this 1914 lecture he argued that philosophy should 'draw its inspiration' from science rather than ethics and religion (Russell, 1953, 96).

Russell thought that those who had sought to practise a scientific philosophy had tended in the past to attach too much importance to the often temporary results of empirical investigation. He thought philosophy should be *a priori* and that its propositions ought not to be provable or disprovable by scientific evidence. He thought also that philosophy should be concerned, unlike the special sciences, with matters of great generality. A scientific philosophy would distinguish itself from traditional philosophy both by the centrality of logic and by its willingness to put forward tentative conclusions. Logical analysis showed, according to Russell, how much of traditional metaphysics was mistaken. Thus the Idealists were wrong in supposing that metaphysics could make pronouncements about reality as a whole. For, according to Russell, there are no propositions of which the universe is the 'subject', hence 'there is no such thing as "the universe"' (Russell, 1953, 107). Logic is not, however, the whole of philosophy. Russell believed, on the contrary, in a piecemeal metaphysics in which conclusions of a general sort were put forward, such as that sense data are 'part of the actual substance of the universe' (Russell, 1953, 170). Russell thought this was something that had to be supposed in order to account for the fact that physics was empirically verifiable.

An interesting feature of this conception of a scientific philosophy is that it seems to outlaw the demand for certainty. Such a demand may be proper enough in mathematics. But a scientific philosophy would need to share with the sciences a certain hypothetical character:

> A scientific philosophy such as I wish to recommend will be piecemeal and tentative like other sciences; above all, it will be able to invent hypotheses which, even if they are not wholly true, will yet remain fruitful after the necessary corrections have been made. This possibility of successive approximations to the truth, is more than anything else, the source of the triumphs of science, and to transfer this possibility to philosophy is to ensure a progress in method whose importance it would be almost impossible to exaggerate (Russell, 1953, 109).

Russell said these words in 1914. And yet, in spite of the near impossibility he claimed of exaggerating their importance, it does not entirely fit either with his own practice or with his other statements of the new 'scientific method of philosophy' he wished to recommend. On the contrary, Russell himself seems to make certainty a goal in philosophy—a goal he does not imagine can be achieved by the empirical sciences. In another paper, also written in 1914, his emphasis is not on encouraging but eliminating the hypothetical scientific philosophy. The purpose of doing this is to avoid an element of needless doubt so often introduced in various branches of philosophy when inferred entities are postulated. For instance, in traditional epistemology material substances were often presented as inferred entities. What we know directly in experience are ideas, or in more modern terms sensedata, and philosophers inferred the existence of material substances as causes of these ideas or sense-data. But, in doing so, these philosophers opened the door to questions about whether such material substances really existed or not.

Russell was familiar with analogous problems in the philosophy of mathematics relating, for instance, to irrational numbers and classes. The solution to such problems, which avoided the postulation of uncertain entities, was to construct the unknown entities out of known ones. This he claimed was an application of Occam's Razor:

> . . . by the principle of Occam's Razor, if the class of appearances will fulfil the purposes for the sake of which the thing was invented by the prehistoric metaphysicians to whom common sense is due, economy demands that we should identify the thing with the class of its appearances. It is not necessary to *deny* a substance or substratum underlying those appearances; it is merely expedient to abstain from asserting this unnecessary entity . . . (Russell, 1953, 148).

Occam's Razor, Russell went on to claim, was 'the supreme maxim in scientific philosophising'. Its virtue was that it eliminated possible sources of error. Now Russell went on to admit that he did not see how inferred entities could be avoided entirely. He admitted there were sensibilia, for example, in places where there were no minds (Russell, 1953, 150). In this way he sought to reconcile the tension between a view of philosophy which puts scepticism at the centre and a view that favours large explanatory hypotheses. The first view implies that science is centrally concerned with avoiding mistakes, with proving things in the sense of establishing truths beyond doubt. The second view of science accepts the risk of error and implies a view of metaphysics as concerned with offering provisional explanations that may be replaced in due course with others that are closer to the truth.

The contrast between these two views brings out what may be a tension in what Russell looked for from philosophy. The second view is the one most consistent with the view that philosophy, like science, satisfies curiosity. We may be curious to know whether the much discussed tree in the remote Canadian forest where no human has been makes a sound when it crashes to the earth. Russell's answer to this speculative question is 'Yes'. But he also seems to have continued to be driven by a desire for certainty that was never likely to be satisfied by such speculation. Here he drew his inspiration more from mathematics.

When Russell rejected Idealism he did not just reject a theory but also a conception of philosophy and a reason for doing it—doing it to derive comfort, support or anything like the benefits of religion. It is natural enough that he should have looked to science to inspire a new identity for the subject. But he seems to have been caught between a mathematics-led and an empirical-science-led view of what philosophy should be and what is the point of our doing it. Perhaps this is why, though Russell has been hugely influential in providing tools for the critique of traditional philosophy, hardly anyone has attempted to adopt his conception of the subject as contained in his redefinitions. Russell's work represents a crisis in the identity of philosophy in which it began to seem clear that philosophy could not be as envisaged by the Hegelians though it was not clear exactly what it could be. Others, independently of Russell, had the thought that philosophy ought to become 'scientific'. This was true of the Vienna Circle, some of whose members were indebted to Russell's critique of traditional philosophy. But the logical positivists had a distinctive view as to what a scientific philosophy would be like.

III

The crisis of subject identity which is noticeable in Russell's writings is reflected also in the writings of many other twentieth-century philosophers. Though some have been content to retain or revive older conceptions of the subject there is a fair degree of consensus that philosophy cannot now be what it has traditionally been. There is, for instance, a fair degree of consensus that it cannot continue to promise its novitiates much by way of comfort and guidance through life. Like Russell, many twentieth-century philosophers have looked to science for hints of what philosophy should be like. Almost invariably, philosophers nowadays would seek to explain what they think philosophy is by relating it to science, even if they thought the first point to make about philosophy was that it was not a science. This is true even of Wittgenstein, who (in his later writings) rejected the idea of a scientific philosophy and came to regard the pre-occupation of philosophers with the method of science as a symptom of a deep-seated cultural malaise.

I intend to say a little about Wittgenstein and the new identity he proposed for philosophy in his later writings since his redefinition of the subject is quite different from Russell's and is in some respects entirely opposed to it. As it happens my own impulse to the subject was for a considerable time affected by what I would now agree was this cultural malaise against which the later Wittgenstein wrote. I do not propose to attempt a summary account of Wittgenstein's *Tractatus Logico-Philosophicus* or of its relations to the later writings. Instead, since I believe I was myself imbued with this cultural malaise in my earlier impulse to philosophy, I can fulfil part of the brief to the lecturers in this series by making some remarks about my own early interest in the subject.

Stuart Brown

My first study of a real work of philosophy was in a school Greek class, where we struggled with Plato in the original language. I enjoyed these classes in spite of not finding Greek easy. Plato's writings, if I remember correctly, attracted me mostly because they seemed to be about a deep and worthwhile subject, one that penetrated to the real, underlying, nature of things. Philosophy, if it addressed such questions as 'What is truth?', 'What is courage?' 'What is beauty?', and so on, was clearly a deep subject. But it was not the only deep subject, and I am not sure that I had a primordial impulse to essentialist metaphysics rather than to any of a range of subjects. On the contrary, I think could easily have been drawn into one of the other deep subjects had it been presented to me in the right way at the right time. I cannot say whether I would then have included physics as a deep subject, though, of course, I should have done. I had earlier been drawn by the deep, reductive, explanatory, character of Freud's writings but was quickly put off the study of University Psychology. At the time I was very interested in the question whether, and if so how, it was possible to be religious in the modern (secular) world and read avidly on both sides of that question. This reading included philosophical and theological figures such as Feuerbach, Bultmann and Tillich but also included writers who would better be classed as sociological.

University philosophy at St Andrews in the late 1950s did not, on the whole, cater to my desire to study a deep subject but I was encouraged to persevere with it partly by reasonably good class results and because it was held to be a suitable preparation for someone intending (as I was then) to go on to the postgraduate B.D. degree. I and my contemporaries were exposed by the variety of staff to a wide spectrum of British philosophy, some of it distinctly pre-War but with a strong emphasis on analytical or linguistic philosophy.[2] My enthusiasm at this stage was captured by logic and by an essentialist programme of logical analysis. We had, of course, heard of Wittgenstein and, to their credit, the Department responded to our request to present us with a course on Wittgenstein—which must, I suppose, have been one of the first of its kind.

We struggled through the newly published *Blue and Brown Books*. My own understanding of what Wittgenstein was trying to say was limited. But I did acquire some sense that his attacks on essentialism, reductionism and deep explanation were directed against an impulse to

[2] Quite contrary to a common stereotype of Scottish University Philosophy of that time—see, e.g., Passmore, (1968) p. 572, n.19—we learnt nothing of Hegel or that tradition of Idealism, apart from the coherence theory of truth as propounded by Joachim, which was introduced to us as one of several theories of truth.

the subject that I recognized in myself. Nor was this a coincidence. In retrospect it was apparent to me that the later writings of Wittgenstein would not have had the impact they had unless the impulse to essentialism, as Wittgenstein himself seems to have recognized, had become well-established in the intellectual culture of the West. I had probably absorbed this more from my general reading than from my formal studies.

The disease of the culture involved an excessive pre-occupation with the thought-patterns and methods of the natural sciences which permeated philosophy. 'Philosophers', Wittgenstein wrote, 'constantly see the method of science before their eyes, and are irresistably tempted to ask and answer questions in the way science does. This tendency is the real source of metaphysics, and leads the philosopher into complete darkness' (Wittgenstein, 1958, 18). The impulse to metaphysics, according to this view, consists in a 'craving for generality', wanting to explain appearances in terms of something hidden. This impulse was seen by Wittgenstein as one philosophers like Russell and, in some measure,[3] the author of the *Tractatus* shared with certain theorists like Freud and J. G. Frazer, Frege and William James. Wittgenstein did not hold that philosophers are a group of culturally marginal oddities who first inculcate intellectual diseases and then set themselves up to cure them. Intellectual malaise is all around us, according to Wittgenstein. This seems to be the point of one of his remarks on the foundations of mathematics: 'If in the midst of life we are in death, so in sanity we are surrounded by madness' (Wittgenstein, 1956, 157). The fault of philosophers was to be, in their own way, part of the madness and carriers of the disease instead of being bastions of sanity who are able to offer a cure.

The later philosophy of Wittgenstein became established as an orthodoxy amongst many philosophers of my generation. Most of us, however, found it both too new and too difficult for us wholly to digest its implications for the practice of the analytical or linguistic philosophy in which we had been trained. We thus tended to combine an acceptance of some of the central Wittgensteinian ideas, like the view of meaning and the rejection of private languages, with practices which, though not explicitly discussed by Wittgenstein, did not fit with a complete acceptance of his way of thinking. I continued to work on some of what Wittgenstein called the 'super-concepts' of philosophy—

---

[3] As Anthony Palmer suggests elsewhere in this volume, the relation between the earlier and later Wittgenstein is a complex one. Sometimes the later views are already anticipated in the earlier writings. My suggestion in this paper is that the converse is also true, that views more consonant with the earlier period are to be found residually in the later.

like knowledge and belief—as if they had an essence which conceptual analysis might uncover. Eventually I came to the view that programmes of conceptual analysis in which I had participated were based upon a residual essentialism.

Having thus arrived at a sensitivity to residual essentialism, it gradually became clear to me that Wittgenstein himself was not entirely free from it. No one was entirely free of the craving for generality and from any residual essentialism would be tempted into the kind of general statement about the nature of philosophy to which Wittgenstein frequently succumbed, such as: 'Philosophy is the battle against the bewitchment of the intellect by means of language' (Wittgenstein, 1953, i, 109). Such redefinitions of the subject are directed in part to correcting his own earlier conception of the subject. But since, in some respects, he took himself to have shared that earlier conception of the subject with Plato, Augustine and others, he was also claiming that the subject he now professed was the legitimate heir of the subject traditionally known as philosophy.[4] To that extent his redefinition involves not merely a proposal of one way of usefully pursuing the subject. It also involves some generalization about what philosophy has been and perhaps about what it can be. In both these respects it seems to fall into essentialism.

It seems that Wittgenstein's earlier interest in philosophy continued to dictate, in some measure, his later conception of the subject. He sought, in the *Tractatus*, to elucidate the essence of language through an account of the nature of the proposition. He came to see the error of this view and to diagnose it as the result of a desire for a quasi-scientific account of something underlying language that somehow explains how it is possible. It is this craving for generality, for the kind of account that science gives in an area where no such account can help us, that Wittgenstein came to see as the root of his own earlier mistakes. But his redefinition of philosophy appears to limit the scope of philosophy to a therapy for the problems that essentialism gives rise to. Enormously powerful though Wittgenstein's vision was and indeed partly because it was so powerful, it was limited by the nature of his own pre-occupation with providing a corrective to essentialism. The later Wittgenstein is still gripped by the essentialist craving for generality about philosophy and the *Philosophical Investigations* contains many statements that, though insightful, are ultimately vitiated in the same way and for the same reason Wittgenstein's own earlier statements about the essence of

---

[4] G. E. Moore took notes on Wittgenstein's lectures in the early 1930s when Wittgenstein explicitly discussed the question of how far he was doing a 'new subject' and how far it was the successor to traditional philosophy. See 'Wittgenstein's Lectures in 1930–33', *Mind,* Vol. LXIV, 1955, Section (H).

language.[5] The therapeutic view of philosophy, when applied to itself, leads beyond itself. For it leads to a recognition that not all philosophy involves the kinds of cramp that are characteristic of essentialist impulses to the subject. Doing philosophy is not a single activity with an essence but a family of loosely related activities.

These points may be seen more clearly through a consideration of the alternative Wittgenstein had to offer to essentialist explanations. He did not simply aim to put a block on seeking any understanding in philosophy. He had an alternative view about the kind of understanding that ought to be looked for. He did not want simply to outlaw wrong motives for pursuing philosophy. Rather, at least implicitly, he sought to transform these into motives that were sanctioned by his new conception of the subject. Russell, the logical positivists and the author of the *Tractatus* were not merely reproved for trying to do scientific philosophy and for wrongly seeking to replicate scientific features that are out of place in philosophy. The impulse to seek one kind of (wrong) understanding was rather to be reformed into an impulse to another (right) understanding.

Central to his positive account of the kind of understanding that ought to be sought in philosophy are phrases like 'clear view' and a phrase usually translated as 'perspicuous representation'.[6] Getting the understanding that philosophy can offer, according to Wittgenstein, is a matter of getting a certain kind of overview. This he thought was to be achieved, not by making new discoveries, but by putting things that we already know into the right arrangement, so that we can move easily from one to another, knowing our way about. To take a simple example, if we are puzzled that such a variety of human activities are all called 'games', we should not look for an underlying essence or common feature shared by everything we called a 'game.' We should not ask—to introduce my own examples—what war games have in common with playing patience with oneself. Rather we should look at a range of examples and try to order them in such a way that it is clear how they all belong in the same family. This means looking, according to Wittgenstein, for intermediate cases. So perhaps we might see better how playing war games and playing patience with oneself are connected with one another by placing between them the game of chess. Chess shares with war games the relevance of strategy and indeed can even be thought of as a metaphor for war, with pawns being captured or killed, and so on. On the other hand, people do play chess with themselves. So chess is an intermediate case that allows us to move from one kind of game to another which seems, at first, to be strangely different.

[5] See, for instance, Wittgenstein (1953), i, 121–133.
[6] See, for instance, Wittgenstein (1953), i, 122.

When Wittgenstein wrote that the task of philosophy was to assemble reminders he seems to have had making such an arrangement of familiar facts in mind. In one sense he denied that it was in any way right to look for an understanding from philosophy. That is what he was rejecting when he said that in philosophy we should do away with all explanation and description alone should take its place. But there is also an understanding of sorts that is produced by offering what he called a 'perspicious representation.' When he ceased to believe in the quest for a quasi-scientific understanding in philosophy, Wittgenstein not only redefined the subject but redefined the understanding that philosophy should aim to produce. His new conception of philosophy might aptly be called a humanistic one because of his oppostion to scientistic conceptions of philosophy but also because of the cultural critique that was integral to his project.

IV

These insights can fruitfully be applied to some questions that are raised by this series. There is not a single impulse to philosophy, I am suggesting, neither is there a single coherent pursuit that is uniquely entitled to the privilege of being called 'philosophical'. There are, as we have seen, conceptions of philosophy that are quasi-religious as in Absolute Idealism, quasi-scientific as in Russell and others or humanistic, as embraced by Wittgenstein and others.

Wittgenstein, as I have already observed, remained essentialist about philosophy. In this respect he was a surprisingly traditional philosopher. But the objections to essentialism *about* philosophy are similar to those it was part of Wittgenstein's achievement to articulate about essentialism *in* philosophy. The craving for generality and neglect of differences gives rise to puzzlement about and distortion of cases which do not obviously fit and which have not carefully been considered. Essentialist views of philosophy often do offer some insight. The problems arise because of their generality. Thus Wittgenstein's philosophy does engage in a profound way with some past philosophy, such as that of Plato. But—not surprisingly, given Wittgenstein's lack of background in the history of the subject—it fails to engage with a good deal of past philosophy.

It fails to engage, for example, with the philosophy of J. S. Mill. Mill's projects of attempting to reconcile deeply ingrained beliefs with relatively new but apparently well authorized opinions do not commit him to essentialism. These projects are open to criticism no doubt. But they seem to survive twentieth-century critiques of past philosophy. The identity Mill gave to philosophy is different again. Although it is a common enough motive for doing philosophy, the desire to achieve consistency in one's beliefs is not one that has been previously mentioned in this lecture.

Whatever the explanation for Wittgenstein's essentialism about philosophy, his critique of essentialism in philosophy suggests a quite different view—namely that philosophy is a family of activities more or less closely related to one another and done for reasons that are sometimes closely and sometimes only remotely related to one another. What I am suggesting that what is recognizable as philosophy is a family of pursuits and that what Wittgenstein had to say about games and family resemblances is true of philosophy itself.

To understand what philosophy is and what people look for from it we need to remind ourselves how various this family is. We may need to find intermediate cases in order to understand how two pursuits can both be called 'engaging in philosophy'. We may of course want to give preference to some of these over others. We may even come to the conclusion that some of these pursuits are basically flawed and largely valueless. I do not wish to deny that or to suggest that we can simply decide to take up Absolute Idealism as if there were no real difficulty in our way. At the same time the objections of Russell and others to that style of philosophy do not place a simple full stop after that tradition. It remains a resource on which some will draw much and others hardly at all. None the less there is some truth in the idea that philosophy progresses by redefinitions and that it never returns to exactly the same place.

On the whole I have given examples of conceptions of philosophy that have been in competition with one another and between which there has been a rational debate. So, if I do not wish to claim that there is a single correct conception of philosophy I am not saying either that anything goes. Being willing to take a fairly liberal view of the admissible motives for pursuing philosophy is consistent with recognizing the difficulties in the way of philosophy fulfilling the hopes that some people place in it. Part of the point of studying the history of philosophy is for us to be aware of what options are already established within the practice of the subject. We may not, in the end, think they are options for us. But that does not mean that we have not learnt something of philosophical value in the process. On the contrary it is a poor philosophical education that does not develop a sense of what philosophy can and cannot do. Since, however, this is not a cut and dried matter and little remains beyond controversy, there is no substitute for doing it the hard way. That means not closing off the options by a doctrinaire presentation of one conception of philosophy as if it were the only one with a legitimate claim to the title. It means allowing that, as philosophy itself can take many forms, so there are many diverse impulses to pursuing it.

Some Philosophers I Have Not Known

FREDERIC RAPHAEL

We have the idea that philosophy is an unemotional way of considering human knowledge and testing its reliable logics. Is it not an essentially impersonal attempt to discover abiding truths and their orderly, more or less necessary, connection? The philosophers we are incited to respect are those whose logic is least susceptible to charges of idiosyncrasy and whose arguments are clean of rhetoric. When Russell remarked 'the worse the logic, the more interesting the results,' was he not warning us against looking to him for entertaining theories or pyrotechnic display? Flashiness, we were intended to gather, is not a happy method in philosophy; the brightest are those who are not ashamed to be dull; our passion is best reserved for the dispassionate. Roughly speaking, one gathers, all philosophical objects are colourless.

The philosophers most commonly admired in the British tradition are, unsurprisingly, those whose practice mirrors what the British like to think of as their own sensible and typically unassuming qualities: the absence of what Byron called 'enthusy-musy' is the happiest warrant of worth. David Hume's lack of credulity in the prospect of—and certainly the arguments for—religious salvation, makes him an exemplary figure among those who, while honouring a trenchant prose style, are wary of dogma and averse to mystification. Dr Johnson may have accused Hume of writing like a Frenchman, but Johnson had not read Sartre or Pierre Boutang, say, whose so-called philosophy is, for the most part, indistinguishable from exhortation or autobiography, not to say rant.

On the British side of the channel, we attribute a certain nobility to those who make it their calling deliberately to saw the branches on which they might otherwise hold head-in-the-cloudsy sway. Russell's centrality, in the present century, at least until the advent of Wittgenstein, owes something to the paradox of an aristocrat who disclaimed aristocracy, while never quite renouncing its usefulness in intimidating those who did not share his low opinion of it. Russell was a leveller who made a point of being seen to have come a long way down the mountain in order to be at one with the common man. 'Tommy loves a Lord' said Byron, sarcastically, of Thomas Moore, as if he himself did not. How sweet are grandees who elect not to be grand with us!

Frederic Raphael

When he allotted a whole chapter in his *History of Western Philosophy* (Russell, 1948) to Byron, we can scarcely doubt that Russell was making both claims and allowances. He was asserting an affinity between himself and that other trouble-making aristocrat whose moral versatility it would not be unglamorous to associate with his own, while also, of course, allowing that a man whose thoughts were scarcely logical, and were certainly never expressed in any systematic sense, could—by his influence at least—be recruited to the philosophical pantheon, even if, like Monsieur Jourdain in more prosaic circumstances, he did his philosophy without ever being conscious of the fact. Russell was also, I think, and more seriously, alerting us to the importance—even to a supposedly 'logical' and 'scientific' discipline—of the general social and artistic climate, to which a popular poet much more than a cloistered logician is likely to contribute, a fact which Plato acknowledged (much less philosophically than Russell) with regard both to Homer and to Aeschylus, whose influence he deplored. Scepticism and the pursuit of 'liberty', the emancipation of philosophy from theology, owe much to Byronic impudence, even if he lisped in numbers rather than making any conscious contribution to the foundations of mathematics.

Russell shows but does not quite state that, while philosophy may indeed aspire to be an impersonal, even abstract activity, analogous to mathematics by virtue of its chaste renunciation of rhetoric and its systematic publicity, it is often flavoured with personal considerations and prejudices and favoritisms which logic may ignore but practice and style confirm. My amateur purpose here is, in part at least, to consider the kinds of elective or unconscious affinities which draw us to one philosopher and alienate us from another, even though we prefer to suppose that our choices have been made on logical grounds, based almost entirely on the quality of arguments advanced or conclusions unarguably reached, rather than on account of more shifty congenialities, such as Bertrand championing Byron, or Ayer Voltaire. I intend to hint at the sorts of reasons which make philosophy attractive to us, despite and because of its aridities or difficulties and despite or because of its failure or inability to deliver ultimate answers to ultimate questions. Despite our sceptical selves and the modesty of at least certain practitioners, the philosopher's stone is something we still dream of discovering in some secret compartment of our chosen champion's luggage, however modest his case.

By 'systematic publicity' I mean simply that unlike poetry or painting, in which privacy privileges the artist to do as he or she pleases, philosophy passes for a common, accessible enterprise where one philosopher may legitimately question the line taken by another; pleasure is not a principle here nor creativity a password. Anything may be challenged, however fancy the brushwork. Logical errors are not a matter of opinion: they are demonstrable, as errors in poetic expression are not. One may wince at a man's rhyme, but one cannot in honour provide an indubitable correction. Plays may have arguments, but they are not right or wrong. The worst daub in the world cannot be refuted. Nietzsche said, 'You say there can be no argument about matters of taste? All life is an argument about matters of taste!' Philosophy and life, in that event, should be studied in different departments.

In the British tradition which was so plausibly propounded at Cambridge, not least by my old supervisor Renford Bambrough, the editor of *Philosophy*, philosophy is not a form of personal expression. 'Mere autobiography' was the standard dismissive formula for statements beginning, 'I sincerely believe' or 'I have always felt'. Intimate convictions do not override an error nor does a famous signature validate a worthless argument. In philosophy, there may be genius, but there is no privilege. The most eminent contemporary or dead pundit may be challenged, and corrected, by a neophyte. What philosophers do is, so the cant argues, a sort of science, perhaps a godless theology, although it no longer lays claim to queendom. Even in the domestic service to which A. J. Ayer once sought to approximate it, philosophy is a discipline whose recruits seek to dispel the dust of centuries and to create a clean, good place in which arguments may be marshalled and their advocates march in reasonable step. Investigation, not speculation, and the evaluation of evidence, not the fervours of belief, were the best means of creating a world of co-operative intelligence which would allow us to banish superstition and band together in the common pursuit of valid methods, rather than of some ultimate Truth. Yet how rare collaboration and how common jealousy is among philosophers! Russell and Whitehead formed the only significant partnership of which I can think.

To speak of a common pursuit is, of course, to allude to what Frank Leavis imagined that literary criticism could or should be. Luckily, this is not the place to discuss whether there can ever be objective aesthetic standards, or whether to assert or deny that objectivity is anything but an exercise in misapplied zeal (it is not), but it certainly seems more plausible to think that philosophers can reason together than that critics can prove that Conrad is better than H. G. Wells. It is more incontrovertible, if I can be permitted such a phrase, that an argument is flawed, if it is, than that (as Vladimir Nabokov insisted) Wells is better than Conrad or, as Leavis did, that Conrad trumps Wells. Philosophy *is* critical, where art can never wholly be, despite the Leavisite presumptuousness which sought to institute a sort of high court of discriminating taste, in which *ex cathedra* rankings would be, as it were, contingently necessary. Leavis could never quite accept a secondary role, although art always precedes what is said about it: as Descartes pointed out, the ivy cannot rise higher than the tree. Leavis's affectations of intimacy with Wittgenstein, to which Ray Monk alludes in his excellent recent biography, suggest how keenly a literary critic can long to be on equal terms with, so to say, the senior service. Similarly, but by no means identically, when Professor Jerome McCann analogises Byron's discursive method in *Don Juan* with Wittgenstein's in *Philosophical Investigations,* we can guess at a desire to dignify the one by reference to the other, as we can at a personal pantheon in which the two utterly different men feature in the same team. Philosophy still dignifies.

The curiosity is that we are constantly piqued by the question of what sort of thing it is. If philosophy is an art, it systematically denies that association, except in raffish cases which, on the whole, do not command respect; if it is a science, then what does it analyse or discover? We do not need to have been subtle students to remember the later Wittgenstein's somehow comforting, as well as forbidding, notion that it has no specific subject matter and that it leaves everything as it is. On this reading, the philosopher becomes a sort of intellectual unsecret policeman, ceaselessly, and selflessly, on the prowl for logical infringements and, if he belongs to the flying squad, outbreaks of metaphysical hooliganism. Such a philosopher is on the beat to detect people pretending to be philosophers in the freebooting manner of those who, with pious phrases, peddle pie in the sky. There is nothing disreputable in the prevention of fraud (nor need one have something to sell of one's own in order to denounce the fraudulence of others), yet this modest view of the philosopher—as a journeyman rather than a pundit, to use Ayer's famously trenchant dichotomy—does little to explain why we attach such importance to finding a congenial or cogent philosophy, or why—despite delusive infatuations or abrupt disillusion—we are disposed, if we are, to take philosophy seriously, indeed—at least in unvexed moments—to regard its study as the very instance of human seriousness.

Philosophy, at least in the tradition which my generation took to be normative, sought to discourage those who looked to it for metaphysical information, whether about the Ultimate Nature of the Real or about the right way to conduct one's life. Ontology could never be a voyage to the essence of Being; ethics could never tell you what to do. The closing of departments dear to continental philosophers testified to the kind of vindictive modesty to which British practitioners were much disposed in the 1950s. Yet the subject retained the lineaments of the majesty from which it sought to abdicate. Nor did philosophers like Ayer and Russell, his paragon, enact the housekeeper's role with any convincingly meek abrogation of upstairs ambitions. I have no polemic purpose in mentioning this; on the contrary, my interest in both men, and in others I shall mention, almost certainly depends on my subjective suspicion—indistinguishable from hope —that they did not mean what they were saying, or denying. A certain duplicity, which has nothing to do with not telling the truth, seems to me to have been essential to the empressing zeal which they, like anyone who bothers to spend his life in argument, undoubtedly harboured and without which they would scarcely have set to sea or assembled a crew. While denying any divine right to command, they were still captains under the god they questioned.

Since I have called this lecture 'Some philosophers I have not known', it is perhaps time for me to give some uncoy indication of why I chose the title and where I mean to go with it. If my preamble was meant to tease, but not to mystify, we are now far enough along my rambling route for its direction and destination at least to be indicated. The title itself is, I hope and fear, at once modest and mystifying; it is both personal and impersonal; it is clear and obscure. In this sense, it parodies the titles which philosophers themselves often elect to give to their papers. A close reader might remark that, if there is an element of self-effacing egotism in the phrase 'I have not known', there is also selective deference in speaking of 'Some philosophers': without affecting to belong to their league, I am, after all, daring to nominate my team.

Part of the purpose of my title is to draw ironic attention to the modern fetish for the biographical treatment of those who, like at least some artists and philosophers, have often gone to considerable lengths to make it clear that they wish to be judged by their work and not by its motivation or provenance. These wishes, one can quite plausibly claim, do not become commands merely by being formulated; philosophy itself, with its fetish for analytic procedures, could be accused of sanctioning that unpacking, to use Gilbert Ryle's term, which leads us to investigate psychological no less than logical structures and links. Yet the reduction of a man's ideas to the possible reasons or predispositions for them is an inadmissible operation in logic, however toothsome it may sometimes be in serialized practice. The fetishism of biographical facts can become ludicrous or prurient.

A man wrote to me recently to say that he had known Wittgenstein in wartime Newcastle, where, it seems, they both frequented the same public lavatories. There is, I daresay, no scandal in that, although my correspondent must have thought that he was breaking hot news; what made his letter so comic was that he imagined that this banality should be communicated to some central authority where, like a piece of a lapsed mosaic, it might add a fleck of crucial colour to a fuller picture of Wittgenstein. I replied that what interested me about Wittgenstein was not what he did or did not do in public lavatories, which was, I supposed, what any number of people did in those days and nights. Such high-mindedness was not, perhaps, what I might have displayed if the letter had offered details about T. S. Eliot's hitherto unknown naughty moments with a couple of leathered Fascists in the 1930s, but there it was: my idea of Wittgenstein denied interest in the kind of little-did-we-know beans which W. W. Bartley III was the first to spill. Since Eliot is, I confess, someone against whom I have some animus—being one of the jews he thought underneath the lot—I cannot deny (although I might hope) that I should be in the market for dirt on him, whereas since Wittgenstein has no demonic place in my personal bestiary I prefer to consider his supposedly aberrant behaviour *sub specie aeternitatis,* sub-section *nihil humanum a me alienum puto,* by which time it has become smaller than small potatoes.

The mention of Gilbert Ryle prompts me to remember an occasion when he came to lecture in Cambridge, soon after the publication of *The Concept of Mind* (Ryle, 1949) made his way of talking memorable enough for 'Category Mistakes' to remain a part of my vocabulary whenever intellectual special forces must be summoned to the aid of the civil tongue. Ryle, for those who never saw or heard him, was a rather brave, grave man whose light was most comfortable under a bushel. He would be irked if I told you of an instance I happen to have been told about when he procured a fellowship for a man of whom he disapproved, because his disapproval of injustice was greater. When I attended his visiting celebrity lecture, I saw only a famous don and a dry stick. He treated us to a rather severe disquisition in which that old truth-functional double-act 'p' and 'q' were soon on the stage. Ryle, whose face was straight to the point of rectilinearity, was considering an instance where p and q ceased to have mutually exclusive characteristics and veered towards each other, so to speak. The problem of definition, its place and use in philosophy, was much in the air (John Wisdom, affecting exasperation in one of his early morning lectures, suggested to some persistent tourist that we define 'good' as 'anything that adds up to an even number—if you think that would help!'). Ryle's examination of blurred areas, where p seemed tinged with q, and q with p, led him to speak, without a trace of unseriousness, of the q-ness of p and, by contrast, of the p-ness of q.

It is not mere puerility, or the memory of ancient sniggers, which leads me to mention this typically pre-sexual revolutionary moment. If we take Ryle's inadvertence—if that is what it was—as an opportunity for facile analysis, it is tempting to suggest that his 'Freudian' flourish at least implied—though it certainly did not entail—a sense of the burden of chastity which weighed on academic philosophers. It requires no large leap to turn this suggestion back on its author by remarking that there is something immature in the notion that those who deal with abstract matters are themselves somehow sublime. What I am hinting at here is twofold: one, philosophy is a subject which may create enormous strains, or even trivial ones, for those who seek constantly to use or fashion a vocabulary divorced from mundane associations; and, two, we—amateurs of the subject—have a tendency to insist on the very aloofness which will sustain our belief that philosophers have an unearthly nobility. We want them to be exempt from vulgarities of which, in another mood, it entertains us, however unworthily, to suspect them. Iris Murdoch, in her novel *The Philosopher's Pupil,* ironises at length on this comedy of expectations, although her fictional philosopher lacks convincing personality or ideas.

This lecture-ramble is trying to attend to two things at once, perhaps because it is easier to do two things badly than one well, but also because the two things may be facets of a single relation, that between the philosopher and his admirer. Thus Ryle's possible Freudian 'error'—there is no evidence that it was a slip—is or was comic, not only because he may not have meant *p*-ness to have the anatomical ring which, to adolescent ears, it did, but also because it was uttered in circumstances, which we—the sniggering audience—wanted to be solemn. Our laughter was a function of our determined belief that Ryle cannot have meant what he said. The sorts of things he meant to say were, we wanted to believe, professorial, pedantic, prim, because these sort of *p*-words were properly associated with the paternal place proper to our needs and hence his duty. Our laughter was at our own expense as much as at G.R.'s. Embarrassment no less than schoolboy derision helped to fund it: we had seen a sort of divinity with his fly unbuttoned. One can well imagine a lecturer, of a different reputation and in another school, whose failure to be outspoken—or even obscene—would come as a dereliction, a failure to inhabit his (or her) assigned role. Imagine, quite simply, a Germaine Greer who omitted to say something shocking. One would be shocked.

Apart from being the editor of *Mind* who, in a *cause célèbre* which, I daresay, is no longer celebrated, refused to review Ernest Gellner's first book, *Words and Things*, Ryle was also the author of a singular little study called *Plato's Progress* (1966). The interest I at least have in this slim volume is due to its stylistic curiosity. Readers of *The Concept of Mind* will not need to be reminded of its author's caustic limpidity. No one could accuse that book of callowness, still less of being slightly embarrassing, even if its central thesis now seems paradoxical to the point, very nearly, of being a kind of impractical joke, but *Plato's Progress,* while never foolish, flirts with themes which are, for want of a happier term, 'psychological'; Ryle hints quite strongly at what he suspects to be Plato's motivation in writing dialogues. If I remember rightly, he suggests that two more or less disreputable appetites fuelled his prolificity. One was his envy of the great dramatists, of whom Aeschylus was his favourite target, and the other was his desire to enrapture what Ryle, in a rather touchingly awkward phrase, called 'sixteen-year-olders'. Now I know nothing and, living a sheltered life, have heard not a word of gossip about Ryle's private life, except for the one instance which, as I have said, suggests a shy, wilfully honourable man. I do not, therefore, incline to the easy, juicy view that Ryle was reading into Plato any desire of his own to emulate Noel Coward or to be the Benjamin Jowett of his generation. It is, however, interesting that a philosopher who refused to send Gellner's perky squib for review, on the grounds that it was largely abusive of other philosophers, and without substantial seriousness, himself wrote a book which, as it were, tested Plato's feet for clay. My interest lies in the implication that Ryle thought that philosophers should not be credited with monolithic and unworldly anatomies and that it was not disreputable at least to hazard plausible guesses about what kept them at it. Such guesses would, of course, vary in each instance and they would not, and could not, damage the force of their arguments. It hardly matters whether Mozart wrote a piece in order to seduce a girl, impress a king, pay a bill or give us intimations of eternity. We have all been promised that a work of art will be as good or bad as it is, whatever that means, regardless of its composer's intentions. Sincerity is not a certificate of virtue among the muses. Plato's philosophical worth cannot be affected by his supposed disappointment at being unable to fill the theatre of Dionysus or make its audience jump out of its skin, as Aeschylus' spectators did, at the discovery of the Furies. If he was jealous or amorous, what difference can it make to the merits of the Theory of Forms? Part of Ryle's claim was, as you will remember, that that theory was no by means held tenaciously by Plato throughout his philosophical progress. He argued for a man's right to modify and abandon aspects of his ideas, an argument which Kolakowski was to dignify in his book in favour of inconsistency. Kolakowski's main thrust was against notions of historical inevitability and the putative 'moral' obligation to align oneself with it. To see that history has no compelling arguments or necessary conclusion is to be spared the pseudo-necessity of siding with, in particular, the kind of inhumanity which, in this century, seeks to make philosophy its accomplice. When it comes to trains of thought, however hectic, philosophers may and should test the links between the carriages, but they should not accept first-class seats, least of all on a gravy-train, as Heidegger did.

Just as Dodds argued that the Greeks were troubled, if not plagued, by the irrational precisely because they were such keen advocates of reason, so Ryle's treatment of the 'case' of Plato argues for a belief, on his part, that philosophers were uncomfortably cornered by expectations of both lifelong consistency and an almost inhuman indifference both to ambition and, to put it plainly, seduction. It does not follow that Ryle was a victim of more or less secret anguish or that he was signalling to us that the supposed otherworldiness of philosophers was a sorry sham. Yet it is not impertinent to suspect a certain impatience with Plato's affectations of impersonality and purity of purpose, if not always of method, which remind one of T. S. Eliot. Eliot, you will recall, deplored the notion of individual talent as against loyalty to a tradition, although his pontifical confidence suggested that, however grey he might be, his eyes were firmly fixed on eminence. Ryle was, no doubt, a competent Platonist, in the Greats tradition, but something irked him in Plato's address and disposed him to 'unpack' his life, in a more or less warranted fashion, if only to make sense of his own feeling that Plato was a more mutable character than his craving for the immutable might seem to indicate.

I am indeed trying to have things both ways, and to do two things at once. This is partly for greedy and impatient reasons, partly because, more nobly, I think that in language and in life two things often do happen at once and that one cannot understand heads without knowing about tails. One of the commonsensical quotations with which we marched into exams was Bishop Butler's 'A thing is what it is and not another thing, to which I am disposed to say now, 'Quite right, my lord bishop, and also, of course, quite wrong: a thing is what it is and also another thing.' The p-ness of q is always there to warn us against too abrupt an assumption of categorical purity. The shameless economy of nature, so offensive to G. B. Shaw, in which one organ serves more than one office, infects and invigorates language too: the richness of speech depends on duplicity, just as drama cannot hold our attention unless at least some of what is happening is, for the moment, puzzling or even unintelligible. André Green, in his *Un Oeil de Trop,* makes the point when he likens tragedy—and *Oedipus Rex* in particular—to the dialogue between his parents which is overheard by a child who both understands (the words) and fails to understand (the significance). André Green suggests that the tragic audience is excited and alarmed by being allowed to spy on the actors, just as the child wishes and does not wish to observe and overhear the sexual secrets of his parents.

One may accept this or not, as one chooses. However, it suggests that there may be reasons beyond logic why certain philosophers become, as they say, familiar to us, while others seem almost inexplicably disagreeable. For some reason, I have never had time for philosophers whose names begin with H, with the exception of Heraclitus, who begins with a rough breathing, one might say, and so escapes sanction. Luckily, this means that Hegel, Husserl and Heidegger are as unpalatable to me as stem ginger; happily, there seem to be good philosophical reasons for not feeling too guilty, but they only lend spurious dignity to prejudice. The charm of Wittgenstein has recently been subjected to more or less venomous challenge. The fury of some of his admirers has been interestingly exaggerated. After all, the 'news', if it is new, that the young Ludwig had homosexual appetites, and may even have been disposed to satisfy them, cannot put his philosophical chastity in question. The rage of the keepers of the flame is understandable only in the light of their idea of W., rather than on Wittgenstein's own behalf. The refusal to accept Wittgenstein's carnal reality, like Jesus' loin-cloth, tells us more about his worshippers than about him. It has a manifest affinity with the quite common notion that members of the royal family propagate their species by loftier means than those available to their subjects. In other words, there is a disposition to play the child's part, at once curious and inhibited, when faced with the sexuality of his parents. It is in this sense, among others, that my title was chosen: the philosophers whom I have known I have also not known, and my respect for their knowledge, my belief in their superior wisdom and impersonal purposes, is at least very like our wilful respect for the parents whom we can never know as they knew each other and who at once excite and inhibit our curiosity. Even if you accept this sketchy analysis, it does not, of course, mean that a given philosopher's ideas become less valuable because a reader approaches him with the hope or fear that he will, in some respects, play the 'pure father', who can have the paternal role without ever having played the two-backed beast. The philosopher as father is more frequent, to say the least, than the philosopher as mother. Hannah Arendt, Simone Weil, Iris Murdoch, Miss Anscombe and Susan Stebbing provide a fairly forlorn quintet of females from whom to cast an ideal mother, which may be put down to the sexism of the profession and its emergence from theology, but suggests, if you like, that those who look to philosophers for ideal parents prefer an asexual genesis of at least that sublime aspect of humanity with which philosophy must or prefers to deal.

In an interesting paper on Addiction to Detective Stories, the psycho-analyst Charles Rycroft proposes, with speculative humour, a theory of why so many people read one mystery after another, although in nearly all cases the books are poorly written, even if they are amusingly constructed. What impels people to repeat the process of bemusement and to seek the solution to more or less factitious puzzles which satisfy them so little that they immediately have recourse to another? Rycroft, being an analyst, offers a not unexpected answer: the addict is drawn to detective stories because, putting himself in the investigator's place, he is warranted to ask questions which normally would be taboo. Crime licenses curiosity of which the analyst's essential instance is curiosity about the primal scene. Rycroft hazards the view, in a fairly light-hearted way, that the victim of the most attractive murder-stories is or stands for the father, as it is in the Oedipus instance where the king himself demands the full investigation which will discover his own guilt.

One may take this or leave it, as one chooses. Rycroft's speculation is not, however, without relevance to philosophical inquiry and our addiction to it, our unwillingness to let go of the hope and fear that philosophers are, as they say, on to something. It is part of the modern style to observe juxtapositions rather than to assert causal connections. Hence to analogise between detective stories and philosophy is not to reduce one to the other or both to nothing very much. However, it is fair to point out that the philosophical paper is, in many cases, a kind of sublime detective story. We are introduced to a problem, however arid, and then to the suspects, those cases where it seems that an exception to the advertised rule is possible. We are usually given an obvious solution to the crux, which we may be sure will not do, and are then introduced to further suspects before being treated to the clinching argument which reveals whatever the author could have announced to us at the outset. If some academic papers are exercises in prolongation, it is clear that the reader cannot be satisfied with the posing of a problem followed by its author's prompt answer. This may happen in mathematics, but it is does not happen in literary philosophy. The fame and fascination of Wittgenstein's *Tractatus*, which partakes of aspects of both declarative brevity and cryptic extension, derive at least in part from the text's remaining puzzling even after the solution has been offered. Wittgenstein is, by the same token, the philosopher whom we do and do not wish to know. You will remember that Heracleitus, whose gnomic style pre-figures Wittgenstein in some regards, alludes to 'The wise one alone who does not wish and who wishes to be spoken of by the name of Zeus'. The oracle, he says elsewhere, neither 'declares nor conceals' but offers a sign. The comedy of philosophy, one might say, especially in a time of competitive incredulity, is that we both believe and do not believe that the philosopher knows a secret and that we both do and do not wish to be initiated into it. We are drawn to those who seem to endorse our scepticism—I am speaking, of course, of my own preference—but we are unwilling to believe that they have told us all they know when they tell us that they know no more than we do. The modesty of the disclaimer becomes as insufferable to us as the pretentiousness of those who proposed grandiose metaphysical schemes. It needs no psychoanalyst to see that we both do and do not want our fathers to be in the same case as ourselves. We wish them, in a sense, to be better investigators than ourselves and also to agree to be our victims (Plato is the father of philosophy who is killed by every generation, unless it prefers to kill Aristotle). Hegel is the Dr Moriarty of modern philosophy, the villain who must be done down, and who rises again in order to horrify and challenge us. We can perhaps take Rycroft's analysis of the detective story addict a little further here. To remark the similarity in anatomy between the philosophical investigation and the search for who killed Roger Akroyd is not wholly impertinent. Just as the addict impersonates the detective, those of us who are drawn to philosophy are drawn to the man who proposes, and seems authorized, to ask ultimate questions. Like the detective, the philosopher often affects puzzlement at the cleverness of answers which do not quite meet the case, perhaps, he suggests ironically, because he lacks the wit to see how they fit with other elements in the puzzle. What is the case of all cases to which all philosophers are drawn and into which all of us, pretty well, wish that we had the licence to inquire? It is, of course, the case of God.

The comedy of modern philosophy is that its modesty and its immodesty are inextricably connected: affectations of incompetence, announced by journeymen like Ayer, never convince us that they do not really know more than they will say, just as a show of certainty, on the part of bishops or politicians, leads us to assume that they know less than they claim. We look for certainty to the sceptic and we badger the dogmatist for confessions of doubt. Yet our desire for a clinching investigation of the ultimate mystery is unabated. We do and do not wish God to be dead; we do and do not wish to have investigators who, themselves above all suspicion, will resolve the primal issue once and for all. We cannot conceive of what a proof of God's existence could be (even if we knew exactly what we meant by the Zeus we seek) nor can we accept that a disproof will ever be final, for what would it be disproving and by what conceivable means? As Pascal saw, we are pitched between one attitude and another and can never be satisfied, not least because what we want is not what we want and never can be, given our natural and linguistic duplicity. We insist on being told lies while maintaining that we want the truth. Our intellectual curiosity mimics that of the child who does and does not want to know what his parents do, or did, in bed. We depute others to tell us what happened in the primal scene even as we avert our eyes from it. I do not, of course, mean to say that philosophical investigation comes down to asking others what they can see through some cosmic key-hole, but I am mundane enough to suspect that our lifelong selection of worthy deputies, whose reports we read as if they might contain the solution of solutions, has something in common with the vacuous addiction to such brave surrogates as 007 or Inspector Morse (how perfect that his very name hints synecdochically at the command of codes!).

Our choice of deputies to report on the cosmic primal scene which we dare not observe for ourselves requires them to have more or less supernatural powers and not to be human-all-too-human, just as—for the faithful—Jesus, although supposedly a man, cannot have sexual desires, or even natural functions, if his divinity is to be sustained. The relation of the pupil to his selected philosopher also has something of this wilful aversion from knowing him as a man, even if not in the Biblical sense: we appoint certain men, and our choices are indeed virtually limited by the canon to males, to be our chaste investigators who, we may hope, will report both that God is dead and that everything remains under control despite His demise. The empty room is, of course, the classic locus for the perfect crime. The Holy of Holies in the temple at Jerusalem was, we are always promised, empty. The life and the death of God are thus indistinguishable on all the available evidence: everything points both ways, just as Heracleitus talked of the road up and the road down being the same road. Our trust in our selected team of philosophers puts them in the father's place, just as Christians believe in the capacity of Jesus to mediate with the Father with Whom, in another regard, He is identical and whom he thus supplants and, in some sense, kills.

The abstract nature of philosophy, the rigour we expect of its practitioners, the lack of partiality to which logic must adhere, can be read as devices for concealing the murderous purposes to which we depute it. I am not sure whether René Girard qualifies as philosopher, but his sense of the capacity of human beings to encode and dissimulate murderous formulae in their social routines is certainly worth a deviation, like a two-star restaurant in the Michelin Guide.

If we had no furtive ambitions, whether for the proof of God's existence or for evidence of his undoubted demise, would we return again and again to the dossiers which grow dusty on our shelves? The selective affinity which we have for this detective inspector or that *commissaire* is not, of course, merely a matter of assuming that he and we, if we had the nerve and commission, would be likely to round up the same suspects. Yet it requires a rare intellect to endure for very long the style of someone, say like Pierre Boutang, who we know will produce findings wholly uncongenial to us. We preserve our illusions of impartiality, if we do, by being determined to make our philosophers men of probity selected on the basis of their dedication to the truth. It is, no doubt, a sign of my natural diffidence that I never called Wisdom John or Ayer Freddie, even when my contemporaries had ventured easily on such intimacies; the reluctance to get too close to other men may have all kinds of explanations, but I suspect that I did not want to discover too much humanity in those whom I deputed, deferentially, to handle the Great Investigation. Just as the French, for all their

reported *franchise* in anatomical matters, still refuse, in polite circumstances, to allow that women urinate, so I, and others perhaps, preferred to have a Wittgenstein who went to Betty Grable movies but not,
not, not to public lavatories. When I declared, latish in life, to Freddie
Ayer that *Language. Truth and Logic* had meant a great deal to me
when I first went to Cambridge, he replied that it still brought him in a
thousand a year. It was rather as if St Paul had remarked complacently
that the Acts of the Apostles was doing well in paperback. We want our
philosophers to be serious and, however keen we seem to be to have
them confess themselves mundane, we look to them to be sublime for
us. We do not know them because we dare not find them to be men very
much like ourselves. We ask them to dispel our illusions about everything but themselves; it suits us to whiten their sepulchres and to refuse
the dirt on them. They are the fathers who kill the Father and whose
sons we can be without the necessity for a primal scene. If we are of a
sceptical temper, we look to them to provide evidence for the certainty
of our uncertainties. The Italians have a saying, '*E certo, cer-
tissimo—ed anzi possibile.*' We ask our philosophers to be no less
trenchant but much more decisive; they will, if they are honest, always
disappoint us, which is perhaps what we want of them, even as we
solicit them once again to set out on their white search for the colour of
all colours.

The Roots of Philosophy

JOHN WHITE

I

Some people think that the impulse to philosophise begins in early childhood: Gareth Matthews, for instance, in his *Philosophy and the Young Child* (1980). His book begins 'TIM (about six years), while busily engaged in licking a pot, asked, "Papa, how can we be sure that everything is not a dream?"' 'Tim's puzzle,' he tells us, 'is quintessentially philosophical. Tim has framed a question that calls into doubt a very ordinary notion (being awake) in such a way as to make us wonder whether we really know something that most of us unquestioningly assume we know.'

Matthew Lipman, Director of the Institute for the Advancement of Philosophy for Children at Montclair State College, New Jersey, also sees the starting point for children's philosophical development in their questionings and wonderings. 'Children begin to think philosophically when they begin to ask why' (Lipman *et al.,* 1977, 35). Children wonder constantly about all sorts of things. They try to cope in various ways—by scientific explanation, by fairy tales and stories, and 'by formulating the matter philosophically' (p. 14). They do so in the latter case when they ask questions like 'What's space? What's number? What's matter? What's mind? What are possibilities? What's reality? What are things? What's my identity? What are relationships? Did everything have a beginning? What's death? What's life? What's meaning? What's value?' (p. 70).

Part of the impulse behind Matthews' promotion of philosophy for children has been the thought that philosophising is an activity which is natural to all of us. He writes:

> I first became interested in the philosophical thought of young children by worrying about how to teach introductory courses in philosophy to college students. Many students seemed to resist the idea that doing philosophy could be natural. In response to their resistance I hit on the strategy of showing them that as children many of them had already done philosophy. It occurred to me that my task as a college philosophy teacher was to reintroduce my students to an activity that they had once enjoyed and found natural, but that they had later been socialized to abandon. (Matthews, 1980, vii).

John White

Lipman, too, first turned to philosophy for children (PFC) through dissatisfaction with teaching philosophy at university. In his case he was concerned about poor reasoning abilities of students (Lipman, 1989). In 1969 he wrote a novel for 11–12 year olds called *Harry Stottlemeier's Discovery* in which children discover logic for themselves (Lipman, 1974). Since then he has used this and other such novels in training programmes for preparing teachers of philosophy in schools.

The literature of PFC stresses the opposition between the idea that young children can be interested in such an abstract subject as philosophy and Piaget's theory. Will Robinson, a British follower of Lipman, says that 'at four years of age my kids would ask me questions that I thought were deeply philosophical; but I knew they couldn't ask those questions because Piaget had said they couldn't!' (Robinson, 1988, 86). He goes on to say that youngsters 'can and do ask important questions which are philosophically substantial' and that 'any day now, even the youngest child may come up with a contribution that is going to be philosophically revolutionary'.

So much for some of the claims of enthusiasts for children's philosophising. How sound are they?

We need, first, to test whether the accounts that theorists give of what children do match the facts. A first issue here is whether children in fact say what they are alleged to say. *Do* young children typically—or indeed ever—ask 'What are possibilities?' 'What is my identity?' 'What's value?'? Since we are given no further evidence we cannot judge, but it is rather hard to swallow.

A second issue is whether the descriptions theorists give of what children say are always well-grounded. Take Tim's question about dreaming with which we began and Matthews' comment on it. It is true that in a certain context this could be a philosophical question—if asked by a philosophy teacher in an undergraduate seminar, for instance. It is true that, in that context, the speaker 'has framed a question that calls into doubt a very ordinary notion . . . (etc.)'. But does it follow that because this is a philosophical question in that context it is a philosophical question in every other context? How in general do we identify a philosophical question? We cannot go by the mere production of a sentence like 'How can we be sure that everything is not a dream?', since a person could be parrotting something picked up elsewhere. We have to presuppose that the speaker understands what he is saying and is saying it with a certain intention in mind, in this case an intention to become clearer about a topic about which he is puzzled or confused. We have to say more than this, of course, for not every confusing or puzzling topic is philosophical. This is not the place to embark on the wild goose chase of producing a non-circular definition of the philosophical. I perhaps need only remark that the person who asks the question about dreaming must at least be affected by doubts of a categorial sort about the distinction between appearance and reality. I am not arguing that any of this must be very sophisticated, such that, say, only those acquainted with the literature of philosophy can be said to ask philosophical questions. But something like this intention, perhaps only in a very inchoate form, must be present.

It *may* be that six-year-old Tim has this intention. I do not want to deny that he does. The issue is only Matthews' warrant for inferring from the data that he has it. Should one go so far, for instance, as to talk of Tim's 'puzzle'? Or of his having 'framed a question that calls into doubt . . . (etc.)' What *I* find puzzling about all this is that professional philosophers like Matthews, who must be acquainted with philosophical discussions about the wealth of intentions that can be hypothetically attributed to the same piece of overt verbal behaviour, can insist without further ado that a philosophical intention rather than some other lies behind a question like Tim's.

When Matthews describes three-year-old Denis, talking about not being able to have bread without butter if it's buttered already, as 'exploring the modal notions of possibility and necessity' (p. 14), the gap between behaviour and interpretation seems very great indeed. If all that Matthews is implying is that such a young child can reason in a logical way, that is not news; but it is misleading to describe this in such a way as to suggest that the child is adopting something of the *higher-order* stance to reasoning taken by philosophers of logic. Lipman, it seems to me, similarly conflates reasoning and philosophising in saying that children begin to philosophise when they ask the question 'why?'.

Philosophers are interested in the criteria for the application of concepts. Another of Matthews' examples records 'an instructive moment of puzzlement over the concept of life:'

> DAVID [aged five] worries about whether an apple is alive. He decides that it is when it's on the ground but not when it has been brought into the house. (p. 6)

We all know that when children are learning new concepts they are often at first uncertain how they are to be applied. But the remarks they make and the questions they ask to reduce this uncertainty must be distinguished from philosophers' comments. Once again, different intentions are at work. Children want to know how to use the concept; philosophers, who have no trouble using it, are interested in mapping it from a higher-order perspective, and usually in the pursuit of larger theoretical enquiries. Needless to say, too, philosophers are only interested in those concepts which present philosophical problems, whereas the point just made about children can apply to their acquisition of *all* kinds of concepts—of cats, rivers, computers. Matthews' example, the concept of life, happens to be one which is of interest to philosophers also. But this is coincidental. David is not puzzled about the concept of life as a philosopher might be who is reflecting on the possibility of survival after death or the ethics of abortion. He is simply on the way to acquiring the concept. Or so it would seem. I do not want categorically to deny that he is really philosophising in something of the way we would describe an adult as doing this. It is just that I see no evidence that this is what he is doing.

To come back to Matthews' comment, in the quotation about his students, that philosophy is something which as children they found enjoyable and natural, but which they had later been socialized to abandon. There is a hint here of the view, often associated with Rousseau, that educators need to strip away the corrupting influences of social conventions and get back to children's 'natural' propensities, when thus unspoilt, to explore their world and make their own discoveries. The same child-centred orientation may lie behind Will Robinson's heady comment that any day we may expect some really young child to make a philosophically revolutionary contribution. (I have begun eavesdropping on our neighbour's toddler in the garden next door, and am almost sure I heard her say 'Slab!', when playing with her bricks.)

Difficulties with this kind of child-centred theorizing are well-known, having been dissected with exemplary clarity by Robert Dearden (1968), and I will not dwell on them here. Whether it is true or not that there is this ideological thrust behind some of the manifestations of the movement for children's philosophising, the latter does seem to suggest that philosophy is something that virtually *all* children would want to engage in, given the opportunity. There are epistemological difficulties here about how one knows that this is so. But there are also ethical considerations. If, as in some PFC courses in schools, it is not only children with a clear philosophical talent—if they exist—who are obliged to participate, but all the members of a school class, then, if the remarks I have made about confusions of purpose in the movement are correct, it is not clear to me how beneficial it will be to the ordinary child to be engaged in philosophical discussion. That is, if we are indeed talking about teaching them philosophy rather than improving their reasoning powers or building up desirable interpersonal dispositions. PFC programmes often have these latter two aims, bringing them under the umbrella of teaching philosophy. But they are surely separable from it. Good teachers in most areas of the curriculum want to develop their students' reasoning abilities and to encourage them to listen with respect to others' points of view. But to come back to the main point, how justified is one as a teacher in obliging young children to engage in philosophising when there are such slim grounds for thinking it suitable for them?

Before we bid farewell to Gareth Matthews, reading his nine-year-old son to sleep with Augustine's *De magistro* (p. 97), one last thought. Advocates of philosophy for children, like Matthews in the quotation from him above, treat children's philosophising as an *enjoyable* activity. If so, that would immediately make it very different from the experience which adults typically have of it. Or, at least, if we talk of enjoyment in their case, it is often only in the broad sense that one may apply to a boxer or a marathon runner. Philosophy often brings bewilderment, despair, painful struggles for understanding. Just as one may wonder whether sitting a class down in an English lesson to write a poem after listening to Honegger's *Pacific 231* may not give them a totally false idea of poetic creation—as something that can be done to order and en masse, so I cannot escape the thought that presenting philosophy to children as a fun activity may impede rather than promote any understanding they may come to have of what philosophy is all about.

II

After writing the last section I came across an excellent article by Richard Kitchener, called 'Do children think philosophically?' (Kitchener, 1990).[1] I commend it as a thorough and scholarly discussion of claims by Lipman and Matthews among others that children can philosophise. Like me, Kitchener is sceptical, on the grounds that young children are by and large incapable of the reflective, higher-order kind of thinking crucial to doing philosophy and that what is labelled 'philosophising' in children is often confused with thinking critically. I will not go over the many points where I find myself in agreement with him, but will focus instead on what seems to be an issue that divides us.

As an expert on Piaget's genetic epistemology (see Kitchener, 1986), he is especially interested in the claim often made by supporters of philosophy for children and instanced above that the existence of young children's philosophising casts doubt on Piaget's cognitive–developmental theory. According to the latter, younger children, say below the age of ten, are capable of concrete operational thought but not formal operational thought. Since philosophising requires critical–reflective abilities impossible before the formal stage, Piaget's stage theory of development must be wrong (see, for example, Matthews, 1980, ch. 4).

---

[1] I am grateful to Professor Matthew Lipman for his kindness and generosity of spirit in sending me a copy of Kitchener's critical discussion of his and Gareth Matthews' work.

Kitchener's arguments that there is no evidence of young children's higher-order thinking, if sound, are enough to rebut the claim that data on children's philosophising have undermined Piaget's theory. But he goes further than this critical move, giving an embryonic sketch of a Piagetian account of the development of philosophical abilities. For this purpose he makes a distinction between 'concrete philosophising' and 'abstract philosophising'. The former is exemplified in the dialogues found in Gareth Matthews and others about such things as death, dreaming, whether plants have feelings, whether computers think, and so on. This thinking remains at the concrete level since young children cannot grasp the principle *qua* principle underlying the concrete case. '"Abstract philosophising" requires the skills underlying concrete philosophy, i.e. the mental operations Piaget characterized as "concrete operations", but also additional ones as well—those involving "formal operations"' (p. 430). Kitchener goes on to suggest that formal operational thinking is not sufficient for doing philosophy since one also needs still higher-order, meta-philosophical abilities, those called in Piagetian circles 'post formal operational skills'. He concludes

> If there is a stage of reasoning higher than formal–operational thinking, then the development of philosophical skills may indeed [proceed] by a stage-like sequence involving lower-order logical skills, higher-order logical skills (formal operational skills) and post-formal operational skills. (p. 430)

This goes further than showing that Piaget has not been refuted and suggests that there may be Piagetian stages in philosophical development just as in other spheres, e.g. in moral judgment or in understanding the physical world. But this raises a difficulty. Is the notion of philosophical development coherent? In some ways of taking the term there are no problems. It may be said of a student that her philosophical skills have developed markedly over the year when all that is meant by this is that she has made great strides in learning the subject. But the Piagetian sense of 'development' is tied to a biological conception of organisms and their powers unfolding from within in the presence of appropriate environmental factors. While we familiarly use this notion in the context of plants growing and the physical growth of young children, it is not at all clear how it can be applied to mental phenomena. The notion of biological development brings with it the concept of some initial state out of which unfolding occurs and also the concept of some mature end-state towards which the unfolding is directed and beyond which it cannot go. But if we apply this to, say, moral judgment, this teleological conception gains no purchase. There is no evidence of a moral seed out of which children's moral learning springs; and ideas of what counts as maturity of moral understanding are very diverse, dependent not least on cultural factors: there is no biologically-based mature state comparable to the fully-grown oak tree which has developed from an acorn. But this is not basically an empirical issue: given what we know of the necessary dependence of moral learning on social involvement, the atomism implicit in the Piagetian conception of individual unfolding is inconsistent with this. Difficulties along these lines in Piaget's cognitive developmentalism in general have been pointed out by other philosophers, notably David Hamlyn (1967, 1978, ch. 4). If this critique is sound, then the notion of philosophical development is a myth; and so *a fortiori,* is the notion of stages of philosophical development.

Although he is a powerful critic of the views of Lipman and Matthews, Kitchener is still at one with them in holding that young children can philosophise, if only concretely and not, as Lipman and Matthews think, abstractly. He writes, indeed, of the 'very insightful and interesting philosophical discussion' that young children can engage in at the concrete level (1990, p. 427). As an example of concrete philosophising he quotes a dialogue from Gareth Matthews about whether cheese is made of grass:

> 'In a way it is true,' said Donald. 'We do not really notice what stuff is actually made of,' suggested Esther . . . 'You know,' . . . [cows] have four different stomachs.' [Donald said] 'It sounds unusual, but grass *is* cheese in a way; it is just the first stage of what becomes cheese— the second stage is milk.' 'Cream!' put in someone as a correction. 'The third stage is cheese,' Donald continued. 'It's all the same really, it's just different stages as it matures.' (p. 428)

Why does Kitchener call this kind of discussion 'philosophical'? His reason is 'the underlying similarities—their family resemblances'— between it and abstract philosophising (p. 430). He does not expand on what these similarities are. He is, of course, entitled to use the word in this way if he pleases: but to me there seems so *little* resemblance between the two, for reasons that I have aleady referred to, and especially over the crucial feature of higher-order reflection, that it is less misleading to restrict rather than extend the use of the term.

I suspect, in any case, that Kitchener's reason for extending it has to do not only with perceived family resemblances but also with a pre-commitment to a Piagetian paradigm. If one takes as a starting point that philosophising is a category of thinking, like moral or scientific thinking, to which cognitive—developmental theory can apply, then one will be understandably drawn to seek out its early manifestations among young children.

One last point on Kitchener. Piaget's own accounts of different kinds of children's thinking are universal in their scope. They are intended to apply to every child: *all* children develop through the stages of moral development or an understanding of space or number. Does Kitchener want to follow this through into the philosophical area? If so, just as we would, within a Piagetian framework, expect everyone—unless there are special internal reasons why their growth is stunted, and always provided external circumstances are favourable—to develop towards higher levels of moral or scientific understanding, so we should expect everyone to move towards more sophisticated levels of philosophising. Usually, however, doing philosophy is seen as very much a minority activity: only a relatively few people seem to come to have the peculiar cast of mind which it demands. Kitchener's view appears to be out of line with this common conception. That is not enough, of course, to show that it is wrong.

III

Is the argument of sections I and II quite fair to the view that the impulse to philosophise begins in childhood? We know that some children do seem genuinely affected by matters to do with the infinite, about numbers going on for ever, or about whether space or time can come to a stop. It is interesting to speculate about why it is issues like these that tend to crop up in this context, rather than questions about, say, logical validity, the objectivity of ethical judgments, or the nature of substance. A plausible answer is that an interest in infinity is continuous with, or grows naturally out of, children's widening understanding of their world, whereas an interest in the other things requires a shift to a higher-order stance. If children's concern with the infinite were to do with the *nature* of mathematical, spatial or temporal infinity, this, too, would require higher-order thinking. But this is not what grips them. In arithmetic they begin with numbers from one to ten, go on to larger and larger numbers and by the time they hit the billions and trillions and quadrillions not surprisingly begin to wonder where it is all going to stop. The same with space: once they move outwards from the planetary system and past the Milky Way, it would be very odd if they *did not* ask themselves what lay beyond. Similarly for time.

I have been suggesting that simply having thoughts about infinite magnitudes is not to engage in philosophising. This may begin when something more is added—some kind of conceptual conflict—between the thought, for instance, that space must go on for ever and the thought that when it was created or came into being it must have been limited in extent. We should not assume that all those children who reach beyond the supernovas—and such children may not be so numerous, we do not know—experience any such conflict: they may just register that space does not stop and turn back to collecting cards of footballers. Some children may well experience some kind of conflict in these situations, but it is likely to be pretty inchoate, since to formulate the issues with any precision depends on resources that we cannot expect many eight or eleven year olds to possess. Whether these children begin to think philosophically when faced with such conflicts cannot be taken for granted. To judge from my own personal experience of children, they are quite likely, even the most intellectually lively of them, to want to put a rapid end to the discomfort of thinking about such headbreaking matters.

This is not to deny that a vague sense of unresolved, deep and important issues may linger with some of them in the obscurer parts of their minds and impel them towards philosophy at a later time. It may be that some children get further than this—that their thoughts about infinity (or something else) start them off down a philosophical road along which, no doubt with tuition, they then make unbroken progress, just as they might make in mathematics, say. What interests me is that, as far as I know, we never hear about any children like this. Do they exist?

One way of throwing light on this, on the topic of children's philosophising in general, and indeed on wider questions about the impulse to philosophise, is to turn to biographical material about how adult philosophers first came into contact with philosophical issues and at what age. I have been suggesting that the number of children who get anywhere near to philosophical thinking is likely to be small. Among them, one might hypothesize, one would expect to find future fully-fledged philosophers and certainly the philosophical stars. Is this borne out in fact?

The earliest age I have been able to discover is five. Colin Radford describes, in his *The Examined Life,* how an older friend tried to quell his fear of cows by telling him 'Cows have got magnifying eyes, so you look very big to a cow and that is why they are frightened of *you*' (p. 3). Radford tells us that

> I suddenly felt—dizzy. There was something wrong, something *terribly, profoundly, wrong,* with what Cecil had said, but although I has stopped, and was grimacing and gritting my teeth in my effort to work out what was wrong, I could not do so.

In fact it was only years later that he was able to sort out the conceptual confusion in Cecil's remark. We cannot, it seems, claim this as an early example of children's engaging in the activity of philosophising, since as he says he was quite unable to cope with the problem. It seems at most an instance of the inchoate awareness of some kind of conceptual conflict that I mentioned above. All this is assuming that his recollection of how he felt and behaved at five is accurate. One can readily imagine that a young child might be fascinated and perhaps frightened by an animal with strange eyes, but it is harder to credit that he could already be operating with a concept of the profound logical wrongness of someone's statement. Of course, there can be different degrees of conceptual understanding and it may be—I would not want to deny this—that Radford possessed this concept in some minimal sense. If you told a child that a certain tree was called a yew tree and the next moment you told her that it was not a yew but a hawthorn, one might expect her to look puzzled and upset. Would one say that she possessed, in some minimal sense, the concept of logical wrongness? Perhaps. The difference between this example and Radford's is that the former is structurally simpler. The child is confronted with an instance of p immediately followed by not-p, and it would be surprising if she did not see a discrepancy. But Cecil's statement, as reported above, is a complex little argument. To see its incoherence one would have not only to grasp how p is presented as a ground for q and q as a ground for r, but also to follow through the implications of having magnifying eyes and see that these would make everything larger, not just oneself, so that one did not look large in comparison to other things. The incoherence here does not leap to the eye as in the former example.

This may raise a difficulty for Radford's description of the case. To see, even at a minimal level, the logical oddness of Cecil's remark seems to involve having traced through—at least at some minimal level—the connections just mentioned. Yet Radford writes that it was many years before he succeeded in working out what was wrong with the account. But perhaps he means by this working through to an explicit, higher-order, understanding of it. And perhaps this is compatible with working through the connections in some more intuitive way at an early age and seeing some kind of logical oddness here. If Radford did do so, this would indeed show that he possessed unusual thinking abilities for his age, perhaps even some proto-philosophical abilities.

How could we ever know? Our only access to the event is Radford's memory and this, as I am sure he would be the first to agree, may be inaccurate. Whether this is indeed the earliest recorded example of a future philosopher's first philosophisings must be left an open question.

Radford is also a contestant for the *second* prize in this competition, for I have found no other contender younger than six, the age at which for the second occasion in his life he encountered what strikes him now as a philosophical problem (p. 15). He was a new pupil at an infants school and found himself behind the other children in arithmetic. Asked to take 48 from 13, he could not do so because he had not come across negative numbers. Recording his bewilderment and despair at not being able to make any headway, he writes

> My difficulties will seem childish misunderstandings, but what I hope to have demonstrated is that the solution requires extensions of techniques and concepts. So my difficulty was not just a consequence of stupidity, or a blind spot for maths, it was philosophical. I did not find it natural to go on, to take the right approach here, on the basis of what I already knew and could do. (p. 18)

Was his difficulty indeed philosophical? If so, it would seem to follow that any learning difficulties that young children have where they need to extend their conceptual schemes can be labelled in the same way. Many children would be facing philosophical problems in learning to read, to count, to talk about things happening in the past or in the future; and those struggling the hardest—the slowest and most handicapped—would be those with most exposure to philosophical difficulties. But this seems to make little sense.

There is a *parallel* between the sort of learning difficulty that Radford describes and the experience of some kinds of philosophising. In each case one feels at a loss, not knowing which way to turn; and in each case this feeling is relieved by coming to see things in a new way. But there is also a difference. Young children—or, for that matter, adults with these kinds of learning difficulties—are aware that even if they are stumped their teachers are not. When Colin Radford 'burst into a further paroxysm of sobs, which allowed me to nestle into the exquisite, warm, firm softness of Miss Davies' right breast' (p. 17), he knew that she knew some way of taking 48 from 13. But when Wittgenstein was wrestling with how the elements of atomic propositions are related to the world, he knew that he was on his own. There are no authorities in philosophy to tell one how to go on.

Perhaps, though, we should compare the subtraction example not with the experience of fully-fledged philosophising but with that of *learning* philosophy. If an undergraduate is thoroughly confused over whether the mental is distinct from the physical or identical with it, she knows—or thinks she knows—that her teacher knows what moves to make to illuminate things. This may well be true, but the philosophy student is still a world away from a young Radford. She knows that her tutor is not privy to the right answer, to the right way of doing things: philosophy is not that kind of subject. She also knows that her tutor has deliberately set up the radical confusion she is suffering, that this is all part of what it is to become a philosopher. Related with this, the headaches she experiences in finding a way out are not wholly painful to her: she enjoys the activity, bewilderment and all. None of these things could be said of the child learning arithmetic.

Radford writes that 'it will be clear to any professional philosopher reading the above that my thinking about mathematics and philosophical problems about mathematics has been influenced by Wittgenstein' (p. 20). Perhaps what he has in mind is that, reflecting on his childhood difficulties in learning arithmetic, he sees in them illustrations of Wittgensteinian themes. They may well provide them, but they can do this without any implication that any philosophising has been going on on the part of the child. The experience of trying fruitlessly to solve problems by following well-worn tracks when a radical shift of perspective is what is required is an object of philosophical interest for a philosopher: the notion of a change of perspective can help to dispel a whole range of philosophical difficulties. These are philosophical difficulties for the philosopher. There is no implication in this that any difficulties which the *learner* faces are philosophical in nature, or at least, are philosophical difficulties *for him or her*.

If these points about the five- and six-year-old Colin Radford are correct, we still have not discovered a clear case of philosophical activity or experience among very young future philosophers.

The next earliest age I have discovered—and this applies to both Collingwood and Popper—is eight. Collingwood found a translation of Kant's *Groundwork of the Metaphysics of Ethics* among his father's books. As he began reading it

> I was attacked by a strange succession of emotions. First came an intense excitement. I felt that things of the highest importance were being said about matters of the utmost urgency . . . Then, with a wave of indignation, came the discovery that I could not understand them . . . Then . . . came the strangest emotion of all. I felt that the contents of this book, although I could not understand it, were somehow my business: a matter personal to myself, or rather to some future self of my own. (Collingwood, 1944, 8–9)

Karl Popper (1976, 15–16) records that he first stumbled on a philosophical problem about the age of eight:

> Somehow I heard about the solar system and the infinity of space (no doubt of Newtonian space) and I was worried: I could neither imagine that space was finite (for what, then, was outside it?) nor that it was infinite. My father suggested that I ask one of his brothers, who, he told me, was very good at explaining such things. This uncle asked me first whether I had any trouble about a sequence of numbers going on and on. I had not. Then he asked me to imagine a stack of bricks, and add to it one brick, and again one brick, and so on without end; it would never fill the space of the universe. I agreed, somewhat reluctantly, that this was a very helpful answer, though I was not completely happy about it. Of course, I was unable to

formulate the misgivings I still felt: it was the difference between potential and actual infinity, and the impossibility of reducing actual infinity to the potential . . . It did not, of course, occur to me that what was worrying me might be an open problem. Rather, I thought that this was a question which an intelligent adult like my uncle must understand, while I was too ignorant, or perhaps too young, or too stupid, to grasp it completely.

It seems this was an isolated experience: Popper remembers similar problems when he was a few years older, about twelve or thirteen.

In accounts of philosophers' early childhoods I have discovered only occasional experiences like these. It is not until we come to the twelve-year-old J. S. Mill that we find hard evidence of philosophising proper. Having been given an extraordinary comprehensive and rigorous education by his father until that age, he tells us

> I entered into another and more advanced stage in my course of instruction; in which the main object was no longer the aids and appliances of thought, but the thoughts themselves. This commenced with Logic, in which I began at once with the Organon, and read it to the Analytics inclusive . . . (Mill, 1873, 15)

Mill is exceptional in the earliness of his acquaintance with philosophy, even among well-known philosophers. There is little evidence of an early interest in philosophy on the part of T. H. Green (Cacoullos, 1974, 26). G. E. Moore became interested in it in his second year at university (Levy, 1979, 51). Russell writes

> I began thinking about philosophical questions at the age of fifteen. From then until I went to Cambridge, three years later, my thinking was solitary and completely amateurish, until I read Mill's *Logic* . . . (Russell, 1959, 28)

Augustine (1909, 51) discovered the subject through reading an exhortation to philosophy in Cicero's *Hortensius* about the age of eighteen. Kant first became interested at university, having shown no signs of philosophical precocity:

> Even those of Kant's boyhood friends who thought they perceived in him the earmarks of future greatness saw then only the eminent philologist-to-be. (Cassirer, 1981, 14–15)

Wittgenstein was considered to be a dull child and did not even start speaking until he was four years old (Monk, 1990, 12) (incidentally, only one year before Colin Radford's philosophical experience to do with bovine vision). At eight or nine he remembered having paused in a doorway to consider the question 'Why should one tell the truth if it is to one's advantage to tell a lie?' and concluded that there was nothing wrong with lying under such circumstances. Apart from this one incident, which—again if his memory is correct—shows him gripped by a philosophical question if not arriving at a characteristically Wittgensteinian answer, there is no further evidence of philosophical interests on his part until after the age of fourteen.

A more comprehensive survey might tell otherwise, but with the exception of Mill, all these philosophers first began to philosophise in their teens, and not always in an organized way. Conflicts of one sort or another often seem to be the first triggers. Russell was affected by theological doubts; Augustine by the unsettled nature of his wayward life. For several of these men, Green, Moore, Russell and Wittgenstein among them, adolescence was a lonely time. Mill's every minute was so taken up with studying that he may not have felt lonely, but in his early years he was certainly much on his own, having been educated by his father—as was Collingwood. I mention all this because solitariness, perceived sometimes, as with Green and Collingwood, as 'indolence' or 'idleness', may be linked with the troubled detachment characteristic of the philosophic turn of mind. Collingwood is explicit:

> I know now that the problems of my life's work were taking, deep down inside me, their first embryonic shape. But any one who observed me must have thought, as my elders did think, that I had fallen into a habit of loafing, and lost the alertness and quickness of wit that had been so noticeable in my early childhood. (1944, p. 9)

The people I have just reviewed all became well-known philosophers. But not all those who begin to think philosophically in their youth make their mark as philosophers, or primarily as philosophers, in later life. Some of them are drawn towards other things. Pasternak is an example. Another great Russian writer, Tolstoy, has left us a vivid description of the philosophical thoughts which began to assail him about the age of fifteen or sixteen (Tolstoy, 1854, ch. 19). His account strikes many a chord in myself and, I suspect, in others of similar inclination. He writes of his solitary interior life, shut in on himself; of his 'weak childish intellect with all the ardour of inexperience' striving to solve abstract questions about man's destiny, the future life, the immortality of the soul; of deciding to live for the present and lying on his bed for two or three days reading novels and eating gingerbread; of fancying that nothing existed in the universe except himself and 'glancing sharply round in some opposite direction, hoping to catch unawares the void where I was not'. For Tolstoy the experience was painful and destructive:

> My feeble intellect could not penetrate the impenetrable, and in that backbreaking effort lost one after the other the convictions which, for my life's happiness, I ought never to have dared disturb.

All this weary mental struggle yielded me nothing save an artful elasticity of mind which weakened my will-power, and a habit of perpetually dissecting and analysing, which destroyed spontaneity of feeling and clarity of reason.

Advocates of encouraging young people to philosophise, please note. He goes on:

My fondness for abstract reasoning developed my conscious being to such an unnatural degree that frequently, thinking about the simplest things, I would fall back into the vicious circle of analysis of my thoughts, entirely losing sight of the question that had occupied my mind at the outset, and thinking, instead, about what I was thinking about. Asking myself: 'Of what am I thinking?' I would answer: 'I think of what I am thinking. And now what am I thinking of? I think that I am thinking of what I am thinking of.' And so on. I was at my wits end.

However, the philosophical discoveries I made vastly flattered my vanity: I often imagined myself a great man discovering truths for the benefit of humanity, and gazed upon other mortals with a proud consciousness of my own worth; but strangely enough when I encountered those other mortals I felt shy of each and every one, and the higher I rated myself in my own estimation the less capable I was not only of displaying any consciousness of merit but even of schooling myself not to blush for every word and movement, however simple and unimportant.

In these examples of future philosophers and non-philosophers the impulse to philosophise is first manifested in adolescence, not in early childhood. No doubt there is more to be said about the conditions in which it flourishes and its origins in individuals' earlier lives, always bearing in mind that it may not be one thing, but may take different forms: some may be drawn into philosophy through religious doubts, others through the quest for a worthwhile life, others—like Wittgenstein, perhaps—through reflections on the nature of mathematics. It may be that some germ of what comes later can be found in early childhood, although I know of no evidence for this. It may also be argued that empirical findings such as I have put forward show very little. The fact that Kant did not start philosophising until late adolescence does not show that engaging him in the activity at eight or nine would have been fruitless. (It might have helped him reach even greater heights.)

This may well be true as a logical point, and I am not ruling out the possibility or desirability of young children's philosophising. All I have been claiming is that the grounds on which these things have been proposed are shaky.

John White

It is interesting to me that it is general philosophers, not philosophers of education, who have been most prominent in advocating children's philosophy. A recurring trigger, found in Matthews, Lipman and others, has been the difficulty of getting undergraduate students of philosophy to think philosophically. But starting them young is not the only way of trying to cope with it, and, in the light of the higher-order nature of philosophy, not the most obvious. Improving secondary education so that more emphasis is put on thinking than on fact-learning across the whole curriculum may have more to be said for it. So, for all I know, may the discouragement of those undergraduate students who show no aptitude for the subject.

The idea that young children can philosophise or naturally are philosophers is arresting. Even more than the earlier idea, associated with Herbert Read (1943) and others, that young children are natural artists, it shocks by its counterintuitiveness. This may help to explain the attention which children's philosophy has attracted—from the media as well as philosophers and educators—in recent years. But does it exist?

Re-engaging with Real Arguments

ALEC FISHER

1. Modern Logic and Real Reasoning

The various 'impulses to philosophy' which are the subject of this series of lectures, include a fascination with the general process of reasoning and argument—with the 'game of logic'. We are all aware of the importance of reasoning in our lives and how difficult it can be to tell 'good' reasoning from 'bad'. For example, which of the following are good arguments

(a) Some people have solved their own unemployment problem by great ingenuity in searching for a job or by willingness to work for less, so everyone could do this.

(b) Only gold will silence him. Gold is heavy. Therefore only something heavy will silence him.

(c) All red boiled lobsters are dead and all dead red lobsters are boiled, so all boiled dead lobsters are red.

(d) 'The Brahmins assert that the world arose from an infinite spider, who spun this whole complicated mass from his bowels, and annihilates afterwards the whole or any part of it, by absorbing it again and resolving it into his own essence. Here is a species of cosmogony which appears to us ridiculous because a spider is a little contemptible animal whose operations we are never likely to take for a model of the whole universe. But still, here is a new species of analogy, even in our own globe. And were there a planet wholly inhabited by spiders (which is very possible), this inference would there appear as natural and irrefragable as that which in our planet ascribes the origin of all things to design and orderly system and intelligence. . . . Why an orderly system may not be spun from the belly as well as the brain, it will be difficult . . . to give a satisfactory reason.' (David Hume, *Dialogues on Natural Religion*)

As I have suggested, some people are drawn to philosophy by a general fascination with reasoning wherever it occurs. Most are probably drawn to philosophy by puzzlement about other things—religion, morality, our knowledge of other minds or of the external world, etc.—but many who become interested in philosophy for these reasons soon discover how central reasoning and argument is to the attempt at resolving their puzzlement and thus soon become interested in argument in general. From either direction, the impulse to distinguish good reasoning from bad has long been of central concern to philosophy.

Now it has long been a common practice to present modern logic as the 'science of reasoning', as the repository of accumulated wisdom about reasoning in general so far as it is possible to say anything about it in general. Indeed, this has often been given as the justification for teaching the subject as part of general and philosophical education.

But suppose we were interested in constructing a general 'science of reasoning' *ab initio*, what would be our starting points? Surely, our 'data' would be nuggets of reasoning—or argument—which people have actually used with a view to persuading others, like examples (a) and (d) above. But modern formal logic pays almost no attention to such reasoning. Indeed, if you look at almost any modern formal logic book you will be struck by the remoteness of its examples from the kind of reasoning anyone would actually use. (c) above is a nice example from Lewis Carroll of the sort of example logicians tend to consider; here's another from Copi's widely used textbook, *Introduction to Logic* (1953).

> If the weather is warm and the sky is clear, then either we go swimming or we go boating. It is not the case that if we do not go swimming then the sky is not clear. Therefore, either the weather is warm or we go boating.

Not only are most of the examples discussed by modern logic remote from real reasoning, modern logic explicitly restricts its attention to reasoning of very particular kinds. For example, it attends almost exclusively to arguments in which the point of view being argued for— the conclusion—is either *true* or *false*, so, for example, reasoning of the kind to be found in most moral arguments and policy arguments, reasoning about what *ought to be done*, is largely ignored. Not only does modern logic restrict its attention in this way, it also pays almost no attention to the fact that in presenting reasons one standardly seeks to *convince* or to *persuade* an *audience* about the rightness of some belief or course of action. For modern formal logic, the object of study is mostly the kind of argument which can be displayed on the model of a mathematical proof, leading from premises to a conclusion, aimed at a universal or no particular audience, and evaluated in terms of whether it 'establishes' its conclusion by generally objective standards, and *not at all* in terms of whether it convinces the intended audience.

But much 'real' argumentation is not like mathematical argument at all. It is about what we ought to do, about clarifying meanings, about whether analogies hold, about the reliability of authorities, etc., and much of it is essentially 'dialogical', i.e., takes the form of an argumentative dialogue, with claims, challenges, defences and rebuttals. It is essentially a *social* activity, to be appraised by standards which apply to conversation, not to mathematics (cf. Grice, 1975).

The implication of these restrictions is that the claim of modern logic to be the 'science of reasoning' is a considerable exaggeration: modern logic pays very little attention to the data that such a science would have to study—to real sequences of reasoning which people have used in order to try to persuade others—and, furthermore, what it has to say applies to very few 'real arguments'. This is not a new complaint; Bar-Hillel summarized the position very well many years ago,

> I challenge anybody . . . to show me a serious piece of argumentation in natural language that has been succesfully evaluated as to its validity with the help of formal logic. The customary applications are often careless, rough, unprincipled, or rely on reformulations of the original linguistic entities under discussion into different ones . . . through processes which are again mostly unprincipled and ill-understood. (Bar-Hillel, 1969, 15)

2. The Development of Logic, the 'Science of Reasoning'

Notice that Aristotle, the key figure in the 'science of reasoning' for two thousand years, was well aware that there are different aspects to reasoning and different kinds of reasoning, and he drew a distinction between 'analytic'—the science of demonstrative reasoning, 'dialectic'—the science of argumentative dialogue, and 'rhetoric'—the science of persuasion. Aristotle's 'analytic' is the beginning of what we have come to call 'logic' and is to be found in his *Prior Analytics* and *Posterior Analytics*. His theory of argumentative debate is to be found in his *Topics* and in *De Sophisticis Elenchis*, and his theory of good and convincing oratory is to be found in his *Rhetoric*. This broad approach to the study of reasoning prevailed for many centuries in the Aristotelian tradition. Medieval philosophers studied Aristotle's theory of the syllogism of course, but they also engaged in 'disputations'—arguments governed by strict rules deriving from the theory of dialectic—and rhetoric too was studied. However, in this respect, Western philosophy has taken a very distinctive course in more recent times and we have now almost completely lost sight of the Aristotelian tradition concerning argumentative dialogue or 'dialectic' and the science of persuasion or 'rhetoric'. For philosophers, the 'science of reasoning' has become 'logic': the science of demonstrative reasoning alone.

It is interesting to speculate about why this has happened to logic—especially since it is very plausible to tell a story which closely parallel's Richard Rorty's account, in *Philosophy and the Mirror of Nature* (1980), of what has happened to epistemology.

The explanation for what has happened to logic, at least on the superficial level, is relatively simple. Demonstrative reasoning is *necessary* reasoning; if you accept the premises then you *must* accept the conclusion. It is the kind of reasoning exemplified in geometrical and mathematical 'demonstrations'. With the emergence of modern science in the seventeenth century, and especially as a result of the impact of Newton's theories, demonstrative reasoning increased enormously in importance, and the study of reasoning became increasingly the study of demonstrative, i.e., mathematical and semi-mathematical reasoning. In the last two hundred years, the study of reasoning has increasingly taken mathematical reasoning as the 'model' of reasoning and has increasingly studied that (so, for example, the study of legal reasoning has largely dropped out of sight among those interested in giving a general account of 'good' and 'bad' reasoning).

Of course, as a theory of *mathematical* reasoning modern logic has been amazingly successful. There is no doubt that the modern logical systems deriving from Frege and Russell give a beautiful, enormously insightful, and largely correct account of the principles of mathematical reasoning (*pace* Brouwer). Furthermore, modern formal logic articulates the principles of mathematical reasoning *in a form which renders that reasoning amenable to mathematical study*—which is just what you might expect mathematicians to want to do with any subject matter—and this led to Godel's amazing results and all the rest. Indeed, modern logic has been so successful in its chosen domain that we have tended to lose sight of its limitations. Clearly, mathematical arguments have some very distinctive features within the whole domain of real arguments in that they are abstract, timeless, precise, concerned only with truth and falsity, concerned with belief and not action, addressed to a 'universal' (or no particular) audience and are definitely right or wrong. But, most 'real reasoning' is not like that at all.

Though this historical story about how the study of reasoning was 'taken over' by 'mathematical' logic is plausible enough, it is harder to explain why this development should have taken such a hold on the imagination and thinking of philosophers. To do this would require historical work of considerable complexity. Part of the explanation must lie in the influence mathematical thinking has had on philosophers over the centuries—ever since Euclid and Pythagoras. It is pure, uncluttered, *a priori*, certain, and true. What a lovely thing to find! And philosophers since Plato have wanted to find such truths. Part of the explanation must also lie in the success of the sciences (especially Newton), and in their deductive structure. Part of the explanation must also lie in the influence of Descartes, and the search for certainty. It would be fascinating to chart this story, but the fact is that by the twentieth century, the mathematical paradigm was dominant, and the 'science of reasoning' had quite lost sight of the importance of 'dialectic' and 'rhetoric'. Certainly for much of this century, if your 'impulse to philosophy' was a fascination with reasoning, you studied modern formal, mathematical logic. More recently, Anglo-Saxon analytical philosophy has been so closely associated with logic, that you could hardly study philosophy without studying logic.

3. Why Teach Formal Logic to Philosophy Students'

For some time it has been common to justify the teaching of logic in philosophy programmes as being necessary for the study of philosophy and as sharpening up the students' reasoning skills outside the logic class. Gilbert Ryle's paper 'Formal and Informal Logic' (Ryle, 1953, ch. viii) was an articulate and influential attempt to describe the relationship between logic and analytic philosophy when that movement was at its height. With the benefit of hindsight it is hard to read Ryle's article without feeling that he was puzzled by the relationship which has so long existed between formal logic and general philosophical enquiries: I quote,

> It is not easy to describe this liaison between Formal Logic and philosophy. The systematic presentation of the rules of syllogistic inference is a very different sort of activity from, say, the elucidation of the concept of pleasure. The Aristotle who inaugurated the former is the same thinker as the Aristotle who considerably developed the latter, yet the kinds of thinking in which he was involved are very widely different. The technical problems in the theory of the syllogism have a strong resemblance to the problems of Euclidean geometry; the ideals of systematization and rigorous proof are at work, . . . false moves are demonstrable fallacies. The problems in, say, the theory of pleasure or perception . . . are not like this. Aristotle debates with Plato and Socrates, and the issues become better defined as the debate progresses, but the debate does not take the shape of a chain of theorems, nor do the arguments used in the debate admit of notational codification. Whether a given philosophical argument is valid or fallacious is, in general, itself a debatable question. Simple inspection cannot decide. More often it is a question of whether the argument has much, little or no force. (ibid. pp. 111f).

All this is true and strongly suggests that formal logic is irrelevant to most argumentation, but Ryle proceeded to defend the relationship between 'Formal Logic' and philosophy by means of a famous analogy;

> In some respects the following analogy holds. Fighting in battles is markedly unlike parade ground drill. The best conducted drill-

evolutions would be the worst possible battle movements, and the most favourable terrain for a rearguard action would entirely forbid what the barrack square is made for. None the less the efficient and resourceful fighter is also the well-drilled soldier. The ways in which he takes advantage of the irregularities of the ground show the marks of the schooling he has received on the asphalt. He can improvise operations in the dark and at the risk of his life now, partly because he has learned to do highly stereotyped and formalized things in broad daylight and in conditions of unmitigated tedium. It is not the stereotyped motions of drill, but its standards of perfection of control which are transmitted from the parade-ground to the battlefield. (ibid. p. 112)

Perhaps he had misgivings about this analogy because Ryle also describes the relationship between 'Formal Logic' and the philosopher as 'rather like what geometry is to the cartographer . . . or . . . what accountancy is to the merchant . . .' It is a tool for the philosopher, but it is only a tool and the philosopher is mainly doing what Ryle calls 'Informal Logic' (ibid. pp. 123f)

It is very common for philosophers to argue by analogy (witness our example from Hume above), though they have not theorized much about doing so. It is difficult to evaluate Ryle's analogy, though it seems to have received general assent when it was published. The claim that the soldier's parade-ground drill is important to his battle-ground performance is partly a claim to the effect that drill gets the soldier used to military discipline, used to obeying orders whatever the circumstances, etc., and it is partly a causal claim. (Indeed, one can imagine military experts devising experiments which aim at testing its truth.) If the analogy is to be taken seriously, Ryle must be saying that learning formal logic helps to make good philosophers partly by getting students used to certain intellectual disciplines and techniques, and partly by giving them the right attitudes in argumentative battle! Perhaps that was plausible when philosophy was mainly concerned with 'necessary' connections and with the 'logical geography' of concepts, but it seems much less so now. [Comment from Martin Hollis: 'Once upon a time the better drilled army won battles because they were set-piece parade ground affairs. Then warfare changed. Did the army stop its stupid drills? Of course not, It cooked up the justification Ryle alludes to . . .'!]

Whatever one is inclined to say about Ryle's analogies, there have long been questions in the minds of philosophers about, on the one hand, the role of logic (and epistemology?) in philosophical and general education, and on the other hand, the nature and structure of reasoning and justification. In this century much of the interest in these issues, and in the connections between them, draws its inspiration essentially from the pragmatist tradition and, in origin, especially from the work of Dewey. Dewey was not only an important figure in the history of philosophical pragmatism, he was also passionately interested in educational issues, and his book about how to teach what he called 'reflective thinking' (Dewey, 1909), is often cited as the philosophical origin of the modern, North American 'informal logic and critical thinking' movement.

Dewey's educational ideas might have lain dormant for even longer had not another, more robust, force came into play in the late 1960's and early 1970's. As Howard Kahane explains in the preface to his *Logic and Contemporary Rhetoric* (1969),

> In class a few years back, while I was going over the (to me) fascinating intricacies of the predicate logic quantifier rules, a student asked in disgust how anything he'd learned all semester long had any bearing whatever on President Johnson's decision to escalate again in Vietnam. I mumbled something about bad logic on Johnson's part, and then stated that Introduction to Logic was not that kind of course. His reply was to ask what kind of courses did take up such matters, and I had to admit that so far as I knew none did. (Kahane, 1971, p. vii)

Kahane's experience was not at all unusual in North America at that time. Indeed, the term 'informal logic', in the sense in which we use the term nowadays, first came into use in the late 1960s and early 1970s in North America, to refer to a new kind of logic course, whose overt aim was to equip students to assess real arguments of the kind typically encountered in the mass media (cf. Johnson and Blair, 1985). The impulse to help their students understand and evaluate real arguments (rather than the invented, artificially neat and tidy examples of the formal logic class) has been growing among North American logicians ever since. A similar impulse, moved initially by a similar pressure from students, has also given rise to the closely related critical thinking movement, which has a broader educational agenda, and draws more widely from philosophy (see Blair, 'Current Issues in Informal Logic and Critical Thinking, in Fisher, 1988).

Rather as one might expect, with the benefit of a Kuhnian perspective, the modern informal logic and critical thinking movement is confused and exploratory. The 'normal science' of modern formal logic, in which the problems and methods of solution are largely agreed among the experts, has given way to the 'abnormal science' of informal logic, in which there are no such criteria for reaching agreement. However, the subject matter on which it focuses is clear. This consists of real arguments—arguments people actually use, or have used, in order to convince others of a point of view. Furthermore, the reasons for focusing on such arguments are clear. On the one hand, workers in this field are interested in teaching students to reason well, and whilst it is clear that teaching formal logic never did that, there are reasons to hope that by engaging them in real (good and bad) argumentation, and dissecting such argumentation, one might achieve this objective. On the other hand, there is a sense that certain traditional ideas about the nature and structure of reasoning and justification are mistaken and need to be re-thought. The modern pragmatist picture presents a radical challenge to traditional epistemology which is closely related to the challenge presented by informal logic to formal logic.

4. Teaching Reasoning and The Nature of Justification: Informal Logic and Pragmatism

There is no doubt that these practical concerns (how to teach people to reason better) are increasingly driving those working in this field to reject the mathematical model of reasoning in favour of a *conversational* and *social* model (which draws on ideas from discourse analysis, argumentation theory, dialogue games, the study of legal argumentation, etc.) just when epistemology is going through a similar experience. Ideas about the importance of objectivity, necessity and certainty are being challenged in both domains in favour of ideas about *coherence, conversation* and *agreement between speakers*. A few remarks from Richard Rorty's *Philosophy and the Mirror of Nature* will illustrate the point.

> If we have a Deweyan conception of knowledge, as what we are justified in believing, then we will not imagine that there are enduring constraints on what we can count as knowledge, since we will see 'justification' as a social phenomenon rather than a transaction between 'the knowing subject' and 'reality'. (Rorty, 1980, 9)
>
> If . . . we think of 'rational certainty' as a matter of victory in argument rather than of relation to an object known, we shall look to our interlocutors rather than to our faculties for the explanation of the phenomenon. If we think of our certainty about the Pythagorean Theorem as our confidence, based on experience with arguments on such matters, that nobody will find an objection to the premises from which we infer it, then we shall not seek to explain it by the relation of reason to triangularity. Our certainty will be a matter of conversation between persons, rather than a matter of interaction with non-human reality. So we shall not see a difference in kind between 'necessary' and 'contingent' truths. At most, we shall see differences in degree of ease in objecting to our beliefs. (ibid. p. 157)

Later, he argues that the holism of the pragmatists arises out of their view 'that justification is not a matter of a special relation between ideas (or words) and objects, but of conversation, of social practice' and that such holism produces, 'as Quine has argued in detail, . . . a conception of philosophy which has nothing to do with the quest for certainty' (ibid. pp. 170–171). For more in the same vein see especially (ibid. pp. 173–180).

5. How Do Philosophers Reason?

We shall return to pragmatist ideas about justification shortly, but a digression into the nature of philosophical reasoning is becoming appropriate. It will be quite transparent that very little, if any, of the reasoning in this paper is deductively valid. To that extent it is just like most arguments which people actually use, or have used, in order to try to convince others of a point of view —what I have been calling 'real' arguments. Of course, philosophers readily acknowledge that most ordinary, everyday arguments are not deductively valid as presented (and are not meant to be), but it is much less common for philosophers to admit the same of philosophical reasoning. They usually aspire to logically compelling arguments in their own field and tend to criticise other philosophers whose conclusions 'don't necessarily follow'. It seems clear to me that this obsession with necessity is fuelled by some commonly held ideas about logic and the nature of argument which are mistaken and pernicious for philosophy, and that though recent philosophical work is freeing philosophy from this obsession, logic has yet to break free and become a genuine 'science of reasoning'.

Many people who are teaching informal logic courses search for argumentative material with which to teach their students and are surprised at the difficulty they have in finding suitable material if their ideas about argument are at all inspired by traditional logical ideas. Since most of these teachers are philosophers, many of them teaching students with an interest in philosophy, you might expect that such teachers would be able to find plenty of philosophical examples of the right kind of argumentation. However, they are not easy to find, and a key reason for this appears to be that philosophers rarely argue their case on anything like the mathematical model—on anything like the model which underlies modern logic. Philosophical writing is much more like ordinary argumentative writing than many philosophers' ideas about the nature and structure of reasoning and justification suggest it ought to be if 'ideology' is to bear any relation to practice. Trudy Govier makes the same point, though in broader terms:

Curiously enough, philosophical arguments are not primarily deductive. They are not, on the whole, valid in virtue of logical form alone, not easily translatable into the technical symbols of formal systems. Nor are philosophical arguments like the arguments studied in inductive logic. In accepting the model of successful argument presumed in traditional logic, philosophers have put themselves in an absurd position, because they are unable to apply what passes as a theory of argument to many of their own arguments. This difficulty would be merely silly had it not such a venerable philosophical history. Scholars have often pointed out that Descartes, Hume, Kant, and the logical positivists all have difficulty in getting their own practise to conform to their own theory. ('Rigour and Reality' in Govier, 1987, 9)

Philosophers tend to write (and speak) much more like advocates than like mathematicians and yet many of them continue to employ a model of reasoning which derives from mathematics. It would be interesting to know what is so seductive about this Jeckyll and Hyde intellectual life.

6. An Example of Philosophical Double Standards?

As Govier's list suggests, it is easy to slip into the error of employing standards which do not apply to one's own arguments. It happens to the best of us. For example, the case I wish to present rests on the pragmatists' 'holistic' conception of justification and the idea of a 'web of belief', which rests in turn on the pragmatists' rejection of the analytic/synthetic distinction; but the classic statement of that case for rejecting the analytic/synthetic distinction is Quine's famous article 'Two Dogmas of Empiricism' (1951) and it even seems to happen there.

Remember, Quine's argument is against the idea that there is 'some fundamental cleavage between truths which are *analytic* or grounded in meanings independently of matters of fact, and truths which are *synthetic* or grounded in fact'. The argument is that statements which philosophers recognize as analytic fall into two classes, those which 'may be called *logically true*', like 'No unmarried man is married' which is true in virtue of its logical form (which can be articulated in the notation of modern logic) and those like 'No bachelor is unmarried'. which can be turned into a logical truth by replacing synonyms by synonyms (in this case 'bachelor' by 'unmarried man'). But, Quine argues, we do not have a well-defined notion of synonomy, clear enough to enable us to decide which statements are analytic in this latter sense. But what is wrong with looking in the dictionary? Quine's argument against doing this is as follows:

> Clearly this would be to put the cart before the horse. The lexicographer is an empirical scientist, whose business is the recording of

antecedent facts; and if he glosses 'bachelor' as 'unmarried man' it is because of his belief that there is a relation of synonymy between those forms, implicit in general or preferred usage prior to his own work. The notion of synonymy presupposed here has still to be clarified, presumably in terms of linguistic behaviour. Certainly the "definition" which is the lexicographer's report of an observed synonymy cannot be taken as the ground of that synonymy. (Quine, 1951, 24)

Quine's argument has been widely accepted in philosophical circles, though notice that it does not employ or pretend to employ 'necessary' connections; it says that we cannot use the work of the lexicographer as evidence of synonymy, because he is just an empirical scientist reporting on what we are really interested in. But what sort of argument is that? Surely, if a court needed to decide whether two English words were synonomous, the evidence of the Oxford English Dictionary would be powerful, perhaps even sufficient, testimony in many cases. And this is because the OED is recognized to be *authoritative*; these lexicographers are experienced and thorough experts. What better evidence could you have in most cases? Of course there must be provision to dispute expert evidence (which is to say that the OED will not always be right) but it is basically well proven. So, practically speaking, a good dictionary *does* record what we want to know in many cases in which the question of synonymy arises.

This looks as though Quine is requiring too much clarity of 'synonomy'; he is using a (philosopher's) double standard to achieve his goal; on the one hand he argues quite loosely and naturally, on the other hand he demands much more of his opponents. Grice and Strawson make much the same point:

It seems clear that we have here a typical example of a philosopher's paradox. Instead of examining the actual use we make of the notion of *meaning the same*, the philosopher measures it by some perhaps inappropriate standard (in this case some standard of clarifiability), and because it falls short of this standard, or seems to do so, denies its reality, declares it illusory. (1956, 146f)

This is the interesting thing about Quine's argument from our present point of view. Arguably, it is an example of double standards, and it occurs at the very fount of modern pragmatism! It is not easy to escape from old ways of thinking, from old paradigms.

7. Pragmatism and The Laws of Logic

So how should real arguments be assessed, if not by ideas inspired by a mathematical conception of argument? There were several elements in the mathematical picture which were misleading about the nature of reasoning. One of the most important is the deductive structure of mathematical theories. Euclidean geometry has had a dramatic effect on the imagination of many a thinker, especially because of the way so much can be deduced from so little. Many other theories have subsequently been cast in the same axiomatic—deductive form, including, very importantly, Newton's mechanics. This structure suggests that there are some basic truths which serve like the foundations of a building, and the other truths of the theory rest on these foundations just as a building rests on its foundations. The axiomatic—deductive way of organizing our knowledge in a given domain is extremely elegant and very useful for some purposes, but it is a mistake to think that the axioms have a special epistemological status. The whole theory stands together—it 'faces the tribunal of experience' as a whole. In general there are many other possible axiomatizations of the same theory which are equivalent in the sense that they yield the same theorems (theorems which are basic axioms in one axiomatization will be derived theorems in another). *This* is the sense in which two statements P and Q in, say, Newtonian mechanics may be regarded as supporting each other (without necessarily being equivalent); there are inferential routes from P to Q and from Q to P in different presentations of the reasoning in that area of the theory. Everyone is familiar with the idea that if one of the 'theorems' of an axiomatic—deductive theory turns out to be mistaken, this error runs back, by modus tollens, to the axioms, but it is not so easy to grasp the holistic character of such theories. The point here is that, even in domains where our knowledge is organized on the axiomatic—deductive model, the structure of the reasoning which supports a particular claim is not linear from basic premises/axioms, but is holistic. Furthermore, not only does the support for a given claim come from many directions, it also comes in many forms ranging from the deductive support which is provided by other elements in the theory, to 'evidence from the world' relating to the particular claim and to the theory as a whole, to probability considerations and considerations about simplicity, etc.

Let us develop this point further with a general question about Quine's rejection of the analytic/synthetic distinction. Supposing that it is right to reject this distinction what now happens to the 'laws of logic'. Quine is sometimes read as believing that logical laws are a special case, to which his general arguments against the analytic/synthetic distinction do not apply. Quine distinguishes in 'Two Dogmas' between two kinds of statement which philosophers take to be analytic, those which are *logically true* and those whose analyticity depends on substituting synonyms for synonyms to yield logical truths;

> Statements which are analytic by general philosophical acclaim . . . fall into two classes. Those of the first class, which may be called *logically true*, are typified by:
>
> No unmarried man is married
>
> The relevant feature of this example is that it not merely is true as it stands, but remains true under any and all reinterpretations of 'man' and 'married'. If we suppose a prior inventory of *logical* particles, comprising 'no', 'un-', 'not', 'if', 'then', 'and', etc., then in general a logical truth is a statement which is true and remains true under all reinterpretations of its components other than the logical particles. (Quine, 1953, 22)

This has often been taken by philosophers to imply that logical truths are immune from revision—because they 'remain true under all rein- terpretations (etc.)'. But I think it is clear that this is to misinterpret Quine—by ignoring the part of the definition of a logical truth which refers to 'reinterpreting its components *other than the logical particles*'. Given the meaning which classical logic attaches to 'not' and 'or', the law of excluded middle is indeed a logical truth in Quine's sense, however, those who reject, say, the law of excluded middle (notably intuitionistic mathematicians) give a different acount of the meaning of 'not' and 'or' from the classical account.

I think it is clear that Quine thinks the laws of logic are revisable, as everything else is;

> Mathematical and logical laws themselves are not immune to revision if it is found that essential simplifications of our whole conceptual scheme will ensue. There have been suggestions, stimulated largely by quandaries of modern physics, that we revise the true-false dicho- tomy of current logic in favour of some sort of tri- or n-chotomy. Logical laws are the most central and crucial statements of our conceptual scheme, and for this reason the most protected from revision by the force of conservatism; but, because again of their crucial position, they are the laws an apt revision of which might offer the most sweeping simplification of our whole system of know- ledge. (Quine, 1952, p. xiv)

8. Pragmatism and Inferential Relations

However, there is a more interesting issue about the rejection of the analytic synthetic distinction: it is this. If this distinction is to be

Alec Fisher

rejected in favour of the holistic conceptions I briefly described above, then the picture we are offered is that some propositions are more central to our belief system than others, and are less readily given up. But now what are we to say about the inferential relations which exist between propositions in different parts of the web? Don't they exhibit a similar variation? Any argument has its corresponding hypothetical statement, of the form 'If [the premises] then [the conclusion]'. The hypothetical statements which correspond to most real arguments will not of course exhibit a valid logical form but why should we not—on Quine's account—have a whole range of such hypotheticals, some of which are very central to our belief system and which we should be very reluctant to give up (they would be very close to what we now call 'logical truths') whilst others would be more peripheral and more readily given up? Corresponding to the 'web' of beliefs which has the truths of logic and mathematics at its centre, there is a 'web' of arguments which has 'deductive' arguments at its centre, but which also recognizes 'warrants' with lesser degrees of inferential strength.

Perhaps Quine himself recognizes this:

> The totality of our so-called knowledge or beliefs, from the most casual matters of geography and history to the profoundest laws of atomic physics or even of pure mathematics and logic, is a man-made fabric which impinges on experience only along the edges . . . Reevaluations of some statements entails reevaluations of others, because of their logical interconnections—the logical laws being in turn simply certain further statements of the system, certain further elements of the field. Having reevaluated one statement we must reevaluate some others, which may be statements logically connected with the first or may be statements of logical connections themselves. (Quine, 1953, 42)

There seems no good reason to deny this picture once we have accepted the holistic picture of a 'web of belief' and once we have recognized that any argument has its corresponding hypothetical. The implication is that pragmatist arguments force us to recognize many different inferential relations, of differing degrees of strength, which should be studied in the contexts in which they occur if we want a general 'science of reasoning'; which is just what the informal logic and critical thinking movement would have us do.

9. Some Kinds of Inferential Relationship

Of course philosophers have long distinguished deductive and inductive reasoning, but this distinction goes down with the analytic/distinction, so the implication of the pragmatist position is that one should look for some kind of array of inferential relations of different strengths and of different kinds.

Some philosophers have done something like this of course, though without much lasting impact. For example, the later Wittgenstein recognized non-deductive, non-inductive inference rules which allow us to make justified inferences from 'criterial evidence'. Hacker explains the idea as follows:

> Kinds of sentences, Wittgenstein suggests, can be characterized by the nature of the criterial evidence which support their assertion. Thus the grammar of material object sentences is characterized by having multiple criterial evidence provided by sentences describing subjective experience (BB p. 51). The grammar of sentences concerning mental states is characterized by the fact that sentences describing behaviour in certain circumstances are fixed as criteria for such sentences. The rules in question are non-inductive, inference rules which allow us to move from an assertion of criterial evidence to a justified though not necessarily true assertion of that which it supports. These rules are fixed by us . . . (PI SS 354–5). (Hacker, 1972, 153)

There is another kind of reasoning, quite different again, but very commonly used, both in ordinary argument and in philosophy, though rarely theorized about as part of the theory of argument and that is argument by analogy. For philosophical examples, consider Judith Jarvis Thompson's famous analogy between the woman who is carrying an unwanted foetus and the person who unexpectedly finds herself hooked up to a dying violinist, or consider Hume's argument ((d) above) against the idea that God created the Universe, or his 'watchmaker' analogy in favour of the idea that God must have done. The negative use of logical analogy—to rebut an argument by citing a parallel but flawed argument—is very common in argument. It often begins with some such phrase as 'But you might as well say that . . .' and then the parallel is produced. The intuition which lies behind this practise is the same as the intuition which lies behind the formal logician's notion of 'counter-example', but the logician has extracted a minimal content from the intuition, and one which is amenable to mathematical study. The general study of the use of analogy is only in its infancy.

A third example, once identified by Wisdom (see Yalden-Thomas, 1974) as the most basic, primary, kind of reasoning, is case-by-case reasoning.

> This reasoning is used, either explicitly or implicitly, in order to show that a word is properly applied to a case. Since both deduction

and induction presume the proper application of words to instances, any kind of reasoning which is a prerequisite of doing this can lay claim to 'most basic' status . . . There may be important disputes in such cases and there is a rational way to resolve them. We find an instance which is clearly a case of negligence, nationhood, being a mobile home, or whatever, and we closely compare and contrast that instance with the unresolved one. In this way, we can argue for a conclusion on the point. Case-by-case reasoning is a species of argument by analogy. The only way to show that terms have been correctly applied is to reason from agreed instances of their correct application. (Two Unreceived Views about Reasoning and Argument', in Govier, 1987, 57)

The core of legal reasoning is, as Wisdom noted, case by case . . . A type of argument of obvious prominence and importance has been widely ignored by theorists. Probably this is due to the fact that it is less prominent in science and in mathematics than in the moral life, law, administration, criticism, and philosophy. We have tended to build up our theories of knowledge and our theories of argument as though all knowledge were logico-mathematical or—empirical-scientific, and then find problems when justification in other areas of life does not fit the models we construct. (Govier, 1987, 64).

What appears to be needed for the general theory of argument is something like Dewey's notion of 'warranted assertability' rather than notions like 'validity', 'necessity' or 'certainty'. Interestingly, this is not only what is needed if one wishes to theorise about the nature and structure of argument, but also what appears to be needed if one is interested in teaching students to reason well.

10. Teaching Reasoning. The 'Science of Reasoning' and Cognitive Psychology

Whether your main interest is in *teaching* reasoning and rationality or in theoretical questions it is surely reasonable to expect any general 'science of reasoning' to take account of what people actually do when reasoning. In recent years cognitive psychologists, notably Philip Johnson-Laird and Peter Wason, have conducted fascinating research into this field with some surprising results. One of the most interesting concerns Wason's so-called 'selection task', and we consider this briefly now.

People make inferences all the time in their everyday lives, and psychologists have long been interested in knowing how human beings do this. Many psychologists have thought that the laws of logic are somehow part of our mental equipment, whether innate or learned, and that in reasoning we do no more than follow these 'laws of thought' (cf. Inhelder and Piaget, 1958, 305): 'reasoning is nothing more than the propositional calculus itself'). One difficulty with this view is that people are often illogical in their reasoning, so if there are innate logical principles, it is necessary to explain why they often fail us. Equally, if the principles of logic are learned, how do children manage to pick them up from adults who often reason so illogically? To assume that children can do this is to assume that they can distinguish valid arguments from invalid ones before they have learned what the principles of valid argument are! So again psychologists are pushed back in the direction of innate principles of logic, and perhaps an explanation in terms of their evolutionary value.

However, there is evidence which suggests that the 'mental logic' account cannot be right, and it comes from Wason's so-called selection experiment. The experimenter lays out four cards in front of the subject, displaying the symbols

E   K   4   7

The subject is told that each card has a number on one side and a letter on the other. The subject is then given the sentence,

> If a card has a vowel on one side then it has an even number on the other side

and is asked to select which cards need to be turned over in order to decide whether the sentence is true or false. The order of dealing with the cards is irrelevant; for each card the question is simply whether it is relevant to determining the truth value of the hypothetical.

Nearly everyone turns over the E card, but very few turn over the 7 card, even though the hypothetical is refuted if the card has a vowel on it! (The other two cards are irrelevant to the truth of the hypothetical, though many people turn over the 4 card.)

But the interesting thing about this experiment is what happens when abstract symbols are replaced by meaningful content. With the cards

Manchester   Sheffield   Train   Car

and the sentence

Every time I go to Manchester I travel by train

Johnson-Laird reports that most people realize that they must turn over the card with 'car' on it (because if this card has 'Manchester' on the other side the hypothetical sentence must be false). In the abstract case, very few people realize the equivalent point. Johnson-Laird also reports that experience with realistic materials fails to transfer positively to abstract materials (cf. Johnson-Laird, 1983, 31)

There have been many replications of the Johnson-Laird and Wason experiments, with varying results. For example, with 'nonsense' hypotheticals like 'If I eat haddock, then I drink gin' performance is much the same as with abstract symbols. With realistic materials which relate to the subject's experience, subjects do much better.

Johnson-Laird concludes that people are far more likely to make the right inferences, even in a simple case like this, if they have a 'mental model' of the relationship expressed in the hypothetical.

> What is crucial . . . is that insight into the task reflects an effect of content on the process of deduction. If subjects already possess a mental model of the relation expressed in the general rule [hypothetical], or a model that can be readily related to the rule, they are much more likely to have an insight into the task. This phenomenon is an embarrassment to any psychological theory that assumes that generalizations are falsified by recourse to formal rules of inference. . . .
>
> The subjects in the card turning task do, indeed, search for counter-examples, but their search is only comprehensive with realistic materials that relate to an existing mental model . . . A mental logic would provide the same formal guide to performance in both cases . . . (ibid. pp. 33–34)

The results of these and related experiments are certainly an embarrassment to any psychological theory which thinks that generalizations are falsified by recourse to formal rules of inference, but why are they of interest to philosophers and logicians? They imply that the existence of *possible* counter-examples to an inference is not a major consideration when people are deciding whether to accept an inference; what seems to matter is whether the picture they are being presented 'fits' with other things they believe (or suppose to be true for the purpose of the argument). The work of Johnson-Laird and others strongly suggests that the 'mental logic' account of the way people reason is wrong and that his 'mental models' account is right. I do not know whether this is true or not, but it is hard to believe that the facts about how people reason do not have serious implications for both a general 'science of reasoning' and for the teaching of reasoning.

11. Conclusion

I have been arguing that something exciting is happening in 'logic' or the 'science of reasoning'—that something like the beginnings of a Kuhnian 'revolution' can be discerned in the theoretical challenge from pragmatism and in the guerrilla activity being mounted by the 'informal logic' movement. A 'paradigm', in Kuhn's sense, is a picture of the way things are in some domain—a picture which is shared by the members of the scientific community who study that domain. It generates what Kuhn calls 'normal science' i.e., research based firmly on some past achievements, which tries to answer the problems generated by the paradigm, and attempts to do so in a prescribed way. In attempting to extend the applicability of the old paradigm, normal science encounters difficulties, failures of fit, falsifying evidence and what Kuhn generally calls 'anomolous experiences'. What I am suggesting is that something *like* this is happening in logic. The old 'mathematical' paradigm, which has the notion of 'logical form' at its core, is proving inadequate in various ways. The old paradigm has run its course, and is in the process of being overthrown. Of course I am not saying that modern logic as we know it is wrong and should no longer be taught in Universities and Colleges. Modern formal logic still has a very important place in our culture and hence in higher education. The ideas contained in modern logic are the very foundation of modern computing technology; they are embedded in most programming languages; they are embedded in the structure of the hardware; they are the basis of the modern information technology industry. That is now the proper home of courses in modern logic. There they have a vital function. But as a general theory or science of reasoning modern logic's time is up.

Just as Rorty has argued that 'Wittgenstein, Heidegger and Dewey have brought us into a period of revolutionary philosophy, in Kuhn's sense of "revolutionary science"' (Rorty, 1980, 6–7), so I have argued that informal logic has brought us into a revolutionary period in the 'science of reasoning'.

Can Philosophy Speak about Life?

İLHAM DİLMAN

1. Does Philosophy have Anything Positive To Say?

Sometimes when artists talk about painting one finds what they have to say interesting: because they are talking about something they have lived with, something in which they find meaning. At other times one feels that it would be better for them to paint rather than talk about painting.

The same is true in philosophy, except for the fact that to talk about philosophy is to *do* philosophy.

I am a philosopher. This means that I have studied the thoughts of other philosophers, tried to learn from them, and in my capacity as teacher of philosophy tried to help others to do the same. But above all it means that I have asked the kind of questions which other philosophers have asked, though not necessarily those same questions. That is what entitles me to try to say something about philosophy. We must bear in mind, of course, that I am talking to philosophers. I am not informing them about philosophy and can take their familiarity with the subject for granted. Indeed, I must be able to do so if I am to say anything worth hearing about it, however much they may disagree with what I say.

With just this situation in mind Professor John Wisdom asked: 'How does anyone say to another anything worth hearing when he doesn't know anything the other doesn't know?' (1953, p. 248). I will not ask this question, but will begin with the more radical question whether philosophy can *say* anything at all or, to put it differently, whether one can *say* anything as a philosopher.

Let me remind you that some philosophers have denied this. For instance, Wittgenstein in the *Tractatus* said, quite starkly, that philosophy cannot itself say anything: it can only show what can be said. No doubt in that work he had a narrow and faulty conception of what constitutes language and, therefore, of what can be said in or by means of it. But in his later and mature work he criticized that conception, so that what philosophy, in his now different conception of it, could *say* was no longer shackled on the side of his ideas of what constitutes saying something. Nevertheless he was careful not to allow what could be said here to become detached from the *work* of philosophy.

In philosophy, Wittgenstein insisted, language is wholly in the service of such work and the remarks it issues are critical and on the whole negative. When they are not negative they take the form of reminders of what we already know, hints, comparisons, similes and analogies which compare the familiar with the familiar.

This gives the impression that Wittgenstein still thinks of philosophy as having nothing positive to say on any matter. Its reminders are 'boring' and only the job of demolishment and demystification is exciting. But it erects nothing new in the site where it has demolished what Wittgenstein described as 'houses of cards' (Wittgenstein, 1953, sec. 118). So one may have some excuse for thinking that for Wittgenstein philosophy is a form of therapy, in the sphere of the intellect, which like behavioural therapy, frees us from what is undesirable, deceptive and an encumbrance, without adding anything to our knowledge. But if this is all that philosophy does, it cannot be a cognitive discipline, and it is an art only in the sense of a skill.

Obviously this will not do: if it were what I found in philosophy I would not have wanted to go on with it. Indeed, as I have come to learn from Wittgenstein's writings themselves, philosophy does have a substantive contribution to make to our understanding.

It is true that Wittgenstein does reject the idea of a special form of knowledge to which philosophy contributes, whether conceived in the Platonic or the Kantian fashion. There is no such knowledge which a philosopher bequeaths to posterity for other philosophers to build on. Indeed, there are no answers, findings, results here which others can accept on the basis of arguments that establish them once and for all, and make them their starting point.

In other words, there is nothing that can stand apart from the *work* which a philosopher has done; each philosopher has to do that work for himself. Having done it, he has to find the best way to present it so that others can learn from it. To learn from it is to make sense of the work itself in the way it has been presented, to ask its questions, to enter its discussions. But having learned from it, one has to find one's own voice and one's own way of working.

Given, then, that in philosophy each person has to find his own starting point and to do his own work, we cannot speak of the progress of philosophy itself: there is no body of philosophical knowledge that grows in the course of philosophy's history. The history of philosophy is the scene of arguments and discussions in which particular traditions are carried on, changed, and sometimes transformed. What we find are 'peaks and troughs'[1] within the tradition: we have great philosophers

---

[1] For this way of putting it I am indebted to Professor Specht of the University of Mannheim.

and original thinking in some periods, and mediocrity and fashions in others. In periods where there is life in the activity of philosophy its questions go deep and they send reverberations in different directions, contributing to the intellectual life of the time.

But though philosophy itself does not progress, this is not to say a philosophical discussion or enquiry cannot do so. Certainly a particular philosopher, or those who take part in a particular discussion, may be getting somewhere in the discussion. They may come to some insight the absence of which was keeping the discusion glued to the same spot or going round in circles.

A good deal of this insight, as I said, is into what one already knows: the familiar grammar of the concepts that trouble us. We misunderstand it only in turning our backs to the workings of the language to which the concepts belong and being lured into abstract thinking. Thus, to give an example, it seemed to Locke that there is more to the familiar objects that surround us than their properties with which, he thought, we are familiar through the 'ideas' we have of them—'ideas' which are their mental copies or representatives. There must be more to them since the properties are what they *have*. But we cannot have any idea of *what* has the properties, because whatever ideas we have will necessarily be of further properties and not of the object itself which has them. It follows that we cannot be acquainted with the object, only at best with its properties—or perhaps only with our ideas of their properties.

This is obviously a disquieting conclusion and it is not too difficult to see that what leads to it has to do with what Locke makes of the subject–predicate form of sentences in which we describe the familiar objects in our surroundings, and of the way he thinks of what entitles us to give these descriptions. These are both conceptual matters familiar to us, even though they hardly seem to warrant the conclusion to which they led Locke.

Understandably disquieted by this conclusion, Berkeley reflected on these familiar matters and, while he rejected Locke's conclusion, drew another one which is equally disquieting. He argued that Locke's notion of a material object hides a contradiction, but it is not *our* notion of it: a material object is the sum total of its sensible properties and those, in turn, are identical with our ideas of them. He thus escaped Locke's conclusion that material objects are beyond the reach of our sense perceptions, but put in jeopardy what Hume called their 'continuous and independent existence', the very thing which distinguishes them from our mental images.

I am not interested now in the details of the arguments of Locke and Berkeley, but in the characer of the issue on which they stood opposed. For it is a characteristic example of philosophical conflict. It revolves

İlham Dilman

around perfectly plausible constructions put on familiar concepts—so plausible, indeed, that while Berkeley described one such construction, Locke's, as the *philosophical* idea of matter, at times he ascribed the faults he found with it to the 'vulgar notion'. That is he, himself, ascribed that construction to the vulgar notion even though he knew that constructions do not appear in the flow of language in our speech and reasonings: 'To those that walk the high road of plain, common sense (he said) nothing that is familiar appears unaccountable or difficult to comprehend' (1950, Intro.). It is when our thoughts turn on themselves and make their own legitimacy the object of their concern, that they become susceptible to such constructions.

Wittgenstein described this situation by saying that here 'language is like an engine idling—not doing work' (1953, sec. 132). But he did not mean to suggest that philosophical questions are somehow unreal or that all we have to learn from the philosopher who raises them is to avoid his mistakes. Where Wittgenstein spoke of language going 'on holiday' (1953, sec. 38), Berkeley spoke of philosophical thought leaving 'the high road of plain, common sense'. He pointed out, much in agreement with Wittgenstein, how when this happens 'we are insensibly drawn into uncouth paradoxes, difficulties, and inconsistences, which multiply and grow upon us as we advance in speculation' (ibid.).

In such a case what we need to do is (i) to appreciate where our thought is being led to an impasse, (ii) to examine critically the constructions and presuppositions that lead it in this direction in the hope that we can discard them, and (iii) to get clear about the ground from which such constructions stem. Thus our thinking is 'demystified' and our understanding of the 'grammar' (as Wittgenstein calls it) of a particular area of langauge is transformed—for instance, what 'the continuous and independent existence' of objects comes to. As a result, not only do we avoid the pitfalls which tripped us in our thinking and feel at home in that language in a new way, but we also become more sensitive to the richness of what is said there.

Take a different example: the idea that there must be a motive for doing whatever we do and that our motives drive us to do what we do. This may raise philosophical questions which lead us to examine what it means to attribute motives to people and what it is we are saying about them when we do so. Such an examination may not only untangle 'knots in our thinking' (1967, sec. 452), but as a result we may come to understand what it means to talk about and reflect on a person's motives in a way we were never clear about before. But more than this such reflections as we ourselves engage in may come to be enriched as a result of our philosophical examination. Indeed, our appreciation of a writer, a novelist for instance, who is concerned with the motives of his characters may be enhanced by what we have gained in our philosophical reflections on 'the grammar of motives'. We are at once freer in our movement in this area of discourse, richer in what we are able to bring to it, and more aware of abuses within it. In fact such insights enrich our whole understanding of psychology.

Let us be clear, however, that philosophy is not an investigation of the grammar of our language in the way, for instance, that psychology may be said to be an investigation of human motives and behaviour. No, philosophy is an investigation of its many diverse questions, of what is asked in them—for instance, whether and how we can know what other people think and feel. These questions are expressions of problems and difficulties which may be characterized as 'conceptual' in the way I have indicated. Philosophy is a struggle with these difficulties.

What we learn, what insight or understanding we come to, is acquired in the course of this struggle; and there is no way of conveying it to anyone except by engaging him in these difficulties and letting him do the work. Indeed, this is the only way of teaching philosophy. We could say that philosophy is an intellectual journey in which we return from positions we are quite naturally tempted to occupy until we are stung by the discomfort of being there. It is the philosophical work which we learn to do that moves us and enables us to make the return. Thus we return, for instance, from philosophical doubt, or from a position which rests on a metaphysical dichotomy—between mind and body, reason and sense, reason and feeling, etc.—which compels us to say or think things which do or ought to leave us uncomfortable: uncomfortable because on closer inspection they turn out to be incoherent.

Philosophy, however, does not merely remove such discomforts to which we are susceptible as part of our philosophical sensiblity. We gain something in losing the discomfort. What we gain is what we learn in moving from the positions we occupied, what we see in the course of the journey. However, we can at best show others snapshots of it and these will never convey the living experience of which what they show are snippets.

One example of such a journey is the one Wittgenstein undertook when he worked his way out of his early views in the *Tractatus* concerning language in its relation to logic and reality. He was already doing a great deal of critical work in that book, especially on some of Frege's and Russell's ideas on logic. But he later came to be dissatisfied with many of the ideas he himself developed in the course of his criticisms or with the stage at which he had left them in their development. The record of this journey is in the various books we have up to *Philosophical Investigations* and beyond. Often quoted remarks such as 'meaning is use' or 'the treatment of philosophical questions is like the treatment of a disease' are only frozen snapshots of the scenes that came to Wittgenstein's view in the course of his journey.

If some of Wittgenstein's remarks on philosophy lead one to think that in his view the abandonment of 'metaphysical myths' does no more than leave us with 'stale truisms', one should remember the exciting insights he offers us in the *Investigations*. Much of what we find there could not have come to view at all from the philosophical perspective of the *Tractatus*. But none of it will be properly in our possession until we actually travel with Wittgenstein. Only then shall we appreciate it in such a way that it enriches and even transforms our intellectual life.

Wittgenstein quotes a line from St Augustine: 'the search says more than the discovery' (1967, sec. 457). If we understand this to mean that the insight lies in the actual search and cannot be separated from it, then we are reminded of what a writer has to say in a novel or a poem. That too cannot be separated from the work and there is no independent statement or demonstration of the truth which a literary work contains. There is this difference however between philosophy and literature. To learn from literature one has to *read* literature; to learn from philosophy one has to *do* philosophy. It is true that reading literature is an imaginative exercise in which the reader takes part in the story he reads. But that is still not the same thing as *writing* the story. Whereas the philosopher, in reading a piece of philosophy and entering into its arguments is, however modest his talents, actually *doing* philosophy. There is no division here between appreciating what someone else has said and thinking it through.

So, in contrast with the sciences, truth in philosophy cannot be detached from the work which opens it up, and it cannot be proved either. One can only lead someone else to it, and leave him to do the work himself. When he has done so what he comes to see stands in a special relation to him. Thus just as a novel or poem offers one person's view or experience, and a different writer could not have written the same novel or poem, similarly a philosopher who may be taking part in an ongoing debate offers his own contribution to it. If he is a great philosopher, he will respond to what *he* finds significant, thereby making it significant for the others.

It follows that the idea of some realm which is the subject matter of philosophy, some realm to which each philosopher stands in the same way, researching to add to the branch of human knowledge which is its province, is a confused idea. There is no such realm which philosophy studies systemically. Instead there are problems, special problems to do with difficulties in understanding and making sense, ways of working on them, and the enrichment in understanding that comes through such work. The problems are thrown up by our intellectual life, by the life of thought and enquiry, discourse and questions, including per-

-sonal ones. There is no area or walk of life which cannot raise philosophical questions for a person who is receptive to them. But the work belongs to the author, just as he belongs to his time, though he can transcend it—as Wittgenstein did in the way he criticized his times and swam against the tide of its thinking.

Philosophy, under attack in a philistine environment, sometimes tries to defend itself by referring to its application in other fields. This is a confused notion if it models itself on the applications of science which has given us the technology which has benefited mankind in many ways. But to benefit from such technology we need *not* know or understand the science of which it is the product. Whereas to benefit from philosophy one has to think for oneself, to do philosophy. Philosophy does not have any products which the public can use or from which it can benefit. In that sense philosophy is useless and should not try to defend itself to those who can see no value in anything except utility. The enrichment which it brings to intellectual life cannot be understood in terms of its utility.

2. Conceptual Clarification and its Substantive Yield

So the kind of work which resolves philosophical problems does throw light on and enriches our understanding not just of the concepts which breed these problems but also of what we think about in terms of them—human language and the kind of life we live with it, the kind of beings we are, how our knowledge grows, the role of reason in this growth. These are, of course, part of the subject-matter of traditional Western philosophy. Wittgenstein who made a substantive contribution to these subjects had, in doing so, something to *say* about them. What he had to say is what he came to in the way he worked with the problems in question.

I shall mention one example—Wittgenstein's detailed critique of the way Descartes had divided 'the inner life' from 'the outer', the mind from the body, and in doing so gave expression to a way of thinking we find easy to slip into. In his critique of it Wittgenstein succeeded in throwing light on the primacy of *human beings* in our understanding of both the mental and the physical attributions we make to ourselves, i.e. to each other—human beings in motion, that is in their various engagements. It is in the surroundings of these engagements that mental concepts have sense and they apply to flesh and blood beings who live the life of these engagements.

As for the body which Cartesian philosophers have treated as an anatomical structure animated by a soul or mind, in causal interaction with it, this is very much a philosopher's myth. A person's body is not to him a physical thing among others, one that he knows by means of sensations and uses as an instrument. He lives, feels, sees and acts through it; indeed, he is not something separate from his body. Nor are other people what he infers from the bodies he sees in motion around him. He sees no such thing; he responds to human beings.

Descartes had recognized the way human beings are separated from the rest of nature by their capacity for thought and intentional action, and the special relation in which each person stands to his own thoughts and actions. But he misrepresented this:

> Human beings are pure centres of consciousness which first of all know themselves. Everything else—the physical world, their own bodies, other people—is outside and known at best by inference from representations produced by them in each person's consciousness. What to such a consciousness is 'the outside world' may or may not exist; but this has no logical relevance to its existence as a consciousness. A person's body thus is not essential to his existence as a mind which primarily lives in its own self-contained world. Nor are other people necessary to the constitution of his inner world.

Wittgenstein criticized this picture of the distinct character of human existence:

> We are physical beings in social interaction with each other and it is this social life that gives us the capacity for thought, imagination and self-consciousness. Our bodies are not something from which we can separate ourselves in the way Descartes found conceivable. Nor are they instruments we use in acting on our physical environment and in coming to know it through perception. We exist as physical beings in a physical environment. Furthermore, the existence of other people is not a contingent aspect of the existence of each one of us. Without them there is no social life and no language and so no knowing and thinking self either. Without a social world in which we attribute significance to things, and thus an arena in which we act, there is no inner world. Descartes' self as pure consciousness, logically separate form everything that exists independently of it, his conception of himself as a purely thinking thing (*res cogitans*) is, therefore, an incoherent notion. Contrary to what he thought the public is logically prior to the private.

Wittgenstein made no such positive statement. He arrived at such insights as I have tried to indicate through a sustained critique of Descartes' metaphysical ideas about 'man's place in nature' and 'each man's relation to others and to the language he speaks'. Certainly Wittgenstein did have something to say on these topics; but it cannot be stated directly in the way I have put it. Philosophical understanding cannot be advanced by such direct statements—any more than what literary works contribute to our understanding of the world can be conveyed through direct statements. But worse still, in philosophy they are hardly meaningful.

If I have made such statements myself, they are meant to point to something *in* Wittgenstein's work, not to be a substitute for it. There is no short-cut to the kind of work through which he expressed what he had to say on topics of philosophical discussion. I simply took Wittgenstein's work as an example and tried to *remind* those already acquainted with it of the kind of positive contribution philosophy can make to 'our understanding of ourselves and of the world in which we live' without making any positive statement about it.

What we have here is a deep-going *grammatical* contribution which clarifies our notion of ourselves as human beings and opens up possibilities of understanding which may have been lost to pockets of our intellectual life. Where the latter is the case, philosophy can make an actual difference to the language and thinking belonging to those areas of our life—for instance to the language and practice of psychology and sociology and to the form of life to which they may in fact contribute. But even if these disciplines and their language remain impervious to philosophy's criticism, such criticism is still an eye-opener on an individual level—that is to the individual who takes it on board through philosophical work. In Wittgenstein's case, as Professor von Wright has pointed out, this is all he, himself, aimed at in his philosophical work (1982, p. 209).

3. Personal Life as a Source of Philosophical Problems

I have argued that conceptual clarification, which involves the criticism and rejection of philosophical presuppositions that shackle our thinking, can have a substantive yield in two directions: the clearing up of conceptual confusion can enrich our understanding of what we use these concepts to talk and think about, and where conceptual confusion actually plays a part in the modification of a language that is becoming current, its criticism is a criticism of a trend in the culture in which we ourselves think. In the first case philosophy clarifies meanings which we already possess and in doing so enriches our understanding; in the second case it reminds us of meanings which are being lost, and it may even, if the ground is fertile, play a role in halting the loss.

I have not considered philosophy in this latter role but I have argued that in either case it is always through a discussion of conceptual problems that it contributes to our understanding of what raises these problems. By and large academic philosophy discusses problems concerned with our capacity to think, to be aware of our surroundings, to speak and communicate with each other, with the nature of our language, the extent to which it creates a world for us, one in which we find ourselves and which we share with others—a 'human world'. It also discusses problems concerned with the character of various intellectual disciplines: mathematics, the empirical sciences, psychology, sociology, and philosophy itself.

When it comes to ethics and religion, the problems considered by philosophers are concerned with what the individual makes of his life in its relation to good and evil, chance, fate and death. This is what I call life in its *personal* dimension—the dimension of life in which the individual is concerned to make something of his life and of himself in that life in his relation to the different forms of significance he finds in things. It is the dimension of life in which the individual is concerned to be himself, to be worthy, to be accepted in his relationships. The problems he encounters here are *personal* problems and how he faces and deals with them shapes him as a person.

This is the dimension of life in which literature is particuarly interested and on which it has something to say. But so does philosophy in its own particular way: that is through a discussion of the philosophical problems which our attempts to understand what goes on here throw up. These are problems connected with the concepts in terms of which we think of what we face, concepts in terms of which we face what matters to us, indeed concepts which shape what we face and in shaping it shapes us. Thus what philosophy attempts to clarify in this connection is the language through which we struggle to be ourselves, attempt to right our relationships with others, the language in which we reflect on ourselves as individuals in those relationships.

It is important, however, that we do not confuse these philosophical problems with the personal ones which are their breeding ground, even when they run into each other. In both sets of problems we are concerned with *sense* or *meaning*; that is why there is some danger of confusing them. But in one case we are trying to make sense of what faces us and of our life in facing it, while in the other, we are concerned to make sense of what goes on in these personal struggles themselves: how are we to understand what goes on here and what the individual is striving towards? Indeed, can we make sense of it: of being oneself, for instance, or finding one's true self, of achieving communion with another person, etc.?

Not everyone has a flair for the language in question. Certainly it is not the language of the markets, not everyday language in that sense. But even those who have a flair for it may find their reflections leading them into paradoxes, so that they feel the need for philosophical guidance: when people have lost their way in life, or have never found it, and they ask 'who am I?', what are they searching for: a piece of knowledge they have lost or a self they have never come to? If the latter, what is this self which they are not or have never been? What is its mode of existence? Or again, what is it for a person to be an individual? Does our being separate centres of responsibility and experience as individuals isolate us from each other? Does it make the kind of togetherness or communion we seek in love and friendship impossible? Or again, does human love involve tendencies which cannot be reconciled with such a desire for communion so that what we seek in love is impossible of attainment? Plato certainly thought so of 'carnal love', but he regarded it as a degraded form of spiritual love. Sartre agreed with him about the impossibility of communion at the level of the flesh, except that he thought of carnal love as the paradigm of all human love, as containing the 'skeleton' of all human relationships.

These are *conceptual* questions, similar to the ones I commented on earlier. To see this similarity let us put side by side the paradox at the heart of our question about love with the one at the core of Berkeley's idealism.

(i) It cannot be that *matter* is not something that exists independently of our 'ideas' or 'sense impressions', nor can it be that it is; yet it must be both. Matter doesn't exist.

(ii) Nothing that is not both earthly and saintly can be love, and yet nothing can be both. Love is impossible.

Berkeley resolved the former paradox by distinguishing between ideas in our minds and ideas in God's mind: matter exists independently of our ideas, but it is nothing over and above ideas in God's mind. Mill eliminated the reference to God's mind by speaking of matter as 'the permanent possibility' of ideas or sensations.

What Berkeley, Mill and later phenomenalists do not recognize is that not every time we perceive physical objects do we have ideas or sense-data by means of which we perceive them. In most contexts of perception there is no logical room for the presence of sense-data. Thus, under normal circumstances, when I look at what is before me I do not see visual sense-data, which may be products of my mind, any more than when I walk in a shopping centre I see hats and coats which may cover automata. That each time we perceive anything what we perceive are sense-data is a philosophical myth or construction. It is only in *special* cases that we can intelligibly be said to perceive sense-data. Once we recognize that normally we perceive physical objects directly, that is without the intermediary of 'ideas' or sense-data, Berkeley's paradox disappears. But such recognition calls for a great deal of philosophical spade work.

Sartre's resolution of the latter paradox was equally reductive. He jettisoned one of the conflicting aspects: spiritual love is a sublimated form of carnal love. But in doing so he made a fundamental kind of communion between human beings, the one sought in love and friendship, impossible. For in suggesting that all love is a form of carnal love he denied one of the conditions required by the possibility of communion: 'respect for the other's freedom [he said] is an empty word' (Sartre, 1943, 479). His conclusion was that 'communion' is only possible on the carnal plane, but it is unstable and short-lived. In that case, what is in question hardly deserves to be called communion—just as what lasts but for a brief span of time may be infatuation, but is hardly what we would call love. It would follow that human beings live alone—a claim that has been presented as a truth by various great literary writers, for instance by Proust.

To be sure Sartre did not deny that human beings make contact with and come to know each other. But in their personal relations, he argued, the form which this contact takes excludes communion: 'Conflict is the essence of our relations with other people' (1943, 502). Thus having successfully negotiated the reefs of Cartesian solipsism Sartre came to grief on what he called 'the reefs of desire' and he fell a prey to another form of philosophical solipsism. I am inclined to call it 'existential' as opposed to 'epistemological' solipsism in that it has its source not in the Cartesian 'privacy of the mind' but in what Sartre calls our 'ontological separateness'—that is the separateness that characterizes our existence as individuals.

I describe this as a form of solipsism because of the way it represents personal relationships as revolving around the self for each person in a way that leaves each 'radically alone'. Thus contrast with Matthew Arnold who, though he said that 'we mortal millions live alone', did not deny the possibility of communion: 'a hand is laid in ours . . . and what we mean we say and what we would we know'. Arnold recognized the difficulties involved in this and emphasized how rarely it is realized: what we call togetherness does not merit that name.

Simone Weil too recognized how much the need we have for another person in both love and close friendship makes it impossible for us to wish the autonomy to be preserved both in ourselves and in the other. But she did not think that this need is incapable of being modified and, unlike Sartre, she allowed the possibillty of true friendship in which 'there is equality made of harmony': 'Friendship is a miracle by which a person consents to view from a certain distance, and without coming any nearer, the very being who is necessary to him as food' (Weil, 1951, 157).

Sartre rejects these conceptual possibilities and turns what is a genuine difficulty into an impossibility: 'togetherness' is an empty word, for it hides a contradiction—much in the way that for Berkeley 'matter' came to involve a contradiction.

I am not now concerned to discuss the kind of solipsism into which Sartre came to be drawn.[2] My point is this: it is not different in kind from the positions which Wittgenstein has dicussed and combated. It is amenable to the same kind of treatment and susceptible of the same kind of yield in terms of understanding. But what is interesting about it is that the conceptual difficulties which give rise to it and which it, therefore, highlights, 'reflect' difficulties which some people face in their *personal* life. Thus where the individual says, 'I do not know how to reconcile my need for her with my wish to keep my independence and to respect hers', the philosopher says, 'these two things cannot be reconciled'. Where the individual says, 'I do not know how to accept some dependence without regressing into childish dependence; I cannot make sense of Winnicott's concept of mature dependence', the philosopher says, 'that concept hides a contradiction'. What the individual faces in examples of this kind is not a philosophical difficulty and it can only be resolved by him in his own life. It is a personal, not a conceptual difficulty, the kind which is depicted in works of literature.

The concepts involved in the *philosophical* difficulties under consideration, however, have their sense in just the contexts in which those personal difficulties arise. Therefore only those who can enter into these contexts imaginatively will be sensitive to the force of the philosophical difficulties in question. What they will bring to such a discusion will thus coincide in part with what writers in literature bring to their works—in terms of experience, insight and sensibility. And what their works, purely conceptual as it is, will yield will be an illumination of an aspect of life. It is in this way, I believe, that a philosopher can speak about and illuminate aspects of life in its personal dimension.

4. Postscript: Philosophy and the Self

The main contention of my paper has been that the kind of critical, conceptual enquiry with which we are familiar in traditional philosophy is not confined to 'academic' philosophy and can be directed to 'existential' questions, that is questions concerned with life in its personal dimension. Here philosophy requires some of the qualities and experiences which enable a novelist or poet to have something to say, and its work can contribute to our understanding of just those matters on which *they* speak.

[2] I do so in *Existentialist Critiques of Cartesianism* (Macmillan, forthcoming).

You may be disappointed with what I have said and complain that I have not gone far enough: 'You have told us that philosophy too, like literature, can speak about life. What we want to know is whether philosophy can address the philosopher's *personal* problems, make a positive contibution to what he makes of them and, through doing so, make a difference to his life.'

To satisfy you on this point I would have to write a new paper. Since I cannot do so now, let me give you an indication of the line I would take if I were to do so. Yes, philosophical reflection can bring one new insight in connection with certain questions about life and this may overlap with what one learns from works in literature. However, there is still a difference between what one learns from philosophy and literature, that is from meeting certain matters in thought, and what one learns from life, that is from meeting them in the course of one's engagements, so that they challenge one's very being. It is notorious how much what makes a difference to one's thinking may fail to make an impact on one's mode of being.

In philosophy and literature one is at one remove from what challenges one's being directly. Despite this, however, it is still possible for philosophy to clear up certain confusions and misconceptions and in the process leave one freer to face certain things in life differently. A first year student doing philosophy told me that the thought that selfishness is inescapable in one's actions had troubled her personally and held her back from taking an active interest in other people's needs. She apparently found relief and release in coming to see the fallacy in her thinking. Certainly philosophy can make a person receptive to ideas he has rejected and these ideas may in time come to change his life. I would not wish to deny the power of ideas to change a person's life. But when they do, they do so by changing the character of his engagements: after all where a person's perspective on things changes they will call for different responses from him.

Perhaps more importantly, however, one needs to make a distinction between what one may gain from the pursuit of particular philosophical questions and what one gains from the pursuit of truth in philosophy—even though, of course, this can only be pursued through the discusion of particular philosophical questions. As far as any particular philosophical question goes, what one gains from its pursuit is by and large confined to one's understanding—except in so far as coming to a new understanding involves the giving up of cherished positions sustained by the will. But the transformation that comes from a serious dedication to philosophy, given the character of its questions, may amount to a spiritual reorientation—as Socrates tells us it did for him. Such a transformation is more than a change in the philosopher's understanding, confined to his thinking; it is a change in *him*, in his mode of existence and, therefore, in his very being.

We must remember, however, that such dedication to the pursuit of philosophy is itself a form of engagement. I mean an engagement of the person as a whole, not merely of his intellect, or to put it differently, an engagement with life as opposed to with objects of thought. One can compare it with dedicating one's life to the service of others. In this sense philosophy is, if you wish, a form of marriage, and so it should not be surprising if it changes the life and perspective of the person who takes it seriously, including his perspective on his own personal problems. And this, indeed, would constitute a change in these problems themselves and thus a change in the person who takes philosophy seriously.

Congenital Transcendentalism and 'the loneliness which is the truth about things'

FRANK CIOFFI

I take the phrase 'congenital transcendentalism' from Santayana who defined it as 'the spontaneous feeling that life is a dream'. 'The loneliness which is the truth about things' is a phrase of Virginia Woolf's. The thesis I will advance is that many expressions of doubt or denial of the shareable world are self-misunderstood manifestations of the state indicated by Woolf's expression. But the loneliness of which Woolf speaks must not be construed as the kind of loneliness which can be assuaged by family, friends, lovers or company. Nor is it the loneliness which a convinced solipsist might experience. It is rather the loneliness of 'that "I" and that "life of mine"' which is 'untouched whichever way the issue is decided whether the world is or is not' (Husserl, 1970, 9).

The earliest manifestation of congenital transcendentalism known to me is the familiar story from Chuang-tse (*c.* 300 BC) of the sage who has increasingly vivid and long drawn out dreams of life as a butterfly until he reaches a point when he can no longer be sure whether he is a man dreaming that he is a butterfly or a butterfly dreaming that he is a man. There is an episode with the structure of the Chuang-tse anecdote in Lewis Carroll's Sylvie and Bruno (a favourite of Wittgenstein's) where at one point the narrator says, 'Either I have been dreaming about Sylvie and this is the reality, or else I have been with Sylvie and this is the dream.' I do not think that fancies like these are the product of philosophical tradition but rather of that ubiquitous feature of our lives known as the 'egocentric predicament'.

Here is one account of the egocentric predicament. It is Samuel Taylor Coleridge's. Coleridge calls the belief 'that there exist things without us' a 'prejudice at once indemonstrable and irresistible', whereas 'the other position . . . namely I AM, cannot so properly be entitled a prejudice (since) the existence of things without us, from its nature, cannot be as immediately certain . . . and as independently of all grounds as the existence of our own being' (Richards, 1950). This apparent asymmetry naturally leads to the impugning of our supposed knowledge of the external world. Philosophical scepticism as to the knowability of the external world must be distinguished from another less theoretical question with which it is often intertwined. This might be described as conspiratorial or Potemkin village scepticism, after the minister of Catherine the Great who (apocryphally) arranged that on her progresses through her kingdom the misery of the populace was concealed by lining the village streets with well-fed peasants, and doing up the fronts of the houses. William James called the fact that at any given moment things are going on which are out of the perceptive range of any one person 'collateral contemporaneity'. It is the 'meanwhile, back at the ranch' order of fact, 'the simultaneous existence of objects not simultaneously perceived' as Strawson puts it. It is a prominent component of what Husserl dubs 'the natural attitude'.

Here is a vernacular expression of the natural attitude from one of the most familiar verses of the North American Continent: 'somewhere in this favoured land/ the sun is shining bright/ the band is playing somewhere/ and somewhere hearts are light/ and somewhere men are laughing/ and somewhere children shout/ but there is no joy in Mudville/ mighty Casey has struck out'. A playful expression of the antithesis to the 'natural attitude' is found in a poem of Housman's: 'Good creatures, do you love your lives?/ and have you ears for sense?/ Here is a knife like other knives,/ that cost me eighteenpence./ I need but stick it in my heart/ and down will come the sky./ And earth's foundations will depart/ and all you folk will die' (*More Poems*, No. 26). The ubiquity of the natural attitude is unquestionable but isn't there something natural in the idea that Housman plays with, too? Isn't this idea of the dependence of worldhood on selfhood both bizarre and familiar?

'Let us imagine,' said the philosopher Ortega to his audience once 'that on leaving this hall when my lecture is over we find that there was nothing beyond, that is, that the rest of the world was not around it, that its doors gave not on the city but on nothing. Such a discovery will shock us with surprise and terror' (Ortega y Gasset, 1963, 64). Ortega does not mention a by no means unimaginable response to the contingency he mentions—that of the congenital transcendentalist—'I knew it! I knew it!'

There are occasions which seem to involve a departure from what Husserl calls the natural attitude and yet are as natural as the natural attitude itself. This fact has been thought to demonstrate the irrefutability of solipsism but I think it means something different.

Here are some examples apparently illustrative of the ubiquity of sceptical doubt: At the end of Mark Twain's *The Mysterious Stranger*, the stranger addresses the narrator:

> *'Life itself is only a vision, a dream.'*
> It was electrical. By God! I had that very thought a thousand times in my musings!

'Nothing exists: all is a dream. God—man—the world—the sun, the moon, the wilderness of stars—a dream, all a dream; they have no existence. *Nothing exists save empty space—and you! . . . And you are not you—you have no body, no blood, no bones, you are but a thought.* I myself have no existence; I am but a dream—your dream, creature of your imagination. In a moment you will have realized this, then you will banish me from your visions and I shall dissolve into the nothingness out of which you made me . . . It is all a dream'

He vanished and left me appalled; for I knew, and realized, that all he said was true.

Here is the same sentiment from a work by someone as different from Twain as is conceivable, Walter Pater: '. . . what pure reason affirmed as the beginning of wisdom was that the world is but a thought . . . the product of his own lonely thinking power . . . as being zero without him'. The same view is expounded by the narrator of Tolstoi's semi-fictional memoir, *Boyhood*, who reminisces: 'By none of my philosoph-ical tendencies was I so carried away as by scepticism . . . I imagined that beside myself nobody and nothing existed in the universe. There were moments when under the influence of this *idée fixe* I reached such a state of insanity that I sometimes looked rapidly round to one side, hoping to catch emptiness unawares where I was not.'

The extent to which these men were drawing on their own reflections which they then imputed to imagined characters is unclear, and even so might suggest that such fancies are confined to febrile men of letters. Here then is a specimen indistinguishable from those cited from the autobiographical memoir of a distinguished physicist:

An event that stands out in my mind must have happened in my early teens. I was paddling a canoe on a clear night and letting my thoughts roam. Suddenly it came over me, and with something of a shock, that maybe everything that I considered most real was pure imagination. The lake, the canoe, the paddle, the stars, the night, the trees, even the feeling of water on my hand, might merely be sensations. Indeed, it might be that I was the only person who existed in the world, that my father and mother, my brother and sister and friends were all just figments of my imagination—that the feeling of the solid earth when I walked on it was only a feeling. There seemed to be nothing to disprove the hypothesis. On the other hand, what would be the sense of such a thing? It occurred to me that possibly this was all a matter of education. Perhaps really I was not a young boy alive here in the world, but one of a group of other kinds of beings, perhaps a God or supernatural being of some sort who is merely going through a course of training; prepared for him by other supernatural beings. At the time, no-one seemed particularly interested in this form of nonsense, but when I studied philosophy in college it was somewhat of a thrill to realize that I was by no means the first to have considered the possibility. (Bitter, 1960, 20–21)

Wordsworth was also prone to sceptical doubts similar to those that afflicted Tolstoi. When a child he would grasp at a wall or tree to assure himself of the existence of the external world. In old age he reminisced, 'There was a time in my life when I had to push against something that resisted to be sure that there was anything that was outside me. I was sure of my own mind; everything else fell away, and vanished into thought.' Is it an adequate response to my patchwork to discuss the cogency of the views expressed? That is, whether Wordsworth and Tolstoi were not making Dr Johnson's mistake when he kicked the headstone in Harwich Churchyard to refute Berkeley? Bitter does not tell us why he concluded his conspiratorial intuitions were mistaken, nor does Tolstoi tell us why he came to regard his sceptical doubts as insane. But we can assume that it was not because of repeated failures to catch nothing at it. And when Cardinal Newman tells us of a time in childhood when 'I thought life might be a dream, or I an angel, and all this world a deception, my fellow angels by a playful device concealing themselves from me and deceiving me with the semblance of a material world,' he may not, as it appears, just be presenting us with a supernatural version of Freud's family romance; his case may be no different from that of the physicist Bitter. What I believe we have in these cases is what John Wisdom described as 'the interpenetration of issues'. It is worldhood itself which these men were, confusedly, calling in question when entertaining such fancies and not just whether the consensual world is the real one. If Tolstoi cannot trust what he sees when his back is not turned to things, why trust what he sees when he sees nothing. Similarly with the metaphysical family romances of Newman and Bitter—what guarantee is there that these supernatural beings who are suspected of producing a simulacrum of reality will not themselves prove ultimately illusory (and thus immediately questionable). What we have in these instances is an incoherent mingling of doubt as to whether things really are what they seem with the more radical doubt whether the way things seem can ever warrant how they really are.

Yet I feel that we would be doing Bitter, Pater, Tolstoi, *et al.* an injustice if we contented ourselves with exposing the incoherence of their solipsism. This is not the way to deal with these utterances because what their authors have stumbled on, in however confused a manner, is Husserl's 'greatest and most magnificent of all facts, that of transcendental subjectivity'. But though the problem explicitly posed by Husserl is, 'How is it possible to drive the intersubjectivity of the world from the intentionalities of my own conscious life' and again,

'How can the world as a world for everyone and the existence of others, be established', this problem masks another—that of the incongruity of our existence as beings both isolated and accompanied, as simultaneously just 'one other among others' and yet the hub around which everything revolves—of our perplexity that, as Wittgenstein puts it, though 'what solipsism means is true . . . it cannot be said'.

The thesis I wish to advance is that the utterances in which the problem of solipsism finds expression are precipitates of something else, more cloudy and indeterminate—the feeling of having stumbled on a momentous but deeply hidden significance, involving the epistemic relation of our being in the world to that of the being of others. The solipsism I want to direct attention towards is not just an apparently counter-intuitive implication of a verificationist semantics. This would only lead to an effort to see how the implication might nevertheless be suspended, or to an acknowledgement that it constitutes a *reductio* of the semantics in question. The solipsism I am talking about requires oxymoron for its expression—it might be called universal solipsism. The feeling of a profound and irremediable solitude which finds expression in solipsistic fantasies transcends scepticism and is unaffected by its refutation. When Ortega tells us that 'human life is radical solitude', he immediately issues an assurance that 'in no sense would I suggest that I am the only thing that exists'. Life is not 'a tenacious and exuberant dream, an infinite phantasmagoria secreted by my mind . . . The radical solutide of human life does not consist in their really being nothing else. There is an infinity of things but . . . (each one of us) is alone with them' (Ortega y Gasset, 1964, 47). This suggests that when this distinctive, unutterable loneliness is expressed as solipsism what is problematic has been distorted *en route* to articulation. What then is this residual problematicality involving the unreachableness of the otherness of others, and thus reciprocally of one's own, which fails to dissipate when the sceptical problem in its various formulations is resolved? Its main feature is a feeling of incongruity between our special epistemic relation to ourselves and the assumptions of our workaday lives.

This is what Wittgenstein has to say about solipsism in the *Tractatus*; 'What solipsism means is true only it cannot be said' (Wittgenstein, 1949, 5, 62). I want to argue for a more intimate relation between this remark and what Wittgenstein calls 'the riddle of life' in *Tractatus* 6, 52 than may initially seem plausible. In *Notebooks 1914–16* he says: 'What do I know about God and the purpose of life? I know that this world exists. That I am placed in it like my eye in its visual field. That something about it is problematic which we call its meaning' (Wittgenstein, 1969, 11/6/16, 72–73). What did Wittgenstein mean by 'the purpose' of life, in this remark? And how is it related to our being placed in the world like the eye in its visual field?

If his remarks on the problem of life are not overdetermined on each or most occasions they certainly meant different things at different times. The problem which involves 'God and the purpose of life' is remote from the problem in *Tractatus* 6, 52 whose solution discovered 'after long doubting' is unutterable by those who have discovered it. If in spite of having arrived at the meaning of life they nevertheless, 'cannot then say in what this meaning consists' it cannot be with them, as with others, because they were persuaded that 'there shall be no more death; neither sorrow nor crying', since this would result not in silence but in proselytization. So we are not dealing with common or garden theodicy as the expression 'God and the purpose of life' suggests.

The question of theodicy can only arise within the natural attitude. The question which Wittgenstein broaches in the *Tractatus* lies outside it or concerning it. It involves the relation between what in the *Notebooks* he called 'the two godheads'—'the world and my independent I' (Wittgenstein, 1969, 8/7/16, 74). But neither is Wittgenstein's problem, as this phrase can suggest and, as J. N. Findlay thought, the problem of solipsism as ordinarily conceived. Doubt or denial of the everyday world are not involved. In his memoir of Wittgenstein Findlay imputes to him

> a deep personal solipsism which is probably among the persistent, secret, and necessarily inexpressible sources of many of Wittgenstein's positions . . . He believed what ordinary metaphysical men would express by saying that he alone was conscious of anything and alone had true feelings and that others were only conscious and had feelings in a different utterly behavioural sense. (Findlay, 1973, 180)

Wittgenstein, says Findlay, 'is one of the few genuine solipsists who ever existed but he suffered the great personal agony that it made no sense to him to avow his solipsism either to himself or anyone else'. We have here the paradox of something which is deemed inexpressible but of which we have a sufficiently clear conception to impute to someone and even to give a role, if an unconsious one, in his ratiocinations. I do not think there was anything particular to him in Wittgenstein's dilemma as Findlay himself concedes in another remark: 'Wittgenstein's secret metaphysical belief—and I am sure many others have entertained the same— was in some egocentric predicament in which each man necessarily treated his own conscious ego as the unmentionable pivot and limit of the world.' Findlay thinks this is merely a conceptual confusion: 'Plainly our understanding and knowledge of the existence of foreign experience and its distinction from and independence of the criteria in virtue of which we establish it is something infinitely better founded than any semantic theory, however ingenious, and the confusion of one with the other, which certain semantic theories entail, is plainly a flat denial of the understanding and knowledge in question' (Findlay, 1973, 180). I doubt that Wittgenstein needed to be told that. In the sense of solipsism which implies doubt or denial of the reality of others it is not a view which there is any reason to think Wittgenstein ever held. And Findlay's view of the issue leaves unexplained why it should cause 'great personal agony'.

Wittgenstein says of the notion of wondering at the existence of the world that it is nonsensical because we cannot imagine it not existing, and a similar problem arises in connection with the experience I have described as the finding of something anomalous about one's own existence. The question naturally arises; with respect to what is it anomalous? T. S. Eliot objected to the use I. A. Richards made of the idea of 'Man's loneliness (the isolation of the human situation)' in the much mocked 'sincerity ritual' expounded in *Practical Criticism* (Richards, 1953, 290). Eliot professed not to understand 'an isolation which is not an isolation from anything in particular'. 'In what sense' he asked 'is man in general isolated and from what?' (Eliot, 1933, 132). In his reply Richards reduced the ambiguity of the expression 'Man's loneliness' by quoting Eliot himself ('thinking of the key each confirms a prison'), thus making it clear that the isolation he was referring to was that of each man rather than of mankind, and that the isolation in question was that of the egocentric predicament (Richards, 1953, 291). This still leaves Eliot's objection of incomprehensibility through lack of contrast unanswered. There is an aphorism of F. H. Bradley's: 'Wherever you are puzzled you have made an assumption and it is your duty to discover what that assumption is', which has sometimes served me well but is difficult to apply to the case at issue. What could the puzzle-generating assumption be in the case of our wonder, and perhaps dismay, at our being placed in the world 'like the eye in its visual field'?

One way of conveying the character of this wonder is to say that it is as if I were capable of imagining a mode of being less personal than that which I have. But how can this be? Here is an analogy which may be helpful. In answer to an interviewer's question as to when he first became conscious 'of his own individual self' Karl Jung replied that it was in his eleventh year. On his way to school he 'stepped out of a mist . . . and I knew "I am". And then I thought "What have I been before?" And then I found I had been in a mist not knowing how to differentiate myself from other things. I was just one thing among other things' (McGuire and Hull, 1980, 381). The mist I am thinking of is analogous to Jung's but it is one which we return to and spend most of our lives in, emerging only fitfully to wonder plaintively what had woken us.

This is Anthony Powell's account of the same dawning of self-awareness:

One afternoon—I was about five or six—we had returned from Kensington Gardens and were waiting outside the door of the flat to be let in. After the park and the street the interior of the building seemed very silent. A long beam of sunlight, in which small particles of dust swam about, all at once slanted through an upper window on the staircase and struck the opaque glass panels of the door. On several occasions recently I had been conscious of approaching the brink of some discovery, an awareness that nearly became manifest and suddenly withdrew. Now the truth came flooding in with the dust-infected sunlight; the revelation of self-identity was inescapable. There was no doubt about it—I was me!

'I was me!'—a statement which makes no sense and which everyone understands. Isn't Powell's 'revelation of self-identity' recognizably akin to the phenomenon to which Husserl is referring when he writes: 'I was a transcendental ego even while living in the natural attitude, but I knew nothing about it' (Husserl, 1970, 15). This is how sense may be given to the obscure conviction that there is something enigmatic and anomalous about our positioning in the world as just a self among selves and yet not just unique but uniquely accessible.

It might seem that the proper response to Wittgenstein's oft-quoted remark is that what solipsism means is not true and that the silence which Wittgenstein enjoins could be appropriately broken by showing that this is so. Certainly there is no dearth of philosophical discourses of the highest order which do, or purport to do, just that; not least Wittgenstein's own. But such discourses are beside the point of that particular remark which addresses a problem which arises just as much for Heidegger, who does not deny worldhood, as for Husserl who suspends it. James Thurber once wrote: 'It occurred to me today that the world exists only in my own consciousness; whether as reality or illusion the evening papers do not say.' If a day comes when the evening papers do say, the problem addressed by Wittgenstein's remark will not have been resolved. This problem persists even after we have allowed Heidegger to persuade us that worldhood and selfhood are given together, or Wittgenstein that 'when the solipsist retreats into his private world the ability to make discriminating references to individuals is something which he is unable to take with him' (Pears, 1988, 230).

In connection with Wittgenstein's later arguments against solipsism David Pears quotes a remark from 1916: 'The I, the I, is what is deeply mysterious' (5 August 1916) and asks 'What has happened to his original feeling for the mystery of the ego?' (Pears, 1988, 226). One possibility is that in Wittgenstein's later dealings with the incoherence of solipsism he is not addressing the question of the mystery of the ego as he originally understood it—the unaccommodatability of the 'I' to the natural attitude; an unaccommodatability which is nevertheless not solipsistic doubt or conviction.

To make the state I am trying to gesture towards more discernible let us imagine the epistemic problems addressed by Husserl and others as arising through our being called on to give an account of how members of a community of intersubjectively related monads are able, each, to assure himself that they do indeed share a common world; we would then have the setting for a debate as to whether it is Heidgegger or Husserl who has given a more correct account of their situation. But the problem I wish to address (or the symptom I want to present for diagnosis) does not arise until I remind myself that I am myself a member of such a community. It also distinguishes the problem I want to call your attention to, that it is blurred when we speak of it as the question why there is something rather than nothing, since I am quite happy to respond, 'Why not?' to that question. But if the question is phrased 'Why is it me in particular who is called on to bear witness that there is something rather than nothing', the response 'Why not?' sticks in my throat.

The difficulty of conveying the experience of being struck by one's own existence constrains us to violate normal standards of intelligibility. One issue raised by Wittgenstein's remark that what solipsism means cannot be said is whether 'saying' is so clearcut a notion that we can be confident that it cannot be done? I have myself gone from thinking Wittgenstein's remark on solipsism nonsense, and quoting with approval Frank Ramsey's 'If you can't say it you can't say it and you can't whistle it either', to finding it extraordinarily penetrating without being able to say why in any sense that I would have previously found acceptable. So perhaps you can whistle it after all. Wittgenstein's later remarks do something to characterize more particularly this meaning which can and cannot be said. In his 1932 lecture on ethics he said, in connection with the experience of wonder at the existence of the world, that this astonishment cannot be expressed in a question and that it was a misunderstanding to think that any formulation we arrive at could correspond to what we meant, but that nevertheless 'the tendency, the thrust, points to something' (Wittgenstein, 1965, 8).

The distinctiveness of this pointing is also stressed by Heidegger. In the *History of the Concept of Time* he writes: 'It is not a question of deducing propositions or propositional sequences from each other but of working out the access to the matters from which propositions are to be drawn in the first place. . .' (Heidegger, 1985, 146). But Heidegger's assertion of the distinctiveness of the issue and its exemption from

Frank Cioffi

normal criteria of intelligibility and cogency has been found unpersuasive by those in the analytic tradition. The passage on 'Nothingness' from Heidegger's 'What is Metaphysics?' which Carnap demonstrated to be meaningless if literally construed might better have been criticized as rhetorically inept. Similarly Heidegger's attempt to convey the situation for which he adapted the term Dasein (being-there)—'the unique ontologic structure which is being in the world'—may require utterances like—'Dasein is the entity which I myself am in each instance' (Heidegger, 1985, 195) and 'It is a matter of an entity to which we have this distinctive relationship, we are it itself—an entity which is only insofar as I am it' (Heidegger, 1985, 149–50).

These remarks are as vulnerable to unsympathetic, literal paraphrase as those on 'nothing' and yet this does not preclude their efficacy in 'working out access to the matters from which propositions are to be drawn'. The trouble is that the tradition insists that we take Heidegger's formulations to other of his formulations, or to the formulations of others, rather than to the 'primordial experiences' which generated them in the first place. Elsewhere in the *History of the Concept of Time* Heidegger speaks of the analysis of being as 'the discovery of the very possibility of doing research in philosophy'. To the state I want to convey, it is as much an *a priori* restriction on the appropriate response to the revelatory experience of 'being there' that it should take the form of research as are 'the latently operative and spurious bonds of the tradition' to which Heidegger scornfully refers. Why must we assume that the disclosure of being would leave us anything much more to say? Why must there be a structure of being to be arduously excavated, taxonomized and architectonically displayed? Moreover do not we sometimes have the feeling that Heidegger himself often expresses his deepest philosphical convictions in a format and in accordance with conventions that contradict them? Might not there be a gross incongruity in passing from the illumination of being to the historical exegesis of Parmenides, Descartes or Kant? Is not it as if one were to announce that Jesus died for our sins and then try to arouse interest in the minutiae of daily life in ancient Palestine?

Certain philosophical illuminations may be like suicide in that once successfully communicated they leave their authors hard pressed for an encore. The relevation of being may be an enterprise of a distinctive, comparatively unratiocinative kind—a matter of finding ways to convey the illumination rather than pseudo-ratiocinative demonstrations; and the gifts required for this task closer to those displayed by Tortelier in his master classes than in ratiocinative philosophy. The right considerations to bring to bear on discourse of this kind may be rhetorical. Wittgenstein's remarks are often too austere, e.g. 'There is indeed the inexpressible. This shows itself; it is the mystical.' In general Wittgenstein's ladder has too few rungs, Heidegger's too many. Whatever the justice of this judgment perhaps it is in these terms that the discussion ought to be carried on rather than in those of logical impropriety.

When I gave the talk on which this paper is based Profesor Griffiths asked me his standard question, of which I had been forewarned, what problem had I raised of whose resolution I was uncertain. I answered then that it was to what degree the questions I was raising belonged to psychology or psychopathology rather than philosophy. Though I would give the same answer if I were asked it now, it is for different reasons. Whereas at the time I was thinking predominantly of the kind of doubt as to the common world avowed by Bitter, Wordsworth, Tolstoi, etc., and described by the last as insane, in which we have a mixture of philosophical and non-philosophical, conspiratorial Potemkin-village scepticism, my grounds would now be my uncertainty as to whether dismay at the fact 'of a prior, primordial, transcendental sphere of peculiar owness' (Husserl) or, as Ortega puts it, that 'each "I" is in its very essence solitude,' is idiosyncratic or demanded by the nature of the relevation. Not only may the problem as I have described it be too idiosyncratic to be generally communicable, but it manifests a puzzling intermittent inertness for the very persons who are troubled by it. Those who address such questions must therefore reconcile themselves to the minuteness of their constituency at any given time and to its inconstancy and fluctuating membership—this kind of problematicality waxes and wanes. The moments of revelation or lucidity are succeeded by judgments as to the banality of the content of the revelation. And yet every once in a while we are struck by our peculiar and distinctive accessibility to ourselves and for some of us this thought has a disquieting hinterland—something distinct from the epistemic conundrums it sets.

In his *Self-Consciousness: Memoirs*, in a paragraph which beings with the single word 'Dasein', John Updike writes: 'Billions of consciousnesses silt history full and every one of them the center of the universe. What can we do in the face of this unthinkable truth but scream or take refuge in God' (Updike, 1986, 36–38). What was there in the notion that 'billions of consciousnesses silt history full and each of then the center of the universe' to make Updike want to scream? It does not make everyone want to scream. It did not make even Husserl want to scream and he cannot be accused of simple obliviousness. Nor do the numerous professional philosophers who discuss the topic of transcendental intersubjectivity show any such inclination—unless from exasperation. Being says 'Boo!' to some of us; but we cannot help but notice that scarcely anyone else is frightened. There is a problem here. Heidegger has suggested one solution: 'Whenever a phenomenological concept is drawn from primordial sources, there is a possibility that it may degenerate if communicatd in the form an assertion. It gets understood in an empty way and is thus passed on, losing its indigenous character . . .' (Heidegger, 1962, 60–61). Thus the jibe, 'Death, to a Heideggerian, is what he lectures on in the Spring term.'

The verbal formulae in which we express these intuitions 'have their dead and vital seasons', in Robert Musil's metaphor, and so not only may they be deployed by those who have never fully realized them, but even those who once have may lose touch with the primordial experience from which they are drawn. Even those who have not lost touch find it difficult to communicate the experience in its fullness by bare statement. At best this is like handing someone a photographic negative and leaving to him the task of developing it.

What more can be done in the way of 'primordial pointing out' than assemble hopefully apposite quotations? 'What has history to do with me. Mine is the one and only world' (Wittgenstein). 'The who of Dasein is not at all the "I myself"' (Heidegger). 'I am not the ego of an individual man. I am the ego in whose stream of consciousness the world itself—including myself as an object in it . . . first acquires meaning and reality' (Husserl). 'There is no such thing as the subject that thinks or entertains ideas. If I wrote a book called the world as I found it . . . it alone could not be mentioned in that book' (Wittgenstein). 'Each "I" is in its very essence solitude' (Ortega). These can only function as reminders for those for whom there are reminiscences to be evoked.

If it were necessary to attempt to convey the dismaying aspects of the experience I am speaking of I would start with an exchange from D. H. Lawrence's story 'The Captain's Doll', in which the eponymous captain compares his dead wife to a caged bird he once owned who seemed to think of the bars of his cage as inside him. 'He thought it was part of his own nature to be shut in. And she thought it was part of her nature. And so they both died.' Thus far Polonious/Heidegger. But when his interlocutor interposes 'What I can't see is what she could have done outside her cage. What other life could she have except her bibelots and her furniture and her talk?' the Captain backslides (whether with or without Lawrence's knowledge I am not sure):

'Why none. There is no life outside for human beings.'
'Then there's nothing?'
'That's true. In large measure, there is nothing.' (Lawrence, 1960, 204–205)

But though this captures one aspect of the revelation it is not particular enough. It veers towards the same ambiguity as the first item in I. A. Richards' sincerity ritual—'Man's loneliness'—which he eliminated in his reply to Eliot. It is not a question of 'we humans' and nothing, but of you, whoever you are, and nothing; and yet not in the sense intended by sayable solipsism. It might help to further specify the fact towards which I am gesturing if I add that broaching to an audience a sense of their own ultimate solitude in its concreteness might be felt as a betrayal because those who assembled did so on an unspoken understanding that they would not be driven back on themselves in this particular fashion. It is unlikely that Fichte's students were at all disturbed when asked to 'think the wall' and then to think of themselves 'thinking the wall', but the kind of reflexivity I have in mind can, if developed, be deeply disturbing. It may help further to characterize this version of the transcendental revelation that, even were its recipients too robustly constituted to experience dismay, its content is such that feeling it too vividly in company would constitute a breach of decorum akin to erotic fantasizing so intense that we erect or lubricate. Perhaps there is a kind of philosophical rumination which should only be engaged in privately. Husserl's suggestion that we could undertake the epoché in the company of others always struck me as strangely improper. (It is pertinent that Ortega connects this ontological revelation with a sense of shame: 'Is shame the form in which the "I" discovers itself?' (1964, p. 179.) Perhaps an ingredient in the satisfaction taken in praying for the souls of all the living and the dead may be mitigation of our guilt at our irrepressible claim to uniqueness and privileged ontological status.

It may further help to characterize the fact I am trying to gesture towards that it was inevitable that I should have been oblivious to it during the bulk of period during which this paper was written and even during the writing of much of it. But why should an idea of which I am oblivious for most of my life seem so momentous on those rare occasions when it presents itself? Why does it seem so impossible to accommodate it within the assumptions on which my daily life is lived? Might it not be some kind of aberration?

In Edmund Wilson's essay on Paul Valery he passes on an idea of Valery's which was prompted by Pascal's reaction of terror before the silence of the infinite spaces. Valery believed that in the future 'our increasing knowledge of the universe will have come to change not merely our ideas but certain of our immediate reactions' and 'what one might call Pascal's reaction will be a rarity and a curiosity to psychologists' (Wilson, 1971, 78). Cannot we imagine something comparable happening to Wittgenstein's feeling that 'the "I" is deeply mysterious'? Professional philosophers do not find it so. Why should what is true of many now not become universally true at some future date so that though Husserl's arguments, say, might remain graspable the centrality he attached to them or better, the peculiar sacramental tone in which he, Ortega, Heidegger and others sometimes adopt would have become inexplicable. This is how Ortega for example introduces the topic of the primacy of the self: 'we are to descend boldly below what each one customarily thinks his life to be and which really is merely its crust; piercing the crust we will enter into subterranean zones of our own living, zones which hold for us the most intimate secrets of being, secrets of our deepest selves, of the pure being of our being' (Ortega y Gasset, 1964, 18). Even more striking because of his normal desiccation are the places in Husserl where our necessary egocentricity is expounded in the rhetoric of salvation ('the greatest of all discoveries', 'the greatest and most magnificient of all facts', 'my true self'). It is as if through the phenomenological epoche we become twice born.

Yet this falls short of the dismay I suggested belongs to the revelation. There is no way to demonstrate that those who take up a clinical attitude towards what they would regard as our problematizing compulsion with respect to selfhood are mistaken, nor even to reasssure ourselves, in those moments when our relation to the natural attitude seems unproblematic, that we have not succumbed to a delusion; that what we have been saying is not merely gabble but morbid gabble. In attempting to respond appropriately to that unsayable truth which solipsism means—which though it can be indicated by words is not a saying by them—we may be dealing with a phenomenon akin to the delusions of reference which psychiatrists have studied (and which Wittgenstein tells us sometimes afflicted him). Wittgenstein speaks in *The Blue Book* of this 'strange illusion' in connection with a musical theme and describes it as the impression that the music seems to be saying something and it is as if we had to discover what it says. He does, however, place one restriction on the delusory character of this sense of imminent revelation—we may licitly look forward to its belated elucidation by analogy or felicitous description—'the word that seems to sum it up' (Wittgenstein, 1958, 166–167). I have said that for me that what sums up the experience of 'the unique ontological structure of being' is Virginia Woolf's: 'The loneliness which is the truth about things.' But of course I know that there are many for whom it does not and for still others it is not even a question of evocative summing up but of a more intellectual, examinable enterprise. Those of us who think otherwise need the courage of our parochialism and to cultivate a more intense awareness of the message-in-a-bottle character of our efforts at communication. There are some lines by Philip Larkin which have a peculiar pertinence to the transcendental loneliness which is the truth about things:—'Saying so to some/means nothing; others it leaves/ nothing to be said.'

Philosophical Plumbing

MARY MIDGLEY

Is philosophy like plumbing? I have made this comparison a number of times when I have wanted to stress that philosophising is not just grand and elegant and difficult, but is also needed. It is not optional. The idea has caused mild surprise, and has sometimes been thought rather undignified. The question of dignity is a very interesting one, and I shall come back to it at the end of this article. But first, I would like to work the comparison out a bit more fully.

Plumbing and philosophy are both activities that arise because elaborate cultures like ours have, beneath their surface, a fairly complex system which is usually unnoticed, but which sometimes goes wrong. In both cases, this can have serious consequences. Each system supplies vital needs for those who live above it. Each is hard to repair when it does go wrong, because neither of them was ever consciously planned as a whole. There have been many ambitious attempts to reshape both of them, but existing complications are usually too widespread to allow a completely new start.

Neither system ever had a single designer who knew exactly what needs it would have to meet. Instead, both have grown imperceptibly over the centuries, and are constantly being altered piecemeal to suit changing demands, as the ways of life above them have branched out. Both are therefore now very intricate. When trouble arises, specialized skill is needed if there is to be any hope of locating it and putting it right.

Here, however, we run into the first striking difference between the two cases. About plumbing, everybody accepts this need for specialists with painfully acquired technical knowledge. About philosophy, people—especially British people—not only doubt the need, they are often sceptical about whether the underlying system even exists at all. It is much more deeply hidden. When the concepts we are living by function badly, they do not usually drip audibly through the ceiling or swamp the kitchen floor. They just quietly distort and obstruct our thinking.

We often do not consciously notice this obscure discomfort and malfunction, any more than we consciously notice the discomfort of an unvarying bad smell or of a cold that creeps on gradually. We may indeed complain that life is going badly—that our actions and relationships are not turning out as we intend. But it can be very hard to see why this is happening, or what to do about it. This is because we find it much easier to look for trouble outside ourselves than within. It is notoriously hard to see faults in our own motivation, in the structure of our feelings. But it is in some ways even harder—even less natural—to turn our attention to what might be wrong in our ideas, in the structure of our thought. Attention naturally flows outwards to what is wrong in the world around us. To bend thought round so that it looks critically at itself is quite hard. That is why, in any culture, philosophy is a relatively late development.

When things go wrong, however, we do have to do this. We must then somehow readjust our underlying concepts; we must shift the set of assumptions that we have inherited and have been brought up with. We must restate those existing assumptions—which are normally muddled and inarticulate—so as to get our fingers on the source of trouble. And this new statement must somehow be put in a usable form, a form which makes the necessary changes look possible.

That is the need that philosophy exists to satisfy. It is *not* just a need felt by particularly highly-educated people. It can spoil the lives even of people with little interest in thinking, and its pressure can be vaguely felt by anyone who tries to think at all. As that pressure becomes fiercer, people who are determined to think particularly hard do sometimes manage to devise a remedy for this obscure discomfort. Time and again in the past, when conceptual schemes have begun to work badly, someone has contrived to suggest a change that shifts the blockage, allowing thought to flow where it is needed.

Once this has happened, the bystanders tend to heave deep sighs and say, 'Aha—of course. I knew that all along. Why didn't I happen to say it before?' (Sometimes indeed they think they have done so . . .) These new suggestions usually come in part from sages who are not full-time philosophers, notably from poetry and the other arts. Shelley was indeed right to say that poets are among the unacknowledged legislators of mankind. They can show us the new vision. But to work the new ideas out fully is still a different kind of work. Whoever does it, it is always philosophical business. It needs, not just a new vision, but also the thorough, disciplined articulation of its details and consequences.

Much of this work is boring, and it can sometimes prove astonishingly long and difficult, but it is absolutely necessary. Any powerful new idea calls for a great deal of change, and the more useful that idea is going to be, the more need there will be to work out these changes fully. For doing this, it really is very helpful to be acquainted with other visions and other sets of changes, to have some background training in the way past conceptual developments have worked. There have been some self-educated philosophers who did not have the advantage of this background—Tom Paine was one—but the work is much harder for them.

Great philosophers, then, need a combination of gifts that is extremely rare. They must be lawyers as well as poets. They must have both the new vision that points the way we are to go and the logical doggedness that sorts out just what is, and what is not, involved in going there. This difficult balancing-act is what has gained them a respect which is of a different order from the respect due to either kind of work on its own. It accounts for the peculiar prestige which philosophy still has, even among people who are extremely vague about what it is or why they might need it.

Bringing these two functions together is desperately hard. Where philosophy is salaried and professionalized, the lawyer-like skills are almost bound to predominate. (You can examine people to test their logical competence and industry, but you cannot test their creativity.) These skills are then no longer being used to clarify any specially important new vision. Philosophy becomes scholastic, a specialized concern for skilled plumbers doing fine plumbing, and sometimes doing it on their own in laboratories. This happened in the late Middle Ages; it seems to have happened in China, and it has happened to Anglo-American philosophy during much of this century.

This self-contained, scholastic philosophy remains an impressive feat, something which may well be worth doing for its own sake, but it leaves a most dangerous gap in the intellectual scene. For it cannot, of course, prevent the other aspect, the poetic aspect of philosophy, from being needed. The hungry sheep who do not get that creative vision look up and are not fed. They tend to wander round looking for new visions until they find some elsewhere. Thus, a good deal of poetic philosophising has been imported lately from Europe and from the East, from the social sciences, from evangelists, from literary criticism and from science fiction, as well as from past philosophers. But of course, this poetry comes without the disciplined, detailed thinking that ought to go with it.

The living water flows in, but it is not channelled to where it is needed. It seeps around, often forming floods, and it finally settles in pools where chance dictates, because the local philosophic practitioners will not attend to it. In fact, the presence of these alien streams merely exasperates them. They are convinced that the public has no business to ask for visions at all, and that unlicensed merchants have certainly no business to supply them.

So we get a new version of the old 'quarrel between philosophy and poetry', a demarcation dispute embittered by modern professional territorialism and by modern academic specialization. Philosophers are tempted to imitate other academic specialists by defensively narrowing their subject. They follow the specialized scientists who claim that nothing counts as 'science' except the negative results of control-experiments performed inside laboratories, and the specialized historians who insist that only value-free, non-interpreted bits of information can count as history. Ignoring the philosophic howlers that are so obvious in these claims, philosophers in their turn also rule that only technical, purely formal work, published in learned journals and directed at their colleagues, can count as 'philosophy'.

Do they still do this? Much less so, I think, than they did a little time back. In the last few decades, the absurdity of over-specialization, the emptiness of the heavily defended academic fortresses, is certainly becoming more clearly realized in many quarters. But unfortunately, these absurdities are built into hiring and firing and promotion procedures that will take a long time to change, even when the need for change is widely understood. Meanwhile, it needs to be loudly and often said that this contracting of territories, this defensive demarcation-disputing among professionals, is not just misguided. It is thoroughly unprofessional and extremely harmful.

Learning is not a private playground of the learned. It is something that belongs to and affects all of us. Because we are a culture that values knowledge and understanding so highly, the part of every study that can be widely understood—the general, interpretative part—always does seep through in the end, and it concerns us all. The conceptual schemes used in every study are not stagnant ponds; they are streams that are fed from our everyday thinking, are altered by the learned, and eventually flow back into it and influence our lives.

This is not only true of philosophy. In history, for instance, ideas about the nature of social causation, about the importance or unimportance of individual acts or of economic and social factors, are constantly changing. Historians cannot actually be neutral on these questions, because they have to pick out what they think worth investigating. Selection always shows bias, and cannot be prevented from having its eventual influence. All that specialist scholars gain by refusing to attend to this bit of philosophy is ignorance about their own thinking, ignorance of their own commitment and of the responsibility it carries. The same thing is true of science. One has only to think of the part that concepts like 'relativity' or 'evolution' have played in our thought during this century to see this.

But of course, philosophy is the key case, because it is the study whose peculiar business it is to concentrate on the gaps between all the others, and to understand the relations between them. Conceptual schemes as such are philosophy's concern, and these schemes do constantly go wrong. Conceptual confusion is deadly, and a great deal of it afflicts our everyday life. It needs to be seen to, and if the professional philosophers do not look at it, there is no one else whose role it is to be called on.

Ought we all to be able to do this ourselves, each on our own, on a do-it-yourself basis? This attractive idea probably lies at the heart of British anti-intellectualism. We do sometimes manage this do-it-your-self philosophising, and there is, of course, a great deal to be said for trying. But it is exceedingly hard to see where we need to start. Indeed, as I mentioned, often we find it hard to imagine that anything definite is wrong with our concepts at all.

This is the crucial paradox. Why are we not more aware of our conceptual needs? The difficulty is that (as I have mentioned), once this kind of work is done, conceptual issues drop out of sight and are forgotten. Systems of ideas which are working smoothly are more or less invisible. (This, of course, is what provoked my original compari-son with plumbing, another service for which we are seldom as grateful as we might be.) While there are no actual explosions, we assume that the ideas we are using are the only ideas that are possible. Either (we think) everybody uses them, or, if there are people who do not, they are simply unenlightened, 'primitive', misinformed, misguided, wicked or extremely stupid.

It is time to mention some examples. But we need the right ones, and this raises a problem. Our disregard of our conceptual schemes is so strong, so natural, that in order to pick on an instance of what I am talking about, we need to choose a notion that is already making too much trouble to be disregarded. I considered discussing the Machine Model here, but it is now wallowing in too many kinds of difficulty to deal with in this article. Let us instead open a related manhole, and look at the idea of the Social Contract.

That was the conceptual tool used by prophets of the Enlightenment to derive political obligation from below rather than from above. Instead of saying that kings must be obeyed because they were appointed by God, philosophers suggested that the only reason for obeying any kind of government was that it represented the will of the people governed and served their interests. At last, unsatisfactory kings were expendable. The only possible source of civic duty was tacit agreement among rational citizens, each concerned for their own inter-est—an agreement regularly tested through voting.

After fierce disputes and much bloodshed, this startling idea was quite widely accepted. Once this had happened, questions about it largely ceased to be noticed and vanished under the floor-boards of many Western institutions. On the whole, we now take contractual thinking for granted, and we are not alone in doing that. The authority of contract is, for instance, treated as obvious by the many oppressed and misgoverned peoples all over the world who are now demanding something called 'democracy'. Yet difficulties about that notion do still arise, and indeed they are on the increase. Lately, distinct patches of damp have been arising round it, and there have been some very dubious smells.

For instance—if we rely heavily on the notion of contract we have to ask, what about the interests of non-voting parties? What, for a start, about the claims of children, of the inarticulate and the insane, and of people as yet unborn? What about something that, till recently, our moralists hardly mentioned at all, namely the non-human, non-speaking world—the needs of animals and plants, of the ocean and the Antarctic and the rainforests? There is a whole great range of questions here which we now see to be vital, but which we find strangely hard to deal with, simply because our culture has been so obsessed with models centring on contract. Again, too, even within the set of possible contractors, we might ask who is entitled to a voice on what? What happens to the interests of people in one democratic country who suffer by the democratically agreed acts of another? What, too, about minorities within a country, minorities who must live by decisions they did not vote for (a question which Mill worried about profoundly in his *Essay on Liberty*)? And so on.

Plainly, social contract thinking is no sort of adequate guide for constructing the whole social and political system. It really is a vital means of protection against certain sorts of oppression, an essential defence against tyranny. But it must not be taken for granted and forgotten, as a safe basis for all sorts of institutions. It needs always to be seen as something partial and provisional, an image that may cause trouble and have to be altered. It is a tool to be used, not a final decree of fate or an idol to be worshipped. It is, in fact, just one useful analogy among many. It must always to be balanced against others which bring out other aspects of the complex truth.

This provisionalness, in fact, is a regular feature of conceptual schemes. None of them is isolated; none of them is safe from the possibility of clashing with others. All of them, if they are successful in one area, tend to expand and to be used on different material. (One can see this happening all the time with intellectual fashions.) Sometimes the expansion works well, but its success is never guaranteed. The cluster of ideas that centres on the image of contract has been very expansive, generating powerful ideas of rights, autonomy, interests, competition, rationality as self-interest and so forth. It has strongly influenced our whole idea of what an individual is—again, something that we take for granted and rarely think to alter when we run into trouble.

Contractual thinking makes individuals look much more separate than most cultures have taken them to be—more separate, surely, than they actually are. It says that there is really no such thing as society, that the state is only a logical construction out of its members. By contrast with older organic metaphors such as 'we are members one of another', contract-talk portrays people as essentially distinct beings, free to make just what contracts each of them chooses and to abstain from all others. It opens the way for thoroughgoing individualism.

This is, of course, particularly revolutionary about personal relations, and it has been meant to be so. The defence of individuals against outside interference has been personal as well as political. It has been seen as a deliberate emancipation from all non-chosen obligations, in particular, from allegiance to parents and from lasting marriage-bonds. Because these institutions really had been used for tyrannous purposes, the axe was laid to them too. Systematic contract thinking makes it possible to rule that personal relationships, like political ones, can only arise out of freely negotiated contracts, and that what is freely negotiated can at any time be annulled.

This conceptual move certainly did make possible much greater social freedom, and thereby a great deal of self-fulfilment. Yet it has some extremely odd consequences. Unfortunately, personal relations, such as friendship, do normally have to be relied on to last, because they involve some real joining-together of the parties. Friends share their lives; they are no longer totally separate entities. They are not pieces of Lego that have just been fitted together for convenience.

People are different from Lego. If you have been my friend for years, that friendship has changed both of us. We now rely deeply on each other; we have exchanged some functions, we contain elements of each others' lives. We are quite properly mutually dependent, not because of some shameful weakness, but just in proportion to what we have put into this friendship and what we have made of it. Of course any friendship can end if it has to, but that ending will be a misfortune. It will wound us. An organic model, which says that we are members one of another, describes this situation far better than a Lego model. And what is true of friendship is of course still more true of those personal relationships which are of most importance in forming our lives, namely, our relations to our parents and to our children. We did not choose either parents or children; we never made a contract with either. Yet we certainly are deeply bound to both.

Is this binding a tragic infringement of our freedom? Some twentieth-century theorists, such as the Existentialists, have said that it is, that any mutual dependence, any merging of individual lives, is bad faith. Freedom itself is (as Sartre told us) the only fixed value, the ideal against which all others must be judged. Here, of course, the concept of freedom too has been radically reshaped. Freedom, here, is no longer being viewed as a necessary condition of pursuing other ideals, but as being itself the only possible ideal. It is seen as consisting—not in ability to do things which we independently know to be important—but simply in heroic solitude. In fact, freedom itself becomes, in this vision, almost synonymous with solitude, the undisturbed life of the Lego-piece that has retired under the sofa, existing according to its own chosen principles without interference.

Now no doubt this is a possible ideal. There are hermits who seem to live by it, though they are not many and, of course, it is not very easy to find out whether that is really what they are doing. But this impregnable solitude is certainly a very *odd* ideal, and there seems no reason why the rest of us ought to adopt it. What has made it look impressive is surely something that very often happens over conceptual schemes. A pattern of ideas has been extended from the political field—where it was quite suitable and successful—into the private one, simply because of its success.

Resistance to tyranny, and resistance to the dead hand of tradition, had proved invaluable weapons in the public context. They obviously had some application in the private one as well, so they began to look like an all-purpose remedy there too. Countless parricidal novels were shaped round them, from Samuel Butler's *The Way of All Flesh* and the novels of revolt about the First World War on to the present day. But the negative, destructive recipe always needs to be supplemented with something more positive, if people are not simply to give up in despair.

This is what limits the value of the individualistic pattern. It tells us how to reject what we have—which may be very helpful—but it has not the slightest suggestion to make about what we should look for instead. In actual living, we normally do not follow such negative patterns beyond the rebellions of adolescence, to which indeed they properly belong. Left to ourselves, without moralistic propaganda, we quite quickly find that the hand of tradition is *not* always dead, but can sometimes be life-giving, nor are all close relations tyrannous. But we are not left to ourselves, because the morality of our age runs so strongly in destructive channels more appropriate to politics.

Individualistic moralities can make nothing of these cheerful discoveries about benign traditions and good relationships. They merely denounce them as disgraceful symptoms of moral cowardice, and because we are prone to guilt, we readily try to believe them. We cannot, however, easily find alternative ways of thinking to replace them. Organic models, which would probably help us, have for some time treated with great suspicion because, on the political scene, they had been misused for the defence of tyranny.

With the rise of concern about the environment, this taboo on organic ways of thinking may now be lifting. It may even become possible for our species to admit that it is not really a supernatural variety of Lego, but some kind of an animal. This ought to make it easier to admit also that we are not self-contained and self-sufficient, either as a species or as individuals, but live naturally in deep mutual dependence. Of course these organic models too will need watching, of course they too can be abused. But if we can once get it into our heads, that a model is only a model, if we can grasp the need to keep correcting one model philosophically against another, then some sort of social life begins to look possible again.

Where is all this taking us? I have mentioned the social contract model as an example of the underlying conceptual schemes that we rely on, and I have so far said two things about it.

First, that this model is merely an indicator of much wider and deeper structures. It is exceptional because it is already making visible trouble, so we are more aware of it than we are of many others. What we chiefly need to notice is the unconsidered mass that lies behind it. I am sorry if that sounds like a rather paradoxical demand to notice what one is not noticing, but really it makes quite good sense—compare the plumbing. The point is, of course, that we need to remember how large and powerful the hidden system of ideas is, so as to be ready to spot any particular elements of it when they do make trouble. People who simply do not believe that that powerful system is there at all really are in a situation much like those who do not believe in the drains and the water supply. The alternative to getting a proper philosophy is continuing to use a bad one. It is not avoiding philosophy altogether, because that is impossible.

Second, I have been saying that this social-contract model, along with all other such models, is partial and provisional. Even the most useful, the most vital of such patterns of thought have their limits. They all need to be balanced and corrected by one another. The strong unifying tendency that is natural to our thought keeps making us hope that we have found a single pattern which is a theory of everything—a key to all the mysteries, the secret of the universe . . . Hard experience has shown that this cannot work. That realization seems to be the sensible element at the core of the conceptual muddle now known as Postmodernism, though it is often obscured by much less useful excursions into the wilder shores of relativism.

This discovery that truth is not monolithic does not really leave us in a sceptical, relativistic welter, because the various patterns overlap and can be related to each other. But it does mean that we need to view *controversy* very differently. An immense proportion of academic time, paper and word-processing power is used on battles between models both of which have their place, instead of on quietly working out what that place is and how to fit them together. Academic imperialism is constantly setting up unnecessary tournaments. Attempts at takeover are very common where scholars are not specially trained to avoid them, and of course these attempts are encouraged when there is a vacuum of serious, wider theorizing. Philosophers themselves may have stopped imitating Hegel, but sages from other disciplines are still at it.

I am, then, using this parallel with plumbing to say that the patterns underlying our thought are much more powerful, more intricate and more dangerous than we usually notice, that they need constant attention, and that no one of them is a safe universal guide. What more should be said about these patterns? Chiefly, I think, that to understand their power we need to grasp their strong hold on the imagination—their relation to myth.

Myths are stories symbolizing profoundly important patterns, patterns that are very influential, but too large, too deep and too imperfectly known to be expressed literally. Sometimes myths are actual stories—narratives—and when they are, these narratives do not, of course, need to be literally true. Thus the social contract myth tells a story of an agreement that was once arrived at, but no-one supposes that this ever actually happened. The story can indeed sometimes be an actual lie, like the forgery of the 'Protocols of the Elders of Zion' and the lie will not be nailed until the essence of the myth—the meaning that has gripped the imagination of myth-bound people—is somehow reached and defused.

Examples like these led Enlightenment thinkers to denounce all myths and to proclaim, in Positivistic style, a new age free from symbols, an age when all thoughts would be expressed literally and language would be used only to report scientific facts. But the idea of such an age is itself a highly fanciful myth, an image quite unrelated to the way in which thought and language actually work. The notion of dispensing with symbols is a doomed one. All our thinking works through them. New ideas commonly occur to us first as images and are expressed first as metaphors. Even in talking about ordinary, concrete things immediately around us we use these metaphors all the time, and on any larger, more puzzling subject we need constantly to try out new ones.

Strictly literal talk is in fact quite a rare and sophisticated activity, a late form of speech, hard to produce and useful only for certain limited purposes. It is not by any means the only language used in science. Scientists constantly use fresh models and analogies drawn from outside their subject-matter, and they need to do this all the more vigorously where they are not doing 'normal science', but generating new ideas. Whole books have been written about Darwin's metaphors, and probably about Einstein's too.

Is all this symbolizing dangerous? Of course it is. Everything fertile and unpredictable is dangerous. Imaginative talk makes it impossible to disinfect thought by confining it in libraries for the use of licensed academics. Thought is incurably powerful and explosive stuff, not safely insulated from feeling and action, but integrally linked with both of them *We think as whole people*, not as disembodied minds, not as computers. All ideas that are of the slightest interest to anybody can have unexpected emotional and practical consequences—consequences that cannot possibly be spelt out in advance. And, without this constant flow of ideas, life would grind to a halt.

Here, if you will believe me, is something more that has made the imagery of water haunt me as suitable for philosophy. Useful and familiar though water is, it is not really tame stuff. It is life-giving and it is wild. Floods and storms have appalling force; seas can drown people, rivers carve out valleys. Then, too, rivers produce fertile plains and forests. Water works at the heart of life, and it works there by constant movement, continually responding to what goes on round it. Thought, too, ought to be conceived dynamically, as something that we do, and must constantly keep doing. The static model shown us by Descartes, of final proofs to be produced by science, proofs that will settle everything, is one more model that has very grave limitations.

So too, of course, does this talk of water. All analogies are imperfect, all of them have faults, all of them do only limited work. I am not suggesting that this one is any exception. I have tried to explain the work that it does do. But to be quite clear about it, we need to look (finally) at the question I raised in starting, the question about dignity.

Is the approach I have been suggesting undignified? The reason why it can seem so is not, I think, just that it is unfamiliar and domestic, but that it postulates *needs*. It treats philosophy, like food and shelter, as something that we must have because we are in real trouble without it. We are perhaps more used to the thought that philosophy is splendid but gratuitous, and that it is splendid because it is gratuitous—something grand and exalted, which people could quite easily live without, but ought to pursue all the same. On this view, intelligent people philosophise because they can see a special kind of supreme value in doing so, and perhaps everybody is capable of seeing this. But this taste is seen as something a bit removed from the rest of life, and independent of it. It is felt that our regard for philosophy ought to be a disinterested one, that there is something mean about dependence.

There really is a point in both these ways of talking, and it is not easy to balance them properly. The idea of disinterested detachment does have its point, but there is a difficulty about it here rather like the one that arises in the case of Art. This talk can sound as if we were describing a luxury, a hobby, an extra. When Socrates said that the unexamined life is unlivable to man, I do not think that he meant just that our species happens to have a peculiar taste for understanding, an unaccountable and noble impulse to philosophise.

That is the way people often do interpret this kind of claim, and it is particularly often brought forward as a reason for doing science. But Socrates was surely saying something much stronger. He was saying that there are limits to living in a mess. He was pointing out that we do live in a constant, and constantly increasing, conceptual mess, and that we need to do something about it. He knew that the presence of this mess, this chronic confusion, is something we do not much want to think about because it indicates the thoroughly undignified fact that we are inherently confused beings. We exist in continual conflict because our natural impulses do not form a clear, coherent system. And the cultures by which we try to make sense of those impulses often work very badly.

So—(said Socrates)—unless we acknowledge the resulting shameful confusions and do something to sort them out, none of our projects, whether grand or mundane, is likely to come to much. This means that we have to look at the confusions where the problems are actually arising, in real life. The kind of philosophy that tries to do this is now called Applied Philosophy. This suggests to some people that it is a mere by-product of the pure kind—a secondary spin-off from nobler, more abstract processes going on in ivory towers. But that is not the way in which European philosophy has so far developed.

Socrates started it by diving straight into the moral, political, religious and scientific problems arising in his day. He moved on towards abstraction, not for its own sake, but in a way that was designed to clear up the deeper confusions underlying these primary messes. The same is true of Kant's preoccupation with freedom, which shaped his whole metaphysic. The direction of metaphysics has always been determined by considerations which are practical as well as theoretical, substantial as well as formal. Metaphysicians who claim to be free from these considerations certainly have not really got shot of them. They are merely unaware of their own motivations, which is no gain at all.

Granted, then, that the confusions are there, is abstract philosophical speculation really a helpful remedy? Are the plumbers any use? Obviously this kind of speculation cannot work alone; all sorts of other human functions and faculties are needed too. But once you have got an articulate culture, the explicit, verbal statement of the problems does seem to be needed.

Socrates lived, as we do, in a society that was highly articulate and self-conscious, indeed, strongly hooked on words. It may well be that other cultures, less committed to talking, find different routes to salvation, that they pursue a less word-bound form of wisdom. But wisdom itself matters everywhere, and everybody must start from where they are. I think it might well pay us to be less impressed with what philosophy can do for our dignity, and more aware of the shocking malfunctions for which it is an essential remedy.

Beyond Representation

ANTHONY PALMER

So stellt der satz den Sachverhalt gleichsam auf eigene Faust dar.

Foreword. Towards the end of this paper I refer to the work of A. J. Smith who died suddenly on 11 December 1991. His last book, *Metaphysical Wit*, was published in January 1992 by Cambridge University Press. I would like this paper to be thought of as a small tribute to the man and his work.

There is in Texas an area known as 'the Big Thicket'. It is an area of impenetratable swamp and woodland. Once, long ago, I heard an American philosopher singing about Wittgenstein's *Tractatus*. His song had the refrain 'O the *Tractatus* is a big thicket'. The general idea was that philosophers, like runaway slaves of old in Texas, had disappeared into it never to be heard of again. I am going to risk it in this paper. But I do hope to emerge with something relevant to say about the theme of this series of lectures: the impulse to philosophise.

What I have to say about the *Tractatus* is set in the general background of how it should be read in relation to Wittgenstein's *Philosophical Investigations*. In his preface to this later work he wrote

> Four years ago I had occasion to read my first book . . . and to explain its thoughts. It suddenly seemed to me that I should publish those old thoughts and the new ones together: the latter could be seen in the right light only by contrast with and against the background of my old way of thinking.

This was generally taken to mean that the *Tractatus* formed a background to and a contrast with the new way of thinking in that it involved a total rejection of it, or a radical assault upon it. The most notable proponent of this view in recent years has been Norman Malcolm. He powerfully expressed it in his last book *Wittgenstein: Nothing is Hidden*. The subtitle, of course, comes from the *Philosophical Investigations*.

The way of looking at the two works was, I think, largely fostered by Russell's introduction to the *Tractatus*, which encouraged philosophers to read it as the final form of the line of thinking that Russell himself developed out of conversations he himself had with Wittgenstein before 1914. These views were developed in a series of lectures given in Gordon Square, seventy-four years ago. They were published under the title of 'The Philosophy of Logical Atomism'.

The curious thing is that we have Wittgenstein's own authority for regarding Russell's introduction as, to put it mildly, misleading, for he wrote to Russell telling him so. His letter must be one of the most crushing letters ever written from one friend to another. He says in it 'When I got the German translation of the introduction, I could not bring myself to have it printed with the work after all. For the fineness of your English style was—of course—quite lost and what was left was superficiality and misunderstanding' (Wittgenstein, 1969, 131). What I have to say in this paper about the *Tractatus* will, I hope, contribute to our understanding of the continuity of Wittgenstein's philosophy.

Wittgenstein began his *Tractatus* by telling us that 'The world is all that is the case', it 'is the totality of facts not of things'. A fact, he said 'is the existence of states of affairs' while 'a state of affairs (a state of things) is a combination of objects'. He also maintained that 'it is essential to things that they should be possible constituents of states of affairs'. He sent the manuscript of it to the greatest logician of the day who, if we are to judge by his reply, does not appear to have been able to progress beyond the first page. This is how Frege replied.

> Right at the beginning I come across the expressions 'is the case' and 'fact' and I suspect that *is the case* and *is a fact* are the same. The world is everything that is the case and the world is the collection of facts. Is not every fact the case and is not what is the case a fact? Is it not the same if I say, A is a fact, as if I say, A is the case? Why then this double expression? . . . Now comes a third expression: 'What is the case, a fact, is the existence of a *Sachverhalt.*' I take this to mean that every fact is the existence of a *Sachverhalt*, so that another fact is the existence of another *Sachverhalt*. Couldn't one delete the words 'existence of' and say 'Every fact is a *Sachverhalt*, every other fact is another *Sachverhalt*'. Could one perhaps also say 'Every *Sachverhalt* is the existence of a fact?' (Monk, 1990, 163).

Although initially we might have some sympathy with Frege's bewilderment, I think that these remarks betray a lack of understanding that has continued amongst *Tractatus* commentators ever since. I shall argue that it is fundamental to the picturing theory of propositions that facts (*Tatsachen*) and states of affairs (*Sachverhalten*) should be kept apart.

Part of the trouble for English readers comes from translating '*Bestehen*' in proposition 2 ('*Was der Fall ist, die Tatsache, ist das Bestehen von Sachverhalten*') by 'existence', although it is clear from Frege's response that the difficulty is contained in the German too. If it had been translated by some such expression as 'the holding of' or 'the obtaining of' Frege's difficulties would disappear. It is not so much that the translation is wrong but rather that it tends to push our thinking in the wrong direction. It is easy to move from 'the existence of a state of affairs' to 'a state of affairs that exists', or 'an existing state of affairs' and this is crucially wrong.

If a *Sachverhalt* is a combination of things it should be clear that a *Tatsache*, the obtaining or holding of *Sachverhalten* could not also be a combination of things. Equally, of course, the existence of combinations of things could not itself be a combination of things. Facts are what are expressed in 'that' clauses. That things are combined in a certain way is not itself things combined in a certain way. A *Sachverhalt* has elements, i.e. the things that are combined. That a *Sachverhalt* obtains does not itself have elements.

This is the point which I take to be central to Wittgenstein's picturing theory of propositions, for it was his contention that propositions are facts that picture other facts not states of affairs that are somehow related to other states of affairs. 'Propositions, which are symbols having reference to facts, are themselves facts (that the inkpot is on this table may express that I sit on this chair).' (Wittgenstein, 1961, 98). This remark from the *Notebooks* shows that Wittgenstein was already hammering this point home as early as 1913. If we are to understand it we must eschew the thesis that the essence of picturing or representing consists in a correspondence between the elements of the picturing fact and elements of the fact pictured since just because both are facts neither has elements. And yet this is precisely how the picturing theory has generally been interpreted. If we think of facts as having elements then we tend to think of them as complexes, as something that can be described by describing their elements. But, as Wittgenstein himself later pointed out, while

> A chain is composed of its links, not of these and their spatial relations. The fact that these links are so concatenated isn't composed of anything at all. (Wittgenstein, 1975, 201)

Although this remark is later than the *Tractatus* it is entirely in accord with what is said in the *Tractatus*. Ray Monk, from whose magnificent biography I have culled the Frege letter, and who kindly supplied me with the full text of the letters, certainly does not realize this for he writes:

> The problem with which he was principally concerned during this time was that of how language pictures the world—what features of both language and the world make it possible for this picturing to take place:

> The great problem round which everything I write turns is: Is there an order in the world *a priori*, and if so what does it consist in?

Almost against his will he was forced to the conclusion that there was such an order: The world, as he had insisted to Russell, consists of *facts*, not of things—*that is it consists of things (objects) standing in certain relations to one another.* (Monk, 1990, 129; my italics)

But facts, according to the *Tractatus*, are not things standing in certain relations. That is what states of affairs are, and facts are the holding of states of affairs.

Monk is not alone in failing to keep facts (*Tatsachen*) and states of affairs (*Sachverhalten*) apart. Indeed the failure to do so is almost universal. Norman Malcolm, for example, in his book *Nothing is Hidden* (1986) does precisely the same thing. The last three sentences of the opening paragraph of chapter one of his book read as follows.

> A configuration of objects is a state of affairs (2.0272). A possible combination is a possible state of affairs. The actual world (at a certain time) is just the totality of existing states of affairs (at that time) (2.04).

This shows how all too easy it is to move from 'the existence of a state of affairs' to 'States of affairs that exist' or 'existing states affairs' which places all the emphasis on states of affairs, not facts. For facts are not states of affairs, even existing states of affairs.

A fact, then is the obtaining of a state of affairs. We cannot describe facts we can only state them. While the holding of a state of affairs does not itself consist of elements standing in certain relations obviously states of affairs that do hold do have such elements standing in certain relations. And while we can talk about the relations between the elements of various states of affairs since this would just involve the holding of other states of affairs, we cannot talk about the relations between elements of facts for facts have no elements.

The idea of picturing or representing enters the story when it is noticed that among states of affairs that do obtain some can be used to represent others. Those states of affairs that are so used will, of course, have elements, although the fact that those states of affairs obtain will not.

What, then, makes it possible for us to use the fact that one state of affairs obtains to represent the fact that another state of affairs obtains?

> 2.161 There must be something identical in a picture and what it depicts, to enable the one to be a picture of the other at all.

What is common to both is what Wittgenstein calls 'pictorial form'. How should we understand this?

Suppose the state of affairs that we want to make a picture of is of one thing on top of another. Let us suppose that it is the state of affairs of a particular cat being on top of a particular mat. In order to make a picture of this you will need something to deputize for the cat and something to deputise for the mat, and the things that you choose will have to be capable of standing in the same relation as the cat and the mat. Although anything capable of standing in that relation will do let us for simplicity sake have a model of a cat and a model of a mat and let us place the first model on top of the second. Let us also suppose that there is an actual cat on an actual mat. We now have two states of affairs, a model cat on a model mat and a cat on a mat. The point that Wittgenstein is making when he insists that states of affairs and facts should be kept apart is that no amount of inspection of the relationships that obtain between the model cat and the actual cat or the model mat and the actual mat will give you an explanation of why it would be correct to say that one is a picture or representation of the other. You might discover lots of new relationships, i.e. combinations of things, but the discovering of new relationships will not take you any closer to understanding representation. Outside the interpretation of the *Tractatus* this point is a commonplace in philosophical writing about representation, i.e. you will not succeed in accounting for representation by any resemblances that might be discovered between a representation and what is represented. To use the vocabulary of the remark from philosophical grammar you would be operating at the level of complexes and no amount of operating at that level would tell you about picturing. A model cat on a model mat tells you nothing about cats and mats. In order to say something about cats and mats the models have to be used. In order to explain this we have to move to the level of the use of the model cats and mats, and when we move to that level we move to the level of facts. We are now not concerned with states of affairs but with the fact that certain states of affairs obtain. The possibility of cats being on mats is already contained in the fact that there is a model cat on a model mat. If it were not possible for cats to be on mats then it could not be the case that there is a model cat on a model mat. Of course that there is a model cat on a model mat does not entail that there is a cat on a mat but it does entail that it is possible for there to be a cat on the mat. (2.203). '*A picture contains the possibility of the situation it represents.*'

This way of thinking about representation is captured dramatically in the remarks in the notebooks for 4 and 5 November 1914.

How does the proposition determine logical place?
How does the picture present a situation?
It is after all not the situation, which need not be the case at all. One name is representative of one thing, another of another thing, and

they themselves are connected: in this way the whole images the situation—like a *tableau vivant*.

The logical connexion must, of course, be one that is possible as between the things that the names are representative of, and this will always be the case if the names really are representative of things. N.B. that connexion is not a relation but only the *holding* of a relation.

In this way the proposition represents the situation—as it were off its own bat. (Wittgenstein 1969, 26)

Here then is an account of representation which does not see representation as a relation. It is not something that in the Russell's symbolism or the symbolism of *Tractatus* could be regarded as a function. There could be no function which mapped the picturing fact on to what it pictures since that something is the case is not a suitable candidate for filling the argument place of a function. That there is a model cat on a model mat represents that there is a cat on a mat. Moreover, even the model cat on the model mat need not be related in any way to a cat on a mat for there may be no cat on any mat for it to be related to. But if there can be model cats on model mats then there can be cats on mats.

If you know that something is the case then you are thereby presented with the means of understanding that something else might be the case. When I place something on something else, i.e. when I make it true that one is on top of another, I am thereby enabled to represent something else being on top of something else. Making something be the case also enables us to represent the world to ourselves. That is how we make pictures of facts for ourselves.

The propositional sign guarantees the possibility of the fact that it presents (not that the fact is actually the case). This holds for general propositions too. For if the positive fact ϕa is given then so is the possibility of $(x).\phi x, \sim(\exists x).\phi x, \sim\phi a$ etc. etc. (All logical constants are already contained in elementary propositions.) (Wittgenstein, 1969, 27)

This stress on the point that pictures are facts not states of affairs and that what pictures picture are also facts not states of affairs helps us to understand what Wittgenstein says about pictorial form and logical form. Forms are possibilities. Just as the form of an object is its possible combination with other objects, so

2.151 Pictorial form is the possibility that things are related to one another in the same way as the elements of the picture.

It follows directly from this that pictorial form is not something that can itself be pictured. The possibility that things are related to one another in a certain way is not itself a fact i.e. is not itself the obtaining of a state of affairs. It is not therefore something which could be pictured by a fact. It is true however that this possibility is contained in a fact. So

2.172 A picture cannot, however, depict its pictorial form: it displays it.

and

2.203 A picture contains the possibility of the situation it represents.

The same argument applies to what Wittgenstein calls 'logical form'. If pictorial form is what facts must have in common in order for one fact to picture another, i.e. they must both contain the possibility that things are related to each other in a certain way, so logical form is

2.18 What any picture of whatever form must have in common with reality in order to be able to depict it, correctly or incorrectly in any way at all.

Hence logical form like pictorial form is not itself something that can be pictured. As Wittgenstein says later it is something that can be shown but not said. It makes itself manifest.

The argument of the *Tractatus* is from logical form to thought and from thought to proposition i.e. a thought made visible to the senses. In all of this development the stress on facts, the obtaining of states of affairs, is central.

2.1 We picture facts to ourselves.

2.141 A picture is a fact.

2.15 The fact that the elements of a picture are related to one another in a determined way represents that things are related to one another in the same way.

3. A logical picture of facts is a thought.

3.1 In a proposition a thought finds an expression that can be perceived by the senses.

3.12 I call the sign with which we express a thought a propositional sign.

3.1432 Instead of 'The complex sign "aRb" says that a stands to b in the relation R' we ought to put, '*That* "a" stands to "b" in a certain relation says *that* aRb'

I am not in this paper seeking to defend Wittgenstein's views. (Although I do think that they can be defended and that once they are they will provide a new perspective on his later work.) I do, however, wish to show how, when they are correctly understood just how revolutionary they are. If they are correct then a whole range of problems, all centring on the conception of representation which at least since the seventeenth century have been thought of as central to philosophy are swept away.

It is arguable that these views of Wittgenstein take us back to ideas about representation which Descartes' writing rendered unintelligible. For the central problem which Descartes set subsequent philosophers was the problem of how we can legitimately move from representations to the things themselves. His question was, How can we move from the knowledge we have of our own ideas, which are the easiest of all things to know, to knowledge of things other than our own ideas? Descartes opened up a gap between thought and reality which philosophers have been struggling to bridge ever since. The questions we have asked ourselves are questions about the relation that must exist between thought and the world if our thought is to succeed in even being about the world let alone true of it. This was the question which Locke set out clearly in the fourth book of his essay.

'Tis evident that the Mind knows not Things immediately but only by the intervention of the *Ideas* it has of them. *Our Knowledge*, therefore, is *real* only so far as there is a conformity between our *Ideas* and the reality of Things. But what shall here be the Criterion? (Locke, 1979, 563)

We have sought a form of argument which will enable us to go beyond representation, which will enable us to station ourselves at a point from which we can view representation and thing represented and thereby make ourselves acquainted with the relation that exists between them. This was the role of Descartes' own proof of God's existence, and it was also the reason why Locke laid great stress on his claim that it was obvious that our ideas of primary qualities of bodies resembled those qualities. In our own century only the vocabulary of the question has changed. Nowadays instead of asking about the relation of ideas to things we ask about the relation of words to things, we ask not about the relation of thought to the world but about the relation of language to the world. But the form of our questions is the same. We may in the twentieth century have turned problems of knowledge into problems of meaning but we have not really changed the problems. It is not surprising, therefore, that Wittgenstein's *Tractatus* continues to be read in that tradition, even by those who see his later work as an attempt to break with it, an attempt which they claim has yet to be assimilated into our thinking. The *Tractatus* is still seen, in Norman Malcolm's words as 'belonging to a traditional framework of philosophical ideas about the relation of thinking and language'. If I am right in what I have said about the theory of representation that is presented in the *Tractatus* then, far from this being so, Wittgenstein's book is a radical rejection of that tradition. In the *Tractatus* there is no gap to be bridged between representation and reality since representations themselves contain the possibility of what it is they represent. There is no need to go beyond representation. As early as 1914 it was already clear to Wittgenstein that in that sense 'nothing is hidden'. The attempt to penetrate the veil of perception, the veil of thought or the veil of language is misbegotten. As he would later say: 'We feel as if we had to *penetrate* phenomena: our investigation, however, is not directed towards phenomena but, as one might say towards the "possibilities" of phenomena' (Wittgenstein, 1958, sec. 90). What needs to be understood is how the urge to think that there is something to be penetrated comes to be well nigh irresistible. Like Berkeley, Wittgenstein thinks that we have raised a dust and then complain that we cannot see.

It is this which provides me with my excuse for talking about Wittgenstein's picturing theory in this series of lectures; for once more entering into the Big Thicket. For there is no single reason why people are led to philosophise. There are many reasons and they are different at different times. Consequently asked to lecture on the theme of the impulse to philosophise I was tempted to stand back from the work I was engaged in and wonder from what impulse it came. When Professor Phillips Griffiths issued the invitation to me I was thinking about the notion of representation and Wittgenstein's views on it in the *Tractatus*. I had also been reading a paper by Virgil Aldrich entitled 'Photographing Facts'. Aldrich argued in that paper that 'a fact, which correlates with "the fact that" ("is true that") and so with a proposition cannot, as such, be photographed' (Aldrich, 1989, 81). It is easy to see that this view links up with my interpretation of the *Tractatus*. I was inclined to the view expressed by Aldrich in his paper that an enormous number of problems in contemporary philosophy come back in the end to our inability to get clear about the notion of representation, and that one impulse to philosophise is an inclination to go beyond representation. At the same time I had been reading the manuscript of a book by A. J. Smith entitled *Metaphysical Wit*. In it Smith endeavours to make intellectually available to us a way of understanding mind body and nature which he saw as paradigmatically contained in the work of the metaphysical poets and in particular in the poetry of John Donne. This way of thinking and this kind of poetry, did not survive the middle of the seventeenth century. His explanation of this seemed to me to be entirely convincing.

The dualism of Descartes, and Locke's exploitation of it, denied a way of thinking which started in the presumption that mind and body, spirit and sense, are wholly interdependent in our nature. For the English metaphysical writers human nature epitomises a universe which works as a living organism and manifests sacred purpose in all its processes. Their conception of a natural order in which spiritual and material natures continually interwork led them to assume that effective ideas are not discrete mental objects but complex interrelationships between seemingly (if not actually) unlike orders of being. Such ideas cannot be developed in a mere succession of words but are to be comprehended in the whole sentence of a poem. Descartes and Locke now fathered a conception of nature which negated these conceptions at every point; and it is a matter of record that metaphysical poetry could not be properly grasped again while it held sole sway. (Smith, 1992, 247)

One way of putting this point is that the wit of the metaphysical poets provides us with a conception of representation which by the middle of the seventeenth century had become unintelligible and was soon to turn into mere whimsy. It was to become what Dr Johnson under the influence of Locke's version of the Cartesian revolution thought it had always been: 'heterogeneous ideas yoked by violence together'. Here was one impulse to philosophise whose seventeenth-century origins and twentieth-century corrective seemed worth exploring in a paper given to the Royal Institute of Philosophy.

My reference a moment ago to Berkeley's remark that we have raised a dust and complain that we cannot see is not the only point of contact between the philosophy of Berkeley and the philosophy of Wittgenstein. If I am right, however, it is not that we are here dealing with two idealist philosophers as is sometimes alleged. I do not think that there is any idealism in Wittgenstein's writing at all. It is true of both, however, that in both the gap between representation and thing represented disappears.

2.151 Pictorial form is the possibility that things are related to one another in the same way as the elements of the picture.
2.1511 *That* is how a picture is attached to reality; it reaches right out to it.

In the canon of our works of philosophy prior to Wittgenstein it is perhaps only in Berkeley's writing that this is true. One way of reading *The Principles of Human Knowledge* is to see him as seeking to re-establish that view of human understanding to be found, if Smith is correct, in the metaphysical poets. Just as Donne

derives the decay of the entire cosmos from the recent death of a young girl; or finds a present enactment of Christ's crucifixion in his journey to visit a friend on Good Friday; or portrays his fevered body as a flat map over which physician-cosmographers must pore as they struggle to chart a particularly hazardous progress . . . (Smith, 1992, 2)

so Berkeley has it that although

the Lord conceal Himself from the eyes of the sensual and lazy, who will not be at the least expense of thought, yet to an unbiased and attentive mind, nothing can be more plainly legible than the intimate presence of an All-wise Spirit who fashions, and sustains the whole system of beings. (Berkeley, 1962, 143)

Berkeley, however, unlike Donne and Wittgenstein, had to do this within a way of thinking and by means of a vocabulary which rendered that view of representation unintelligible. Berkeley, although he was bitterly opposed to the philosophy of the moderns in which the gap between thought and the world seemed unbridgeable, could do no other than speak their language. He was obliged to operate within the Cartesian cum Lockean way of ideas. If the gap between ideas and things had to be denied then things had to become ideas. The consequence was a philosophical system, which he called immaterialism and others called idealism, that was simply greeted with incredulity and which had scarcely any influence.

Donne's poetry was written before that way of thinking was invented and was ignored when that way of thinking became the modern orthodoxy. Wittgenstein, on the other hand, developed his views on representation at the point at which the Cartesian way of thinking had fallen into disrepute, at least where the subject matter of logic was concerned. He did recognize that what he had to say about representation was capable of generating analogous difficulties.

4.1121 . . . Does not my study of sign-language correspond to the study of thought-processes, which philosophers used to consider so essential to the philosophy of logic? Only in most cases they got entangled in unessential psychological investigations, and with my method too there is an analogous risk.

The subsequent handling of his picturing theory of propositions has shown that that risk is all too easily incurred.

Scenes from my Childhood

BRYAN MAGEE

Until I was five I shared a bed with my sister, 3½ years older than me. After our parents had switched out the light we would chatter away in the darkness until we fell asleep. But I could never afterwards remember falling asleep. It was always the same: one moment I was talking to my sister in the dark, and the next I was waking up in a sunlit room having been asleep all night. Yet every night there must have come a time when I stopped talking and settled down to sleep. It was incomprehensible to me that I did not experience that, and never remembered it.

When I confided my bafflement to my sister she was dismissive. 'Nobody remembers it,' she said in tones of confident finality, as if that were all there was to it. I remained dissatisfied. *How does she know?* I thought? *All that means is* she *doesn't remember it. I bet she's never talked about it to anybody else.* So I set myself to keep a keen watch on myself, so that I would know when I was falling asleep, in the same sort of way as people try to catch the light in a refrigerator going out when they close the door. But it was no use. Everything continued just as before. One moment I would be chattering away to my sister in the darkness on, say, a Monday evening, and the next thing I knew I would be waking up in broad daylight and it would be several hours into Tuesday. That going to sleep was something I did every night yet never experienced was for years a source of active mystification to me.

I retain a vivid memory of myself, two or three years after that, when I was seven or eight, standing in a shaft of sunlight in the corner of the kitchen by our back door, between a barred window and a green wooden wall, focusing my eyes keenly on the index finger of my right hand, which I held pointed upwards in front of my face. *I'm going to count to three*, I was saying to myself, *and when I say 'three' my finger's going to bend*. Then I counted: *One, two, thr*—and sure enough on *three* my finger bent. How did I do it? I did it again. Then I thought: *This time I'll count to four*. And on *four* my finger bent. Next time I counted to five. My finger bent on *five*. I tried dragging out the counting so as to catch my finger out: *one, two . . . three . . four . . .* [wait for it] *. . . five!* But on *five* my finger, not caught napping at all, bent. I could bend my finger whenever I liked. Or not, just as I decided. Yet no matter how hard I concentrated I could not grasp

165

anything at all about how I did it. How could something that was so completely within my command, solely and entirely a matter of my own conscious decision, be a nothing for me, just simply no experience whatever, and yet happen? From that day to this the problem has fascinated me.

When I was a teenager, and had acquired the concept of willed activity, and knew that the decision to crook my finger was something taking place in my head, I tried all ways I could think of to catch, in experience, whatever it was that was happening between my brain and my finger. The result was always total failure. I would take the decision inside my head to crook my finger and *simultaneously* my finger would crook; and between my head and my finger there was an emptiness. The simultaneity presented me with an additional problem: why was not there a time lag? How could a decision be the cause of something that happened at the same time as itself?

For a period of two or three years between the ages of about nine and twelve I was in thrall to puzzlement about time. I would lie awake in bed at night in the dark thinking something along the following lines. I know there was a day before yesterday, and a day before that, and a day before that, and so on, as far back as I can remember. But there must also have been a day before the first day I can remember. I know I was born on 12 April 1930, and there must have been a day before that. And a day before that. And so on—and so on—and so on. Before every day there must have been a day before. So it must be possible to go back like that for ever and ever and ever. . . . Yet is it? The idea of going back for ever and *ever* was something I could not get a hold of: it seemed impossible. So perhaps, after all, there must have been a beginning somewhere. But if there was a beginning, what had been going on before that? Well, obviously, nothing—nothing at all—otherwise it could not be the beginning. But if there was nothing, how could anything have got started? Where could it have come from? Time could not just suddenly pop into existence—bingo!—out of *nothing*, and start going, all by itself. Nothing is nothing, not anything. So the idea of a beginning was unimaginable, which somehow made it seem impossible too. The upshot was that it seemed impossible for time to have had a beginning and impossible for it not to have had a beginning.

I must be missing something here, I came to think. There are only these two alternatives, so one of them must be right. They cannot both be impossible. So I would switch my concentration from one to the other and then, when it had exhausted itself, back again, trying to work out where I had gone wrong; but I never discovered. I became enslaved by the problem, and started to get lost in it not only in bed at night but increasingly during the day. There were adults who I thought at first might be able to help me, so I put it to them, but their responses left me more bewildered than before. Either they admitted they could not solve it, and then went on to talk about other things, as if this particular question were not interesting enough even to discuss, or else they actively pooh-poohed it with superior little laughs and remarks like: 'Oh, you don't want to go wasting your time worrying about things like that.' I could not make this out. If they were as unable as I was to answer the question, how could they feel superior to it? Why were not they disconcerted, and why did not they find it even interesting? After several perplexing rebuffs I stopped talking to people about it and just got on with thinking about it by myself.

I had realized almost immediately, of course, that the same problem operated forward as backward. After tomorrow there would be another day, and then another day after that, and then another; and it was inconceivable that time should ever end—for what was there for it to end *in*, if not time (perhaps another time, or a different sort of time) and so one would always be able to ask what happened after that. On the other hand, it was inconceivable that time could go on for ever and ever and ever and ever—for that would be eternity in this world, in fact it would be the eternity *of* this world. As I thought about it more and more, what came to me were not possible answers but more problems. One of these was that if it were necessary for infinite time to have elapsed before the present moment were reached it would be impossible for us ever to have reached it. Another was that for something to *exist*, it must have some sort of identity, and that meant there must be something it was not, and that meant it must have limits, so it could not both *be* and *be endless*, or *be* and *be beginningless*. I became convinced that a beginningless or endless time was impossible—yet on the other hand I was no nearer grasping the possibility of a beginning or an end.

Again, almost immediately, I realized that a similar problem existed with regard to space. I remember myself as a London evacuee in Market Harborough—I must have been ten or eleven—lying on my back in the grass in a park and trying to penetrate a cloudless blue sky with my eyes and thinking something like this: 'If I went straight up into the sky, and kept on going in a straight line, why shouldn't I just be able to keep on going for ever and ever? But that's impossible. Why isn't it possible? Surely, eventually, I'd have to come to some sort of an end? But why? If I bumped up against something eventually, wouldn't that have to be a something in space? And if it was in space, wouldn't there have to be something on the other side of it, if only more space? On the other hand, if there was no limit, endless space couldn't just *be*, any more than endless time could be.'

After a lot of puzzling about this I began to think that perhaps my key mistake was to suppose that what I could not conceive of could not be.

Bryan Magee

Perhaps there was a difference between what I could think and what could be the case. For after all, there was a sense in which I could think about something going on and on for ever and ever because I could always keep on asking: *What next? What next? What next? What next?* But still it seemed to me self-evident that this was only something I could think and not anything that could actually be. I could think infinity, but infinity could not exist. For instance, there could not actually be an infinite number of stars . . . Or was I now falling back into the mistake I was trying to climb out of? In any case, whatever the truth about this—even if something I could think could not exist, and something I could not think could exist—it would not help me solve my real problem, because it did not tell me what the truth was about whether time did or did not have a beginning. Which of those two alternatives was the truth?

The more I thought about time and space, the more the problems proliferated. One thing that came to puzzle me very much indeed was that the future was specific yet unknown. The thought first came to me in connection with a football match. It was a Friday evening, and the following day my two favourite teams were going to play against each other. My over-excited impatience to know the result bordered on the uncontainable. At first it was merely to calm myself that I said to myself: 'This time tomorrow I'll know the result. Only three things can have happened: either Arsenal will have won, or Spurs will have won, or it'll be a draw. And whatever it is I'll know it for the rest of my life.' But then I found myself thinking: 'Whatever the truth is, it's true *now*. If Spurs win, then it's true *now* that Spurs are going to win. And if the score is 3-2, then it's true now that the score is going to be 3-2. These things'll have been true since that beginning of time that I was unable to imagine. If an ancient Roman or an Old Testament prophet had said them thousands of years ago they would have been just as true even then. So why can't I know them the day before? They'll have been true from the beginning of time, and they'll be true till the end of time, and yet I shall only be able to know what they are at some particular moment tomorrow afternoon.'

And then, inevitably, the fact struck me that the same applied to every event throughout the whole of time: whatever was true of it was true now, and always had been true, and always would be true. Some of these truths we knew and some we did not, but all of them were equally true. The fact that we knew some and not others seemed to be, so to speak, a fact about us and not a fact about the truths, which were all equally eternal. Those we knew we called the past, those we did not know we called the future; but that seemed scarcely anything more than *our* way of dividing them up. In fact the dividing point actually *was* us: *we* were the shifting division between past and future. For anyone who had lived in the past, the period between his time and mine was future for him, past for me—unknowable by him, knowable by me. But my own future, unknowable by me, would be in the knowable past for people in the future. Yet the truths themselves were all in the same boat. How come we were in this strange position of knowing some and not others—and of different people knowing, and not knowing, different ones? It seemed essentially a matter of *our* situation as individuals.

The more I thought about this the more frustrated I became. It was during these reflections that the terrifying thought occurred to me that if everything was true now, nothing we did could ever change it. It was true *now* that everything that was going to happen to me during the course of my life was going to happen to me. It was also true *now* that nothing else apart from those things was ever going to happen to me. It was true *now* that I was going to do everything I would ever do. And it was true *now* that I would never, ever, do anything else, apart from those things. It seemed, then, that everything was fixed and unalterable *now*. But if that was the case there was no such thing as free will. I was a helpless object at the mercy of fate. I found this thought so frightening that it had a seriously disturbing effect on my equilibrium. I felt real terror every time it entered my mind, and I started trying to prevent myself from thinking about it.

That was the first problem of this kind ever to crop up in my reflections that upset me emotionally. Most such problems I found frustratingly absorbing, infuriating yet fascinating; and therefore, in spite of their unsettling nature, pleasurable to think about in some inexplicable but deep-lying way.

One day when I was throwing a ball around, it occurred to me that at any given moment the ball must be some actual where. At every single instant it must, whole and entire, be in some actual position. At no instant could it be in two places, nor could its position in even one place be ambiguous or blurred. But in that case I did not see how it could move. Obviously, though, it did move. Again, something that, it seemed to me, must happen was not happening; and whatever it was that was happening was something I could not find a way of getting my mind round.

It was during these same years, about the ages 9–12, that what had long been the pleasure of listening to music on the gramophone became an addiction. Once, when I was playing records, I found myself imagining a rod sticking out from the turntable with a sideways-on cup at the end. And I imagined a ball perched on a golf tee at the right distance from the edge of the turntable for the cup to catch it as it spun round. And I imagined ball, cup and rod as being made of an absolutely hard

169

material—or, as I might put it now, I imagined them as being perfectly inelastic. What happened when the turntable was spinning at top speed and the cup scooped the ball up? Did the ball change instantaneously from being at rest to moving at the same speed as the cup, without passing through any of the speeds in between? That seemed impossible, and impossible in the same way as those earlier things: impossible to imagine, *unthinkable*. On the other hand, if the cup and the ball and the rod were all 100 per cent hard there was no alternative: it *had* to happen, it was the only thing that could possibly happen. So here yet again, there was something I found it impossible to conceive of as happening, and yet impossible to conceive of as not happening.

And so it went on as the years went by. The more things I thought about, the more problems I acquired. But I never seemed to acquire solutions. And yet, it seemed to me, solutions there had to be. Something or other must be the case with regard to each one of these questions, if only I could find out what it was. Furthermore, if something just self-evidently did happen, like a ball moving, then there had to be something wrong with any way of looking at it that said it could not. And there had to be a flaw in any argument that said it did not. This being so, it seemed highly peculiar to me that I could never discover what any of these mistakes were, no matter how hard I thought. I came to see the ordinary world I was living in as a place crammed with self-contradiction and mystery. Whatever you thought about you were almost immediately led into paradox and inconceivabilities. And this gave me a thirst to understand. This drive became almost as strong as my strongest other instincts, like physical thirst or hunger, and as compelling. An ever-present curiosity became for most of the time my strongest felt emotion, sometimes the mode I lived in.

Perhaps I should make it explicit, in case there are people here whose own beliefs or whose own experience of childhood cause them to assume otherwise, that none of this had anything in my mind to do with religion. No such connection entered my head. All the problems that plagued me were questions about the situation in which I immediately found myself. Some of them were questions about me, some were questions about the world around me, but all of them were practical questions, that is to say questions about how things are, to which something had to constitute a true answer, or so it seemed to me. To none of these questions would the existence of a God have constituted an answer, and I never felt any inclination, no matter as how young a child, to believe in one. There is a story that G. E. Moore, when asked why he had never addressed himself to questions about God, replied that he had never seen any reason for taking such questions seriously, and the same applied in those days to me. The postulation of a God seemed to me a cop-out, a refusal to take serious problems seriously; a facile, groundless and above all evasive response to deeply disturbing difficulties: it welcomed the self-comforting delusion that we know what we do not know, and have answers that we do not have, thereby denying the true mysteriousness, indeed miraculousness, of what is. By sheer chance I had the good fortune to grow up in a family in which religion was never mentioned. I have just said that there was never an age at which I believed in God: still less have I ever been a Christian. But perhaps even more important than either of those things, I have never felt any need to react against such beliefs. That is something for which I am deeply grateful. There was a good deal of carry-on about them at school, but my attitude to anything to do with school—or rather to anything organized by the authorities, such as classes and religious services—was one of boredom and indifference. None of it seemed to me to have anything to do with real life and I never thought any of it mattered, and so never gave any of it a moment's consideration outside the classroom. And it was outside the classroom that everything real and exciting was waiting with open arms to sweep me up into itself as soon as the bell rang. Nor did it ever occur to me to think of any of the problems I have been discussing as abstract or theoretical, still less as other-worldly. They were real, gripping problems, and they were problems *about* reality, about the actual world I was living in, and the life I was living, and me. And I *had* them, whether I liked it or not; there was no choice about it. I had got these problems.

Although none of these problems had anything in my mind to do with religion or religious thoughts, it just so happened that it was in the school chapel, in the middle of a hymn, that the realization came to me that if I closed my eyes then the visual scene of hundreds of boys facing me in that huge, high-ceilinged building, with all those vast paintings and windows, simply disappeared. *They* did not disappear, of course, but the visual image of them did, the scene. And when I opened my eyes, the scene came back again. *They* had been there all the time, and would have been there just the same if I had not been in the chapel at all, but the only apprehension I had of them consisted in the seeing of them plus the hearing of them, and those were in my head. If I stopped my ears and eyes they ceased to have any existence for me. Up to that moment I had always taken it for granted that I was in immediate contact with the people and things outside me, and that their presence was something I experienced in an unmediated way; but now, suddenly, I realized that their existence was one thing and my awareness of it something radically other. Their existence was out there, independent of me: but all the awareness and experience and knowledge I could ever have of it was inside my head, and that could pop into or out of existence irrespective of them, provided of course that they were there.

I could make it come and make it go whenever I liked, simply by opening and closing my eyes. With a horrible turning over of my stomach I realized that the natural way of putting this into words was to say: 'When I close my eyes they disappear.'

Even now, after all these years, what I cannot put into words is how indescribably appalling I found that moment of insight, how nightmarish. I was inundated by crashing great tidal waves of nausea, claustrophobia and isolation, as if I were for ever cut off from everything that existed—apart from myself—and as if I were trapped for life inside my own head. I thought I was going to throw up or faint. I was overwhelmed by panic and a need to escape from the situation—just get out. Groping and blundering, I lurched along the row of boys in my pew, and under the eyes of the whole school that rose up above my head in serried ranks on both sides—they faced each other four hundred to four hundred across a centre aisle—I veered distraught down the channel between them and out of the building. What everyone commented on afterwards was the colour of my face, which was apparently green—so no one doubted that I had felt ill, and therefore no one questioned me about why I had walked out.

From that day on I wrestled with demons for at least a part of every day of my life, especially when I was alone and otherwise unoccupied, which meant most of all in bed at night in the dark. The prospect of going to chapel induced panic, and often I used to hide in the lavatories when the bell for it rang. When I did go to the services I was twanging with tension, sometimes literally shaking. Often the prospect of going was so dreadful that I willingly accepted punishment instead. And there was no way I could explain any of this to anyone. I considered trying to explain it to the school doctor, and asking him to get permission for me to be excused chapel; but he was a hearty extrovert of the old-fashioned public-school type, and I knew he would never understand. In fact I was afraid he would think I was mad. So I kept my terrors to myself.

There was one occasion when I myself thought I was going mad because of this. I was coming out of a cinema one afternoon during the school holidays and suddenly, in the foyer, I was engulfed by the realization that, for me and for the whole of my life, absolutely everything in so far as I could ever possibly be aware of it—not only my own life and thoughts and memories but other people too, and the whole of the present-day world, whatever I read about in the newspapers, all history, all art, the cosmos itself, *everything*—existed only in my head; that this always had been so, and always must be so; and that I should never, ever be able to have any consciousness of anything at all other than of what was in my own mind. The thought was not solipsism—not that everything existed only in my mind—but the opposite: that everything (except, of course, for my experience) existed *outside* my mind, and I was cut off from it for ever and always, unrescuably alone, trapped for life inside the tiny box of my skull, never, never, *never* able to get out and be part of the rest of everything there was. The feeling, again, was one of total, permanent and unsalvageable isolation from everything and everybody, combined with intolerable claustrophobia, a waking nightmare of being locked up inside myself. I tried to flee these terrors by forcibly distracting my thoughts, but then the second barrel of the shotgun went off: *nothing you can ever do can make you experience anything other than the deliverances of your own consciousness*. The only alternative to them is oblivion. I felt about to explode as the only way of breaking out of myself and escaping my own confines, in the way a hand grenade shatters its own casing when it goes off. In that moment I really did believe I was going out of my mind.

And all this was the result of seeing reality in a certain way. Everything, I thought, exists independently of me in a framework of space and time, which exist also independently. The only way I, as one of the objects in that space and time, can get to know about any of the other objects in it is if it impinges on one of my senses, and that conveys a stimulus to my brain which is translated into a sensory image. So the only conscious awareness I can ever have of any part of reality other than myself is of images—which are always, and can only ever be, in my head—and I have to infer back from these images to the existence of the objects of which they are representations. And the representation is the only conception I can form of the *nature* of the object. With objects themselves I had no means of direct, unmediated contact. They existed permanently on the other side of an uncrossable frontier constituted by the limits of the possibility of awareness.

The next insight I had following on from this way of seeing things was that there was no way in which objects could be 'like' my perceptions of them. This came to me for the first time in the living room of my parents' flat, when I was about thirteen. In this room there were two armchairs facing each other with a sofa between them on one side and a fireplace on the other, and beside one of the armchairs stood a tall standard lamp. I was sitting in the armchair opposite the lamp, looking at it. There it was, with a dark brown, square wooden base out of which grew a stem of the same colour and material, culminating in a conical lampshade made of a soft textile of lighter brown. That was it, the standard lamp: and I could not conceptualize it in any other terms. And that is how it would be for an observer anywhere else in the room, except—it suddenly struck me—in one unique position, namely the position occupied by the standard lamp itself. In that room it was only if you *were* the standard lamp that you would not be able to *see* the standard lamp. And in the absence of mirrors, you would have no conception of what you looked like. In other words, whatever your conception of yourself was it could not possibly take the form that for me and anyone else was the only form it could take. I sat there trying to imagine what it was to *be* the standard lamp—putting myself in its place, so to speak. And the same thoughts re-asserted themselves. It could see everything in the room except itself. And no matter where it was it would never be able to see itself. This made me realize that I knew what my own face looked like only because I had seen its reflection in mirrors and windows, and photographs of it—in other words, because I had seen images that were other than myself and extraneous to myself. From inside my face I had no way of knowing how my face was. So if you *were* something you were not it in the terms in which everyone else perceived it and, as a result of that, conceived it. And what is more you could not be. Looking at the same situation from the other end, everyone perceiving or conceiving anything *had no alternative* but to do so in terms in which it was not possible for that thing to *be*. So things as they were in themselves must be unimaginably different from any idea we could form of them.

For a couple of years I was constantly trying to imagine what it was to be an inanimate object, and always with this contradictory thought that it must be unconceptualizably different from anything I could imagine . . . What was it to *be* that building, what was it to *be* that rugger boot? There they were, they existed, they had being. What was that being? Not what was it *like* but what *was* it—for the one thing I was certain of was that it could not be like any image or conception I was able to form of it. Although I knew that my attempt to put myself in the place of that book, that tree, that piece of furniture, was in this very way self-contradictory, I could not stop myself from doing it. *Being*, it seemed to me, was the ultimate mystery, *the ultimately unconceptualizable*. And yet there was not anything that was not. Everything was. So how could it be a mystery? Here, it seemed to me, was the last word in paradoxes: everything that actually exists is unknowable, and the whole of whatever it is we experience is image only, with no existence independent of our experience.

In my middle teens I came across a book in the school library called *The Bible of the World* containing the main writings of the world's great religions. Out of curiosity I read it all. The only part of the book that stirred my imagination really deeply was the Upanishads. Here, to my astonishment, I found it said that the entire world of human knowledge and experience consisted of images only, which were fleeting and had no abiding reality, whereas *real* reality, that which existed permanently, was something we could have no direct knowledge of, and therefore could form no clear and determinate conception of. I was astounded to see my own thought there before me on the page, and in writings thousands of years old. The Upanishads then went on to offer an explanation that had not occurred to me. They said that what presented this indefinite number of variegated images to our minds was not an equal number of ungetatable somethings corresponding to the separate images but just one big something. We became differentiated from it when we came into existence as individuals, and we dissolved back into it when we died; and that, actually, was ultimately all there was. It was only images that were disparate, individual, separate. And because images *were* images, and were subjective and ephemeral, and above all because we had a natural tendency to mistake them for independently existing things, they could not unreasonably be classed as illusions. Separate things, then—separate *any* things, including people—were illusions. In reality everything was one.

This intrigued me as an idea without involving my emotions. It neither commended itself nor failed to commend itself to my intuitions, and I felt agnostic about it. I did not see how we could know it to be true even if it were. But it did drive home to me one essential fact, namely that without realizing that I was doing so I had continued to assume that reality was 'like' our conception of it in one fundamental respect, namely that it was variegated—and that I had no grounds for this assumption. In fact, on consideration, it seemed to me that I had no basis whatsoever for any beliefs about what ultimate reality might be.

However, no matter what it was that existed, it seemed to me extraordinary beyond all wonderment that it should. It was astounding that anything existed at all. Why was not there nothing? By all the normal rules of expectation—the least unlikely state of affairs, the most economical solution to all possible problems, the simplest explanation—*Nothing* is what you would have expected there to be. But such was not the case, self-evidently. And yet although it was impossible to know what there was, and therefore impossible to *say* what it was, and perhaps therefore even impossible to assert that there *was* any *thing, something was unquestionably going on.* Yet how could anything be going on? In what medium? Nothingness? Impossible to conceive: and yet undeniably something was happening.

Although more and more given to talk and discussion and argument as I grew older, for several years I never encountered anyone who felt the same fascination as I did towards these questions. By the time I had grown into adulthood I had become familiar with a number of general attitudes to experience that seemed to embrace among themselves most people, at least most of those that I ever met, but none of them was at all like mine. There seemed to be three main groupings. First, there were people who took the world for granted as they found it: that is how things are, and it is obvious that that is how they are, and talking about it is not going to change it, so there is no purpose that perpetually questioning it is going to serve; discussing it is really a waste of time, even *thinking* about it much is a waste of time; what we have to do is get on with the practical business of living, not indulge in a lot of useless speculation and ineffectual talk. That seemed to be roughly the outlook of most people. Then there were others who regarded that attitude as superficial, on religious grounds. According to them, this life was no more than an overture, a prelude to the real thing. There was a god who had made this world, including us, and had given us immortal souls, so that when our bodies died after a brief sojourn on earth the souls in them would go on for ever in some 'higher' realm. Such people tended to think that in the eye of eternity this present world of ours was not all that important, and whenever one raised questions about the self-contradictory nature of our experience they would shrug their shoulders and attribute this to the inscrutable workings of a god. It was not that they used this as the answer to all questions, because what such people said seldom answered any actual questions: they felt under no pressure to do so. God knew all the answers to all the questions, and his nature was inscrutable to us, therefore the only thing for us to do was to put our trust in him and stop bothering ourselves with questions to which we could not possibly know the answers until after we died. It seemed to me that this attitude was at bottom as incurious as the first; it just offered a different reason for not asking questions; and equally obviously it did not really *feel* the problems. There was no awareness in it of the real extraordinariness of the world: on the contrary, people who subscribed to it were often marked by a certain complacency, not to say smugness. They seemed to be happily lulling themselves to sleep with a story which might or might not be true but which they had no serious grounds for believing.

Finally, there were people who condemned both of these other sets of attitudes as uncomprehending and mistaken, on what one might call rationalistic grounds. They critically questioned both the way things are and traditional religious beliefs, and challenged the adherents of either for proof or at least good evidence, some justification or at least good argument. These tended in spirit to be either children of the enlightenment or children of the age of science, and in either case to have a kind of outlook that did not begin to exist until the seventeenth century. They seemed to believe that everything was explicable in the light of reason, that rational enquiry would eventually make all desirable discoveries, and that in principle if not altogether in practice all problems could be solved by the application of rationality. Most of my friends and fellow spirits seemed to fall into this third category, and indeed I tended to agree with their criticisms of the other two. My problem was that their own positive beliefs seemed to me manifestly untenable, and their attitudes—well, perhaps not quite as comfortable and complacent as those they criticized, but comfortable and complacent none the less. They seemed to think that the world was an intelligible place, and I did not see how in the light of a moment's thought this belief could be entertained. Their faith in the power of reason seemed to me almost unbelievably unreflecting and misplaced in view of the fact that it was the application of reason that perpetually gave rise to insoluble problems, problems that were brought into existence by thinking but could not be removed by it. With many such people, belief in the power of reason tended itself to be a sort of religion or ideology. They never reflected at all seriously on the narrowness of the range within which reason is applicable, or its propensity for self-contradiction, or its manifest inability to solve most of the fundamental questions about experience. Any attempt on my part (or anyone else's for that matter) to draw their attention to these things smacked to them of religion, which they equated with superstition, and of which they tended to be contemptuous. It was self-evident to them that this world of our experience is all there is, and anything we do not as yet understand about it we can reasonably hope to discover in the course of time. All meaning and all purpose inhabit this world: value and morality are created by human beings, which in practice means that value and morality are created socially and historically. Any suggestion that reality is hidden was to them unintelligible, and therefore any suggestion that the significance of our experience might lie outside the range of our understanding a kind of gobbledygook—and again, crypto-religious. What cut me off most deeply of all from this attitude, and what I also found hardest to understand about it, was its lack of any sense of the amazingness of our existence, indeed of the existence of anything at all—the sheer miraculousness of everything. After all, you do not have to reflect deeply, you do not need even to go beyond what a child is capable of thinking, to realize that our experience is unintelligible to ourselves in its most general and basic features—and yet the sort of people I am talking about seemed not to have made that discovery. To them it seemed self-evident that some sort of commonsense view of things must be, by and large, right, whereas I saw it as self-evident that common sense could not possibly be right, since reasoning logically from it as a starting point led one almost immediately into a morass of incomprehensibility and self-contradiction. In fact, to put it baldly yet truthfully, they found the denial of the commonsense view of the world ridiculous whereas I found the acceptance of the commonsense view of the world ridiculous. Their whole outlook was one that could survive for only so long as they did not reflect on its foundations. Not only was it superficial in the extreme, it was also detached, floating in mid-air, unsupported and unsustainable. Any fundamental questioning of it by anyone else was dismissed as uninteresting and pointless. If one drew their attention to the fact that there seemed to be no way in which our reasoning powers could make sense of this or that basic feature of the world or of our experience this was seen by them as a reason for not raising the question. What they wanted to do was confine their lives to the domain within which they *could* make sense of things. So at an only slightly deeper and more critical level they really turned out to share most of the attitudes of the first of the three groups.

Growing to adulthood as I did, absorbed by a sense of wonder about the world, and engrossed in some of the seemingly insoluble problems it presented—especially problems connected with time, space, our perception of physical objects and their intrinsic nature—this to a small extent had the effect of cutting me off from other people. Not only did I never find anyone I could discuss these questions with, I learnt that I was likely to be looked on as peculiar if I raised them. I was not a solitary, for there were other aspects of life in which I was a highly social creature—I always had friends, and after the age of seventeen love affairs; I hugely enjoyed partying, besides being a voracious music-lover and theatre-goer—but my baffled absorption in the whole meta-physical dimension of experience was something I learnt to keep to myself, even though I lived with it daily. What more than anything else made it a source of isolation was its overwhelming importance. These questions were fundamental to our nature, and the nature of the world we lived in, and I could never understand why not everybody was fascinated by them. It seemed to me bizarre that I should be associating all the time with intelligent people yet as if under some sort of informal ban on discussing the most crucial and interesting questions of all.

Until I went to university it never entered my head to associate any of these questions with the word 'philosophy'. I shall never forget the sheer incredulity with which I discovered that this is what they were, and that they had been addressed by some of the greatest geniuses of mankind over a period of 3,000 years. Every one of the problems I have mentioned turned out to be familiar in the history of philosophy. Some of them even had names: my bafflement that a ball could move was known as 'Zeno's arrow' Wittgenstein, it turned out, had dealt with the same point regarding death as had puzzled me so much about falling asleep when I was five: we expect it to be an experience but it cannot be, he said, because, by definition, we are not conscious through it, and therefore not conscious of it. Above all, though it was some time before this happened, I made the discovery that I had grown up a natural Kantian, beginning with the antinomies of time and space and going on to the unconceptualizability of things as they are in themselves inde-pendently of our modes of experience. My undying sense of astonish-ment that anything exists at all was first put into words by, so far as I know, Leibniz, and given its most dramatic and compelling expression by one of Kant's most immediate followers, Schelling. It pervades the work of Kant's most illuminating successor, Schopenhauer, in which I also discovered what in most essentials are the same doctrines as I had stumbled across in the Upanishads—though arrived at in Schopenhauer's case, as for that matter in mine, by considerations not of a religious but of an essentially Kantian nature, and therefore (in his case) by a mode of thinking in the very centre of the mainstream of Western philosophy.

Before and apart from all that, there was the problem of free will, and the question whether an act of will was the cause of a willed action or the same event apprehended in a different way. And from what Hume had to say about the nervous breakdown he experienced when he was young, and its connection with his philosophical reflections, I suspected that his terrifying psychological experiences had had some similarity with my own. Especially given the nature of his philosophy, that seems to me likely. (It is striking, incidentally, how many famous philosophers had breakdowns in youth.) Like the character in Molière who discovered to his astonishment that he had been speaking prose all his life without realizing it, I discovered to my astonishment that I had been immersed in philosophical problems all my life without realizing it. And I had been drawn into the same problems as great philosophers by the same desire to understand the world and my experience of it, followed hard-on-heel by the same realization that these were inexplicable in terms of common sense—which, on the contrary, spawned self-contradictions where it did not remain unhelpfully silent. The chief difference between me and them, of course, was that whereas they had something to offer by way of properly worked out solutions to the problems, I had been unable to find my way through to anything more than a few tentative and incomplete conclusions. In consequence I fell on their work like a starving man on food, and it has helped to nourish and sustain me ever since.

Professional philosophy as I discovered it for the first time in the Oxford of the early 1950s was not greatly concerned with any of this, at least not with much of it, except perhaps for our perception of material objects, having pretty well abandoned philosophy's traditional task of trying to understand the world, and therefore having very largely turned its back on the subject's past. But that failed to deter me from anything, except becoming a professional philosopher in the contemporary mode. Unlike such people at that time, I actually had philosophical problems, real ones, which were about the nature of reality and of my relationship to the rest of it, and indeed about the nature of my self;

and these were not just confusions into which I had fallen as a result of misuse of language. All my life since, I have been wrestling with them, and late in the day I have begun to hope diffidently that before I die I may be able to contribute something either to the solution of one or two of them or to a deeper understanding of why it is that they remain so obstinately unsolved.

Metaphysics and Music

MICHAEL TANNER

In a once-famous article, 'The Elimination of Metaphysics through the Logical Analysis of Language', first published in 1932, Rudolf Carnap (1959) wrote:

> The harmonious feeling or attitude, which the metaphysician tries to express in a monistic system, is more clearly expressed in the music of Mozart. And when a metaphysician gives verbal expression to his dualistic-heroic attitude towards life in a dualistic system, is it not perhaps because he lacks the ability of a Beethoven to express this attitude in an adequate medium? Metaphysicians are musicians without musical ability.

So presumably Mozart expressed what Spinoza attempted to put into words in the *Ethics*, and Beethoven conveyed, in his characteristic middle-period works (one takes it) the 'heroic dualism' which Descartes senselessly propounded in the *Meditations*. And Nietzsche is given credit by Carnap for abandoning metaphysics and expounding his world-attitude in poetry in *Thus Spoke Zarathustra*.

It is a strange, if in some respects gratifying conclusion to Carnap's alleged demonstration of the senselessness of metaphysics. What cannot be said, because it has no 'cognitive significance,' can be, *pace* Ramsey, composed, either as music or poetry. But one's pleasure at the recognition by a hard-nosed logical positivist that music (and I'd rather leave *Zarathustra* out of it) can express attitudes to life is modified by unease about how Carnap or anyone else can know what Spinoza or Descartes were trying to say in their metaphysical works if they were devoid of meaning. And that quite apart from the fact that Descartes's dualism, a view of the ontological separateness of minds and matter, seems to have little relationship to the heroic variety espoused by Beethoven, which is much more of an ethical or religious affair, a striving on the part of the indomitable individual will against Fate or some other, more obviously grapplable-with phenomenon, political tyranny, for instance, or fast-encroaching deafness. Even so, Carnap's is an attempt to explain the appeal for both the authors and the enthusiastic readers of metaphysical works; if metaphysicians are ungifted composers, their admirers are presumably ungifted listeners. Both want something that no set of assertions can yield: a validation, in terms of the nature of the world, of attitudes towards the whole of existence—attitudes which some composers, such as, I suspect, Mozart, would have been surprised to have attributed to them, while others, such as Beethoven of Mahler, would not.

It would be much more surprising now to find a philosopher, at least one who could plausibly trace his lineage back to Carnap, making a comparison or contrast between metaphysics and music. Metaphysics, if not of Spinozistic pretensions, has made a come-back, but one would be hard put to it to make even the most superficial analogies between what is being produced in books and the journals, and any kind of music. For current metaphysics is only respectable because of its putative cognitive content, concerning such matters as the relation between meaning and truth-conditions, the ontological status of events, the nature of the mental, and various controversies between 'realists' and 'anti-realists', which are not of a kind to lead its practitioners to make suggestions as to the kinds of attitude—stoic, aggressive, celebratory, or whatever—that we should take to the world. It is almost universally agreed that music, however significant it may be in some sense—and this is not a subject on many philosophers' agenda—is not cognitively significant; or if it is, only in ways that are far too modest for it to be regarded as comparable in scope and depth to metaphysical truths.

Even so, there are very many lovers of great music of the Western tradition who feel, from time to time consciously, and perhaps most of the time implicitly, that there must be some connection between its greatness and the way the world is, in its most general aspects. Such people are likely, if they have any philosophical sophistication, to dismiss the feeling, because any attempt to establish a genuine link seems so obviously doomed to failure. So they are driven back to something very like Carnap's account of music (at least some music): it may express—though this too will be the work of many laborious pages to clarify and make precise—a general attitude towards life, but that is something to be kept private, because such attitudes—optimism or pessimism, a sense of cosmic harmony or of the world as an inveterate battleground—belong at best to that area which Strawson has said contains 'truths, but no truth.' That goes with a general view of works of art as not being in conflict with one another, or if they are, only in a rewardingly irresoluble way. If one finds Brahms wonderful and Mahler disgusting, that is not because one of them has a closer relationship to the truth than the other, but because of one's temperament. And temperaments are not right or wrong (those terms do not apply) but at most fortunate or unfortunate. They may lead one to make some specific true or false judgments, but very general judgments will be true only if they are generously pluralistic or inclusive, for instance 'There's a lot of good and bad in the world,' in which case the temperament that prompts them will be, as it were, notably untemperamental. As soon as one encounters a temperament which leads its possessor to produce considerable amounts of re-interpretation of the phenomena he encounters, in order to bring them into line with his general view of things, then one has come across something which is interesting in part because it leads to false views. The only philosophical statement which is certainly true is 'Everything is what it is and not another thing', and a person whose temperament was in accord with that remark (there are, of course, such people) would be a cosmic bore. And if he were a composer, his music would be so intolerably bland that it would instantly be hi-jacked by airlines for playing during take-off. Actually there is such a composer, and his name is Vivaldi; but I shall leave that judgment undefended, since I am concerned to advance on a more abstract front.

As I've suggested, when one hears certain pieces of music the temptation to make a validity-claim for the attitude that they express towards life may be, in spite of one's philosophical inhibitions, irresistible; or rather what is irresistible is the claim that to be able to have such an attitude towards life as the music expresses, it is required that the composer should have had certain experiences which receive some justification from the way things are. A paradigm instance of this is the last movement of Mozart's *Jupiter Symphony*. As is well-known, this movement is often, and mistakenly, described as being fugal; the fugal elements in it are a significant but comparatively small part of the whole movement. But it is supremely contrapuntal, its material consisting of five brief themes, or mere motifs, which during in its course undergo combinations and expansions of exhilarating complexity and seeming inevitability, and reach three climaxes (if the movement is played with no repeats) which achieve such heights of exaltation that the process of backward inference—to write such music Mozart must have had certain experiences, to have had such experiences he must have encountered deep features of the world—is one which, I'm inclined to say, one must feel impelled to make if one is to appreciate the music properly. And yet the inferences are not valid.

In the first, psychological place, the processes of musical composition, as of artistic creation in general—but I suspect that this is especially true of music—are sufficiently obscure and mysterious for our never to be in a safe position to posit *a priori* the having of specific experiences on the part of the artist. Nietzsche's claim, made repeatedly in his later works, that one can tell from a work of art whether it was created from superabundance or out of need, is alluring but finally unacceptable. It may be at least as important a part of the artistic temperament that it creates for itself imaginations of the experiences that it expresses in artistic form as that it creates art out of experiences it

Michael Tanner

has actually had. Wagner's celebrated letter to Liszt, in which he writes 'Since I have never in my life enjoyed the true happiness of love, I intend to erect a further monument to this most beautiful of dreams, a monument in which this love will be properly sated from beginning to end: I have planned in my head a *Tristan* and *Isolde*, the simplest and most full-blooded musical conception', is as candid an admission as one could want of the wish-fulfilling nature of some of the greatest art.

But there are other, in some respects more penetrating, objections to the process of backward inference that I said we are, and even should be, tempted to make. One of the chief sources of the power that some art has over us is that it presents us with a comprehensive sense of existence—gives a particular colour to the whole of life—that, while we are under its spell, brooks no contradiction. Music, I think, does this with the especial force because of its very freedom from concepts, its absence of reference to particulars. Listening to the last movement of the *Jupiter Symphony*, one is not likely to have any specific events or objects in mind, but rather to feel the irrelevance of individual events and objects. The astonishing feats of combination that Mozart achieves in that movement, the sense he gives that anything can be made to fit with anything else, and the whole lot raised to a peak of irrefutable affirmation, seems to make absorption in particulars petty and irrelevant. And yet we only get this sense from the movement (if we do) because we are so familiar with conceptual activities which we require to characterize it by analogy. As Wittgenstein puts it in *Zettel* (1967, 31):

> Does not the theme point to anything outside itself? Yes, it does! but that means:—it makes an impression on me which is connected with things in their surroundings—e.g. with our language and its intonations; and hence with the whole field of our language-games.
>
> If I say for example: Here it is as if a conclusion were being drawn, here as if something were being confirmed, *this* is like an answer to what was said before,—then my understanding presupposes a familiarity with inferences, with confirmation, with answers.

So with a great deal of music, certainly in fugues, contrapuntal music and that in sonata form, we understand it by thinking in terms of the processes of argument, but the content of the argument is the mood, or the variety of emotions, that the elements of the piece express, so that it seems as if argumentative processes were being undergone by kinds of item that we do not normally think of as being susceptible to them. Every proof registers a triumph, as Nietzsche remarked, rebuking Socrates for use of the dialectical method and the optimism to which it gives rise—though not, in fact, when Socrates himself is practising it. But what might be called the 'Q.E.D. feeling'—something which Russell tells us he found so overpowering that he sometimes had to abandon work on *Principia Mathematica* from sheer emotional exhaustion—is undoubtedly something which can be conveyed by music, more clinchingly than by any other art-form. The music critic Cecil Gray described that last two bars of Sibelius's *Seventh Symphony*, in which the strings rise in unison from B to C, as 'a gigantic Q.E.D.'. But what does it sound as if it is the assertion of the proof of? A heterogeneous sequence of feelings—in the particular case of this symphony a remarkably wide range, constantly verging on disintegration—out of which Sibelius welds a climax of extraordinarily intense affirmation, and then clinches.

What it comes to is that music, at least during the high period of development between the late sixteenth and the early twentieth centuries, when tonality reigned supreme, achieved on the one hand enormous expressive powers. How music expresses feelings is happily something that I need not go into here, but I take it that it unquestionably does, and not only feelings, but moods and attitudes. On the other hand the purely musical modes of development, whether fugal or more generally contrapuntal, and then the Classical Style, as exemplified in sonata form, above all, do have, as the passage from Wittgenstein affirms, an analogous effect to that of an argument. The joint result of these developments, which were by no means independent of one another, meant that music, especially instrumental music, could be said to present a logic of the emotions, so that one could feel that by the end of an integrated musical work of considerable complexity a goal had been reached, and the steps that led to it had a kind of validating rigour, *sui generis* but strongly reminiscent of more familiar procedures. But it remains profoundly dubious whether that feeling can be substantiated, whether, that is, the analogy with argument is any more than something that it gives us a great deal of satisfaction to experience.

Until the beginning of the nineteenth century, it would not have occurred to composers to claim that they were, in a loose sense, 'making statements' in their instrumental, or even their vocal works, with the odd exception, such as Haydn's *Farewell Symphony*, where a highly specific context is fed to us before we listen to the piece. They employed music to celebrate the greatness of God when they wrote passions, masses, motets; or to celebrate the greatness of monarchs when they wrote coronation music or operas called 'La Clemenza di X'; or to celebrate or denigrate their beloved, depending on how she was behaving, in songs; or to give entertaining or instructive pictures of life among the gods or human beings in (mainly) mythological operas. The statements—what possessed truth-values—were pre-existent, and the vocal music these composers wrote expressed their attitudes towards a truth non-musically expressed and established. But the sheer security of their faith coloured the music in which they bodied it forth. Thus in the 'Dona nobis pacem' of the *B minor Mass*, one of Bach's most glorious fugues, the sheer weight and momentum of its musical process makes it an overwhelming consummation of the work (even though he had already used it for the 'Gratias agimus' of the 'Gloria'). The only insecurities in Bach's music are those of the sinner whose place in Heaven is not assured. His instrumental music, which either derives from dance-forms or manifests his craftsmanship in contrapuntal writing, inhabits the same world as the vocal music. As has often been remarked, the divide between the religious and the secular gains no purchase here. Hence the non-Christian is in the satisfying position of being able to gain spiritual nourishment from the Well-Tempered Clavier or the 'Cello Suites without being required to make any commitment to transcendental beliefs. The carry-over from the religious vocal works, the heart of Bach's achievement, provides the credit, as it were, on which to draw.

In the period immediately following Bach, even to some extent during his later years, when he was considered old-fashioned, instrumental music began to assert its autonomy. Its forms ceased to be derived from the dance or religious music, and independent forms evolved, above all the symphony, the concerto, the string quartet and the piano sonata. Thanks to the genius of Haydn and Mozart, these forms progressed at an almost alarming rate, though in the vast majority of their compositions in these forms there is nothing that one would be inclined to call *weltanschaulich*. The *Jupiter Symphony* is an exception, as are its predecessor, one of the tensest and most insecure works in the repertoire, and certain of Mozart's piano concertos, especially those in minor keys. But still, to adapt Carnap, one would hardly say these were by a musician with metaphysical abilities. The first composer who virtually demands categorization in those terms is of course Beethoven, and he has certainly received it. It was fashionable to make fun of those works, such as Paul Bekker's and J. W. N. Sullivan's books on him, which made explicit metaphysical claims for certain of Beethoven's profoundest compositions (it is striking how natural it is to lapse into calling them 'utterances', though most of them are purely instrumental), above all the last five Piano Sonatas and the last five String Quartets. If that mockery is no longer fashionable, it is because it does not seem a task worth bothering to perform.

Bekker's and Sullivan's strategy, though not explicitly announced as such, is essentially that I delineated briefly in talking of the last movement of the *Jupiter Symphony*. They take these works to communicate states of mind, in some cases states that it is very difficult to see could be communicated by instrumental music; they then infer that such states are the result of experiences which vouchsafe truths about the nature of the world. Though the fallacies involved in such claims are obvious, one might try to defend a weaker but related position. Using R. K. Elliott's well-known terminology, one might say that if one experiences these works 'primordially', that is, takes the states expressed in them to be one's own, then one is driven to say that one could not be in such a state unless one felt in a certain way about existence. To adapt one of Bekker's claims, though it is hard to do so without introducing a mild note of parody, one might say that experiencing the *Grosse Fuge*, opus 133, primordially, one's state is such that one can only say one has apprehended the reconciliation of Freedom and Necessity. But how does one know what that state feels like? Presumably it is one of advanced exaltation, but would it be a state of more advanced exaltation than if one had solved the Mind–Body problem? To be in an exalted state and know why, there must be, if it is a matter of having solved a problem, propositional content to the object of one's state. But one could only claim that that was the case if the *Grosse Fuge* itself somehow indicated to one that it was concerned with the reconciliation of Freedom and Necessity, and it seems clear that a piece of instrumental music could never do that. Stretching charity still further, one might alternatively suggest that the *Grosse Fuge*, experienced primordially, made one feel an exaltation that was only appropriate to having solved the most difficult problem that one can conceive, and that there is only one problem that answers to that description. But once more one has to point out that one can experience the exaltation appropriate to a given situation without actually being in that situation. So the most that could be claimed is that one knows what the state of exaltation is, thanks to the music, but there is no warrant for claiming that it is justified.

None of this is controversial—quite the reverse. But I have spelled out the familiar at some length because it does indicate that certain pieces of music which have achieved canonical status during the past two centuries, as those by which all else is judged, are liable to lead us to try to have our cake and eat it. On the one hand, we would deny that they have cognitive content; on the other, some of us allow ourselves to respond to them as if they did. Although music lovers indulge in a great deal of hand-wringing about the ineffability of music, tormenting themselves about their incapacity to say, in terms that do not seem absurd, why and how they can move them so deeply, they also often, I suspect (and here my first autobiographical confession emerges) allow themselves a lot of strictly private meditation on what the music means, and means to them. However firmly one insists, with all due solemnity and sincerity, that the glory of music is its self-sufficiency, its untranslatability into the verbal medium, its capacity to move us without our committing ourselves to anything beyond the autonomous experiences which it vouchsafes, one still finds oneself unable to accept that it is so moving, or could be, unless it were telling us something that goes beyond any pattern of sounds, however marvellous. That may be because we are unwilling to admit that our most valued experiences are unrelated to truth, our highest value. Certainly artists themselves, including composers, as they become ever more ambitious for their art, are liable to move towards making truth-claims for it. Not that that provides any evidence that they are justified in doing so. But the pretensions that their art itself assumes—including, as the nineteenth century progressed, ever greater length, and unremitting seriousness— entail that the criteria by which we judge it are correspondingly demanding. Nothing in the history of the arts is less coincidental than the fact that as composers felt less inclined and able to write explicitly religious works, their instrumental compositions took on an ever greater weight of spiritual concern. And the tone of these works is undeniably exploratory; the needs for which they can find no answers in pre-existing dogma or metaphysics had themselves to be expressed in their art, together with an adumbration of what might satisfy them. It seems to me pointless to admit that that was so for the artists them- selves, but for us to accept their art in a quite different spirit, as if they were absolute musicians in the most absolute sense.

Another non-coincidence, I believe, is the near-simultaneity of the enormous flowering of instrumental music from the middle of the eighteenth century to the early decades of the twentieth—that is, of the music that achieved and has retained the greatest popularity; and the rise and climax of the realistic novel. They fulfil complementary needs, and are unquestionably the supreme distinctive achievements of the period in which they flourished. The novel was unequalled in portray- ing the mundane, the prosaic, but also the most refined states of mind of characters whose convincingness is powerful enough to withstand with scornful ease all the attacks on the 'Classic Realist Text' made by the now fast-waning school of deconstructionists bent on telling us what we already knew, that they are verbal constructs of the high bourgeois age. Instrumental music covers a vast range, but is above all concerned with battles waged within the soul for which language is no longer deemed adequate, and furthermore achieves victories and states of serenity or ecstasy which novelists hardly dared to allot to their characters. Dostoevsky is the obvious counter-example, but his rela- tionship to realism is so complex and strained that I do not think his astonishing works undermine my generalization. Not surprisingly, novelists looked with envy at what musicians alone could do, above all by way of achieving a unity of form and content which makes those terms virtually meaningless in relation to pure music. And 'pure' musicians, especially those whose ambitions for their art were unbounded, felt impelled, at crucial moments, to employ words, in case the urgency and specificity of their message might be missed.

So we have on the one hand Flaubert, whose obsession with perfection of form was so overpowering that he wrote to a correspondent that he wanted to compose 'a book about nothing at all, a book without any external connection, and which would support itself entirely by the internal force of style.' What emerged from this endeavour was something very different, namely *Bouvard et Pecuchet*, which is not about nothing at all, but about two extremely trivial characters spending their time in occupations which earn their author's withering disdain. It is as if Flaubert had committed the mistake of thinking that if his subject-matter was small enough, that would be the next best thing to inexistence. On the other hand there is Beethoven, finding it imperative that he conveys in words a message which, if left purely as a melody, might be misinterpreted. So he rejects, in the last movement of the *Ninth Symphony*, the themes of the first three movements, and then welcomes the theme of the last not for its own sake but because if fits the words of Schiller's 'An die Freude'. And over the beginning of the last Quartet, slightly less famously, he writes 'Muss es sein?' and replies 'Es muss sein!' The dualistic–heroic attitude has finally to be expressed by a musician without metaphysical ability.

It is characteristic of the realist novel in its heyday that it investigates the condition of man in society, and tends to locate the greatest value in life in personal relationships, and the failures of those relationships as the greatest tragedy that can befall us. Yet the most ambitious and penetrating of these novelists have intimations, expressed through their characters, that even the most complete fulfilment in a relationship— and such fulfilment will only come about, it is axiomatic in this context, in a relationship of passion—is not enough. Thus Levin, completely happy in his marriage to Kitty in *Anna Karenina*, has to hide his gun from himself. For he, like several of George Eliot's characters, has the need to aspire to an impersonal good as well, which may include but must also transcend the level of 'relationships'. The century during which the constraints on fulfilment through passion were being removed also found that the ideal of Romantic Love was not enough. Its profoundest psychologists even came to an apprehension that the ideal was inherently contradictory. But in an age which increasingly rejected the transcendental, where could people look for something more satisfactory? The dominant morality of the period, utilitarianism, all too evidently encouraged the pursuit of states of mind that were evanescent, founded in shaky contingencies, and only sustainable, at best, if one turned a blind eye to the quantity of unrelievable misery in the world. But lacking, for the most part, the courage or conviction needed for the erection of metaphysical systems which would be satisfying precisely because, like all the most nourishing ones of the past, man's station was enhanced in relation to the total order of things of which he was a comparatively insignificant part—the central paradox of metaphysics—what sprung up instead were innumerable vulgar off-spring of a Christianity which could no longer be believed. Spiritual-ism, theosophy, Christian Science are only some of the most obvious debris of an age which could no longer subscribe to a view of things that sanctioned a full-bloodied commitment of profound minds operating at their furthest reach.

Throughout my argument to date, I have been drawing no distinc-tion between metaphysics and religion, and this procedure clearly stands in need of defence. In sketching one, I shall be finally homing in on the subject of this course of lectures, the impulse to philosophise. I know that I am not the first speaker to point out that there is no single impulse to philosophise, and it may well be that every speaker has—it is so obvious. But I take it that there is an implicit suggestion that one talk about the impulse that led *one* to philosophise, and for me, as for many others, that impulse grew out of an intellectual need to work out the basis of my religious beliefs. In my own case, they were short-lived, but intense. Like many people's, they coincided with the various tur-bulences of adolescence, and, especially, with strong feelings of guilt, which I found were most effectively assuaged by ritual and the possibil-ity of confession. I say possibility, because I was brought up as a milk-and-water Anglican, and felt drawn to the Roman Catholic Church, then still firmly in its pre-Vatican Two days. So there was plenty of ritual to attend and modestly participate in. Since my parents would not allow me to convert to Catholicism, it seemed to me inappropriate to go to confession. Anyway, magnificent as I found every aspect of the Catholic Church under Pius XII, when I discovered that there was an official Catholic philosophy I was still more captivated, though I found, when I embarked on reading Aquinas's *Summa Theologiae*, that it was the general project rather than the details which appealed. But I did study the traditional arguments for God's existence very closely, and subscribed to the Church's insistence that it was required for salvation that one believe that His existence could be rationally estab-lished. When at the age of seventeen I read Hume and Kant on the traditional arguments and was convinced by their criticisms of them, I abandoned my Christian beliefs, and was promptly told by several people that that only served to show that I had never genuinely held them. Whether or not they were right, it had certainly felt as if I did. But perhaps the most pressing motive for my Christianity had passed—I no longer felt guilt.

However, the satisfactions of subscribing to a view of the world which comprehensively explained it and my place in it had provided me with too strong a taste of what it was like to have the possibility of such order and significance in one's experience for me to be in the least inclined to abandon the quest. My first interest in philosophy, then, was as the handmaid of theology, but when the subservience of philosophy had to be given up, the obvious solution was to accept the autonomy of rational enquiry, and to attempt to work out *a priori* the nature of existence. Searching through the shelves of the local public library, I found to my delight that there were two volumes with that title, by McTaggart (1988), and set about reading them. Not surprisingly, I once more grew impatient with the detailed analyses and proofs, and jumped, temporarily, to the end of volume II to see what McTaggart's conclusions were. I was staggered to find that, having begun austerely with the two premises that something exists and that what exists is differentiated, he established by pure deductions that the true end of existence was a republic, not a monarchy, of immortal selves, and that the final stage of the C series is such that

> We know that it is a timeless and endless state of love—love so direct, so intimate and so powerful that even the deepest mystic rapture gives but the slightest foretaste of its perfection. We know that we shall know nothing but our beloved, and ourselves as loving them, and that only in this shall we seek and find satisfaction.

I was sufficiently energized by this concluding paragraph (McTaggart, 1988, 479) to begin volume I a second time, and to work through, a willing follower of the chain of argument, and a stunned and largely uncomprehending spectator of McTaggart's centrepiece, the establishing of the Principle of Determining Correspondence. I could not, and still cannot, imagine a much more exciting and rewarding enterprise than the rational rigour combined with the satisfaction of one's deepest cravings that it seemed that McTaggart offered.

Even so, and even with the glow of that sumptuous final paragraph, the whole enterprise struck too abstract a note for me. What I felt was needed was an artistic rendering of what McTaggart had provided in conceptual terms; and it so happened that my close study of him over the summer holidays coincided with a broadcast from the Bayreuth Festival of *Tristan und Isolde*. I studied the score and some commentaries in preparation and then listened—and, as Nietzsche puts it in *The Case of Wagner*, 'from that moment I was a Wagnerian'. I had read some of Wagner's prose works, and accepted one of his views of Beethoven's *Ninth Symphony*—roughly the one I sketched, that he was forced into words to make his message unambiguous. McTaggart was not musical, I believe; but to my eclectic mind it seemed as if he was supplying the rationale for Wagner's opus metaphysicum, Nietzsche's phrase for *Tristan*. For in that work, as in *The Nature of Existence*, there is no god—the only divinity invoked is the Goddess of Love, and I took that to be Wagner's way of referring poetically to the fundamental force of the universe. The oppositions in Wagner's work, between Day and Night, the code of honour and duty versus love, and the illusions of individuality as opposed to the reality of oneness, were not by any means precisely what McTaggart had in mind. Wagner himself derived them from Schopenhauer in a way that can most charitably be described as idiosyncratic. But the contrast of the world of appearances, devoid for me of mystery and passion, and the true world, which consisted of nothing else, was broadly similar enough for me to be satisfied that McTaggart and Wagner were purveying a single view of things which satisfied the imperatives of both my reason and my emotions.

I could see—I still can—no reason for refusing to call *Tristan* a religious work. It registers a conversion from a set of values which are serviceable only in this world to the embracing of a view that puts them at a discount, just as the traditional religion that I had previously accepted did. It demonstrates the arduousness of the path which seems inseparable from any genuine religious striving. And, most significantly, it portrays the nature of the ecstasy which is the whole point of the enterprise. The intensity of conviction which it establishes from the opening notes of the Prelude is something that is found elsewhere only in religious art celebrating more traditional values. Its demands are absolute. Once it has been experienced, nothing in life can be the same again, unless one undergoes a rigorous and heart-breaking course of de-toxification. The words which Bruno Walter used to Thomas Mann as they walked home after he had conducted a performance of the work seem exactly right, but also just wrong: 'That is not even music any more.' For what that remark betrays is a failure to see how much more music could be than anyone before Wagner had ever realized. Whether it is good or healthy to achieve in music what Wagner did is another, interminably debatable matter. But one of the things that his revolutionary mehods made possible was the setting of words, and the portrayal of an action, which in any previous or different idiom would have seemed simply absurd or merely pretentious and comic. His extraordinary resources of dramatic and musical skill enabled him, in *Tristan und Isolde*, to present a couple of characters—the eponymous central pair—with whom in the First Act we can identify with no more difficulty than with those in a middle-period play of Ibsen's, for all the medieval trappings of the setting, and despite the mention and use of wonder-working potions. Indeed the First Act is such potent drama, involving a clash of wills and its resolution into abandonment to a long-unacknowledged love, that one might feel it is self-sufficient, and that one could draw the implications of it without anything further being enacted. It is only through the agency of music that the world-tran-scending passion of Act II can be worked towards without seeming unintelligible. When, at one of its climaxes, the lovers finally join voices and sing 'selbst dann bin ich die Welt' ('Then I myself am the world') one recognizes that these lovers have moved beyond anything pre-viously understood as the meaning or purpose of love; and in the final stretches of the duet they take their metaphysical sentiments still further, explicitly exchanging identities and reaching a peak of ecstatic union rudely interrupted by the arrival of the other characters, so that their flights give way abruptly to all-too-human reproaches and regrets, and Wagner enforces for us the gulf between what Tristan and Isolde have come to recognize as the only realm of experience which they can acknowledge as unconditionally valid, and the world of Day, con-temptuously dismissed by Tristan as 'deceiving and barren.'

The most robust and simple line to take about Act II of *Tristan* is that it demonstrates, what many people have long suspected, that you can get away with any nonsense you please if you set it to sufficiently seductive music. That is the line that Nietzsche, patron-demon of all anti-Wagnerians, came to take, not without a great deal of reluctant admiration for the skill and conviction with which Wagner had done it. The implications of Nietzsche's many-pronged attack on Wagner might be said to be: Look what happens when musical gifts fall into the wrong hands. Anyone with a metaphysical or ideological system which they wish to persuade up-market searchers of would do well to hire a composer of Wagner's rhetorical and expressive gifts, and get him to set their texts to music. The charge is not in itself original, but Nietzsche was making it against a particular species of music which lends it much more force than it had ever had before.

Odd, though explicable, that Nietzsche did not subject Bach to a comparable onslaught. For, as the Antichrist, Nietzsche might have argued that the insistences of Wagner, which he found so wearing when not seductive, were not rhetorically superior to the calm affirmations of the Christian faith that Bach deploys throughout his work. In a striking passage in *The Importance of Nietzsche*, Erich Heller (1988, 16) writes 'Time and again we come to point in Nietzsche's writings where the shrill tones of the rebel are hushed by the still voice of the autumn of a world waiting in calm serenity for the storms to break . . . In such moments the music of Bach brings tears to his eyes and he brushes aside the noise and turmoil of Wagner.' Which only goes to show that, as all expert rhetoricians, emphatically including Wagner, know, quiet, unassertive tones can be the most persuasive, to some extent because it does not sound as if they are trying to persuade. The doctrine of the Incarnation is not less paradoxical than that of two people merging their identities—indeed, it has to do with three. Bach sets it to music of hushed intensity, partly, no doubt, because he felt that near-silence was the appropriate response to such an event; partly because he was telling people something they already knew, but which, valuing it as they did, they wanted re-presented to them in the most serenely confident tones possible.

The creators of the great, violently revisionary metaphysical systems, or those that operate as supports for religious beliefs, disdain rhetorical devices—present their views in as unmusical a way as possible, as it were, always excepting that involuntary artist Plato. In this respect the contrast between music and metaphysics appears to be extreme. In general the metaphysicians offer their self-evident axioms, or go through an elaborate process of discarding the bogus to reach the genuine article, and proceed according to the dictates of ungainsayable logical principles. Self-advertisingly they eschew all methods of persuasion other than the seemingly coercive force of logic itself. So even if it is only Spinoza, or Descartes briefly in the Replies to the Objections to his *Meditations*, who overtly put their thoughts in Euclidean form, most of the great system-builders want us to gain the impression that what they are doing amounts to the same thing. Yet which of them concludes with results that he wishes were otherwise, or that he is indifferent to, or is even amazed by? If there is anyone who answers to those descriptions, it is Hume, whose account of the anguish that the conclusions of his deliberations cause him is a *locus classicus* primarily because it is unique. And in any case with so wily an ironist it is not clear that the impotence of Reason wherever it functions, or rather fails to function, in relation to what we most care about, is not a built-in device of demoralization. For the rest, the determination to get where they want to, on the part of philosophers, is so blatant that it ought to be a scandal. Nietzsche thought it was, as indeed he thought was the general desire to build systems. But his remarks on that subject have been largely ignored, and so has his claim that it is the moral views of philosophers which have always been fundamental for them, and that although they have devoted themselves to presenting more or less abstract accounts of the world, from which their morality allegedly follows, actually their motivation has been in the reverse order to their procedure.

By 'moral' Nietzsche clearly means something wider than the use of the term in most contemporary discussion: something more like taking up a general attitude to the character of the world and our place in it from which moral values and actions in the narrower sense will proceed. Metaphysics, in other words, even if it has not always been the handmaid of theology, has behaved as if it were; in this way it bears a striking resemblance to moral systems which reject the idea of God the lawgiver, but retain the notion of a moral law—which is to say, most morality. Indeed, the more that a philosopher is concerned to reject belief in God, or a transcendent realm of Being which imposes patterns of attitude and conduct on us, the more he is liable to insist that such ontological omissions are irrelevant to the pressure of morality upon us. Hence is conjured up the strange claim that moral values have an absolutely binding force on us, though those who make that claim are usually at pains to locate morality within a general view of man and society. Similarly, metaphysicians who do not crown their systems with a morally concerned Deity (and there are few who have been interested in any other kind) none the less proceed, as Hume himself does, to produce oughts out of ises at an impressive rate. For a, if not the, fundamental impulse to philosophise is to answer Plato's question 'How should we live?' and no plausible answer to that question will be forthcoming if we are not provided with an account of what kind of creatures we are, and what our environment, in the widest sense, is like.

There is nothing questionable in having as the driving-force of one's philosophy the urge to find out how one should live—it would be far more questionable to have any other. And Nietzsche would certainly not have disagreed with that. What he pointed out is that philosophers have typically had their answer to that question ready in advance, but pretended that they reached it only after strenuous investigations of a value-free kind. And what Nietzsche felt impelled to do, if only sketchily (it is one of the things that post-structuralists have devoted much labour to, some of it profitably) was to show not only how they manipulated the evidence at their disposal—inventing, suppressing, distorting alleged 'facts'—but that their so-called logic rests, more often than not, on a variety of moderately ill-concealed rhetorical devices.

Whatever may be one's verdict on Nietzsche's maxim 'There are no facts, only interpretations', it is hard to resist its force when one is dealing with the 'facts' as philosophers select and deal with them. And whatever Nietzsche's standing as a philosopher, it is impossible to deny the overtness of his rhetoric—he made sure that no-one would ever mistake him for a *soi-disant* purveyor of the unvarnished truth about things. Part of the point of his frequently hilarious autobiography *Ecce Homo* is to stress the kind of factor which influenced his philosophical outlook: he traces his genealogy (in the ordinary sense), the climate in which he grew up and felt compelled to leave, even details of his diet. Since philosophers, perhaps even more than most people, dislike being teased, they have found it convenient to categorize *Ecce Homo* as the work of a man evidently on the verge of or undergoing, breakdown. That he actually was only makes the more poignant, as well as triumphant, his tactic of exhibiting his temperament, and some of the factors that were responsible for it, to such an unexampled degree. But his aim, in violating canons of philosophical good taste so exuberantly, was to bring home to philosophers that they do *have* a temperament, and that they attempt to disguise it, in their philosophical writings, at their peril.

It should by now be a commonplace that the temperament of a philosopher is as evident in his writings as that of an artist in his works, and yet commentators go on commentating as if it were either imperceptible, or could be discounted while one examines the validity of the philosopher's arguments. That they can continue to do this is, no doubt, largely due to the presence, in almost any philosopher's work, of areas of argumentation where his temperament does not obtrude—but then that is as true of artists. In almost all art except the most insistently expressionistic there are areas where it is sustained by what might be called the common pool of craftsmanship available at the time, which is the analogue of the argumentative devices available to the philosopher.—And it may well be that in philosophy such areas are more extensive than they are in art.

It could also be the case that, though, say, one can speedily identify which of the great, and many of the not so great philosophers one is reading other than by the views he is arguing for, that is not relevant. The same may be true of many physicists—I have no idea whether it is or not—but that does not affect the objective standing of their work. But in philosophy, where so much of the time it is not a matter of deductive argumentation leading to a single conclusion, but rather of weighing inconclusive considerations, the mode of presentation makes a big difference to just how heavy they feel. Alternatively, a philosopher may rest his case on the mode of presentation. A blatant case of that is the *Tractatus Logico-Philosophicus*, where very often Wittgenstein is content not to argue at all, but rather to produce statements so lapidary that they serve also to petrify the reader's mind. This is the ultimate rhetoric of the aphorist, someone who couches his thoughts in a manner that makes one feel a fool to question them. Aphorisms, like their extreme opposite, chains of deduction, are a form of reader-intimidation. And if they fail in their intended effect, they produce the same reaction too; one pounces on a *non sequitur* in the same way as on a misfiring aphorism, with triumphant contempt.

It is characteristic of the great philosophical systems that they capture their readers' imaginations in the first place, even if one has to follow their chains of reasoning for that to happen. That is something that is widely acknowledged, at the same time as the uneasy relationship of that truth with the view that philosophy is mainly a matter of ratiocination is left unexplored. For the majority of philosophical practitioners do not possess their own imaginative vision, but take over that of someone else, or shop around in the philosophical supermarket, or alternatively remain agnostic as to the outcome of the major philosophical debates, contenting themselves with exposing the weakness of all the chief known positions on a given topic. Philosophy as a discipline, especially as practised in the universities and the official parts of conferences, tends to bear a close relationship to literary criticism, as conceived on broadly traditional lines. In one way that sounds a strange claim, because discussing a play by Shakespeare is *prima facie* very unlike discussing *The Critique of Pure Reason*. In the first case, one might think, the play remains what it is, while students of it try to find out what that may be. In the second case—what seems to constitute the glory and misery of being a student of philosophy—one enters the lists, taking Kant as an immensely imposing figure but not an authority. A serious study of the *First Critique* will involve showing that Kant made some grave mistakes of reasoning; that he therefore failed to establish some of his central claims; however attracted one may be by the whole structure, one's intellectual conscience will compel one to concede that the architectonic is in large measure a farce; that, on the other hand, Kant succeeds in undermining key positions in both empiricist and rationalist epistemologies, and that some parts of the work constitute major advances: or at any rate's one's thought will proceed along those kinds of line. The text remains intact, but the system does not. One takes what one can from it and adds it to the stock of philosophical truths which one has already amassed—every student of philosophy being a potential contributor to a common area of debate, as in the natural sciences.

And yet it is not the case that the great works of philosophy occupy the same position in relation to us as the great works of science do, which is what that account makes them sound like. One could only make that claim if one could point to decisive respects in which philosophy has progressed, and though there are people around who make that claim, they seem to be blinkered optimistic scientistic philistines. To return to Shakespeare: even the finest criticism of his work is not, for obvious reasons, considered to be continuous with it. And yet Shakespeare is not—this is the element of truth in some of the extravagant schools of contemporary criticism and critical theory—merely there, inviolable and separate from our perceptions of him. The significance of his works is different for us now than it was for anyone in the eighteenth century, and their awareness of him was different from that of his contempories. It is the great mischief of categorizing him as a classic that it prevents genuine response, including finding some much-admired works tedious or dated. And the finest insights into what his plays mean do achieve a kind of continuity with them—one absorbs a valuable critical aperçu into one's experience of the play. So I repeat: the activity of literary criticism is closer to that of the philosophical critic than one might suppose, and the activity of the philosophical critic is less like that of the natural scientist than one might wish.

Of course if one takes a strongly Kuhnian line about science one might say that the activity of the scientist is more like that of the literary critic than Popper, say, would ever accept. But that is a matter I have not time to discuss, so I will merely register my disagreement with the Kuhnians. It may be that in the great exploratory enterprises of mankind, of which I will mention only the natural sciences, philosophy and the arts, there is always an element of intrusion by the practitioners, but my claim is that in the natural sciences not only is it at its smallest, but that it is desirable that it should be, and that it is checkable, to a very large degree, how far it is. In the arts the interplay of registration of the material the artist has to deal with and the sensibility and temperament of the artist himself—a great spirit encounters great subject-matter—is at its most complex and fascinating: that is a considerable part of the inexhaustible interest that the arts have for us. In philosophy, at least as traditionally practised, the aspiration is to achieve scientific or super-scientific status, the reality much more like art. Hence the relationship of philosophers to their subject and its history is in a perpetual state of crisis.

New philosophical movements, like new artistic movements, tend to be heralded by and accompanied by propapaganda attacking the last dominant one, now to be decisively displaced. It is not that a major philosophical viewpoint is found to need so many qualifications that the best thing to do is to abandon it altogether—though that does happen. But the small print of philosophical works is never decisive for their rejection or acceptance, though it is important for the self-image of philosophy that there should be a lot of intricate and minute investigation and argument. It is rather that philosophical, like artistic movements, lose their momentum, so that the element of creativeness present in the most remarkable philosophical minds can find no more stimulus in working within that idiom. That is not the only factor, since philosophical endeavour is fertilized from so many directions. 'Inter-textuality' can no more wholly account for changes in philosophy than for changes in the arts. At any rate, at this stage in the history of the subject we find a tendency that those who would like to believe that it really only got off the ground twenty, or forty, years ago must feel very uneasy about: the tendency, namely, to select a salient figure or doctrine from the past and name him or it as one's patron. Who would have credited, thirty years ago, that in the most advanced Anglo-American philosophical circles there would be a renaissance of essentialism, or pragmatism? More likely they would have been presented to a sceptic about progress in the subject as two of the doctrines that have been decisively refuted. Yet varieties of both are now touted by some of the most influential figures on the international conference-attending scene. One might characterize the major philosophical views as 'permanent possibilities of return to fashion'.

I am not either being cynical or advocating cynicism about the value of doing philosophical work. No society which has any degree of intellectual sophistication can be considered healthy if it does not ask a certain type of question, even if it is unanimous and confident in its answers. And in respect of some philosophical issues, such as that of freedom and responsibility, drastic practical consequences may ensue on those answers. I am not suggesting, either, that some philosophical theories are not vastly superior to others. But I am suggesting that the respects in which they are superior are to be compared more to the qualities which we prize in the arts than those of the sciences.

That clearly leads to the question: Which qualities do we prize in the arts? And I have not time left to give anything like a satisfactorily full answer. Furthermore, what we prize about the arts is closely connected with what we feel can be achieved in other areas of human endeavour; and our views on that undergo, both biographically and historically, enormous shifts. One enormous historical shift has been, during the last two centuries, the triumph of disciplines concerned with means and the collapse of the institution that was, whatever else one may say about it, devoted to ends. That was merely a vague way of putting the banality that Christianity has declined while science and technology have accelerated at a pace which most people will grant is unassimilable. The spiritual vacuum that has ensued, diagnosed with the utmost originality, precision and finality by Nietzsche, could perhaps only be filled by something with the pretensions of Christinanity; and some metaphysical systems, McTaggart's for example, certainly possess that. But while Christianity, at its peak, was a brilliant combination of faith and reason, metaphysics alone demands exclusive faith in reason, and in the capacity of reason to produce a set of conclusions which can command all the faculties of man in the way that belief in Christianity could. That has not been forthcoming, and one can say with depressing confidence that it will not be. So we are left with the painful task of cutting ourselves down to size. Yet, as the remarkable Spanish novelist Juan Goytisolo recently remarked (1991, 14) 'Only by aspiring to transcend the human can we attain human dignity; if we are happy just to be human we descend into subhumanity.'

But what can be our image of transcending the human? For me it can be found best, perhaps only, in music. The great music which has been created during the catastrophic period of our imminent descent into nihilism at least conveys to us states of consciousness so sublime, and so immune to the critical intellect, that it gives us the nearest we can hope for to heaven on earth. Our natural tendency, which I discussed at some length early in the paper, is to think that such states must be connected to adequate statements. The alternative seems to be that they are not about anything, and are therefore empty. But need peace or exhilaration be about anything? Could not it be that the Christian God, perhaps the most bizarre creation of man, was called into being to answer the need we have to celebrate and praise, that therefore we become all too firmly attached to the idea that these are intrinsically transitive activities, and only degenerately self-sufficient? Metaphysics, either seeking to provide the rationale of faith, or creating its own transcendent beings, inveterately optimistic, panders to this need as well. And so does all art that represents and praises. Perhaps the time has come when Rilke, in his Sonnets to Orpheus, the unstoppable singer, can be seen as inaugurating a new age rather than being parasitic on a dead one he writes:

> Praising, that's it! He was summoned for that,
> and came to us like the ore from a stone's
> silence. His mortal heart presses out
> a deathless, inexhaustible wine.
> Neither decay in the sepulchre of kings
> nor any shadow fallen from the gods
> can ever detract from his glorious praising.

Perhaps, in that light, we can say that musicians *are* metaphysicians with musical ability. I am not suggesting that metaphysics should be displaced, or replaced, by music. But in metaphysics we are perpetually dissatisfied, and are therefore led to continue our endless argument. Music accomplishes for us, among its other rewards, a temporary cessation to our debates, and leaves us, sometimes, knowing what it would feel like to reach a conclusion.

Philosophy and the Cult of Irrationalism

BRENDA ALMOND

Philosophy, as I conceive it, is a journey and a quest. Conducted individually, it is nevertheless a collective attempt on the part of human beings from differing cultures and times to make sense of the arbitrary contingency of human existence, to find meaning in life. So understood, the impulse to philosophise needs no explanation or apology. It belongs to us all, and it exerts its own categorical imperative. Here I may quote the words of a wise woman, an invented contributor to this debate, who spoke of the common mind, the common store of wisdom which has the power to outlast the individual. 'For this', she said, 'is what philosophy is: not an esoteric discipline, but the common endeavour of the human race to understand and come to terms with its own perilous, fragile and ultimately ephemeral existence' (Almond, 1990, 185).

It is an interesting irony that it was philosophers committed to respect for ordinary language—philosophers who made what the ordinary person would say the final court of appeal in conceptual analysis—who rejected this popular perception of the goal and purpose of philosophy. And I, like all my contempories and most of my successors, began my academic pursuit of philosophy by learning from my tutors that philosophy was not to be understood as an attempt to find 'the meaning of life'. It is a further irony that A. J. Ayer, the most prominent of those tutors, ended his life and career with a book of that title—not, of course, a deathbed conversion, but a very typical parting gibe at the popular conception (Ayer, 1990).

An alternative title for this paper then, might well be 'The rape of "philosophy"'. For I would suggest that the term has, in a sense, been hi-jacked by professional teachers of the subject and that in fact the ordinary person had it right. Philosophy is the pursuit of meaning in a deeper and richer sense than that which might emerge from looking up 'meaning' in one of the new dictionaries of philosophy that current practice has made indispensable to twentieth-century students. Moreover, by failing to pursue meaning in the sense of 'meaningfulness'—pattern, structure, cohesion, continuities—professional academic philosophy has opened the door to the cult of irrationalism which represents the truly *popular* philosophy of today. This irrationalism pervades all the main spheres of philosophy: epistemology, ethics, philosophy of science, and it runs rampant with disastrous consequences in practical areas which, again in the popular sense of the term, depend upon an underlying philosophical perspective: education and medicine, politics and personal relationships.

As a consequence of this, we have two of the most threatening phenomena of our age: ethics divorced from moral sensitivity, religion divorced from humanity and reason. More exactly, secular moralists limit their options to a narrow form of utilitarian calculation, while at the same time we see the rise of fundamentalist forms of religion which depend on the suspension of critical faculties—on developing the Alice-in-Wonderland capacity to believe six impossible things before breakfast every day. These developments are to be seen against the background of a generalized and ubiquitous rejection of the notion of truth, an entrenched relativism which asserts the essential dependency of ideas upon their sources, and regards intellectual assent to a proposition as submission to the social power of its author. Ideas, arguments and beliefs are portrayed as pawns in the power-struggles of human beings. Against this background, the continuing preoccupations of philosophers in the analytic tradition with the philosophy of language, narrowly conceived but verbosely propounded, can be seen as a case of virtuoso violin performance in a context of conflagration, or, as the plain man or woman might prefer to say: fiddling while Rome burns.

The modern—or should I say Postmodern?—way to describe all this is as the rejection of the of the Enlightenment and its values. The story is by now well-documented, most recently by Alasdair MacIntyre in his iconoclastic attack on contemporary Western culture with its enthronement of that universalistic conception, the liberal individual. The evolution of this chameloen-like creature, first sketched by MacIntyre in *After Virtue*, is subsequently traced by him through four major philosophical traditions (MacIntyre, 1981, 1988). It was relatively recently, he suggests, that the idea took hold that there could and would be a diversity of views about the good, and that politics was about how people with these diverse conceptions might live together. Of course, MacIntyre himself repudiates the irrationalism implicit within this approach—the abandonment, that is, of the idea that there are right and wrong answers, true and false gods—by arguing that rationality can and must be embodied in a tradition. He sees himself, however, not as a relativist, which this might suggest, but as a historicist. One might flesh out this description by calling him a fallibilist Hegelian—Hegel transmuted by Popper and Kuhn—for his account makes use of the notion of 'epistemological crises' in traditions—crises capable of bringing about their downfall and their replacement by new, more robust traditions.

The modern project, however, has been to found a culture and a social order free from the contingency and particularly of traditions, appealing to universal standards and universal moral norms. It has also pursued a notion of truth as laboriously constructed on foundations which are as secure as the honest and unflagging application of reason can make them. MacIntyre, however, is one of many who have come to believe that it is not possible to make your reasoning appeal, as John Rawls and other liberal theorists have attempted to do, to *any* rational person—to individuals conceived of as abstracted from their particularities of character, history and circumstance. While he himself believes an alternative security is to be found in the acceptance of an established tradition which provides guidance in the various contexts of human life—family, education, social relations—philosophers who have followed this line of reasoning but have not found such a resting-place end with conclusions closer to pragmatism.

The Unity of Philosophy

I have already, in this preliminary sketch drawn together the notion of truth in an epistemological context and truth in the area of values. I am aware, however, that many philosophers would share the view recently expressed by David Wiggins that these conceptions are best kept in separate compartments by avoiding, as Wiggins (1991, 63) puts it, the unwanted comparison between 'the aspirations of first order morality and the aspirations of first order science'.

I am not persuaded, however, that philosophy is such a fragmented enterprise as, in particular, this separation of ethics and epistemology, values and science, implies. It is surely not without significance, for example, that in Plato's metaphysics, the culmination of the pursuit of knowledge was awareness and recognition of the Form of the Good—a destination arrived at by way of scientific, mathematical and logical enquiry. Indeed, Plato's account embodies a yet more striking suggestion: that the end-point of enquiry is not the end-point of activity—that those who have made the journey should in the end return from the heights of metaphysics to the prosaic ground of the practical and the applied, from the world of philosophical contemplation to the world of politics and public affairs. This is not to deny, of course, that scientific or practical reasoning is methodologically distinct from moral reasoning and both, again, from logical reasoning. It is to say, however, that underlying these diverse enquiries, despite their necessary differences of approach, is the problem of the gulf between what there is to know and our knowledge of it. This gulf opens up whether what is at issue are everyday empirical statements, logical or mathematical assertions, or scientific claims that go beyond current experience. It is not intrinsically different when the issue is moral or religious truth. The recurring questions are: How is error to be avoided? How is certainty to be separated from mere opinion? What distinguishes irrational dissent from legitimate diversity of views?

Traditionally, the answer has been sought either in observation (the empiricist solution) or in reason and intuition (the rationalist answer). Today it is necessary to incorporate the Kantian insight that we cannot separate our perception of truth from the fact that it is *our perception*. As Hilary Putnam has remarked (1981, 128): 'The idea that truth is a passive copy of what is "really" (mind-independently, discourse-independently) "there" has collapsed under the critiques of Kant, Wittgenstein and other philosophers even if it continues to have a deep hold on our thinking'. The question is, however, what weight to put on this. Certainly it is not to be equated with the facile assertion that truth is simply a matter of one's point of view. For this last position is essentially self-refuting. Lurking behind it is some version of the paradox of Epimenides. In other words, it is fundamentally incoherent both to hold a point of view and at the same time argue that no point of view is more justified or right than any other. And, as Thomas Nagel, has said (1986, 89): 'a view deserves to be called skeptical if it offers an account of ordinary thoughts which cannot be incorporated into those thoughts without destroying them'.

At the root of such sceptical views lies the yet more radical idea that meaning itself is fluid: that the very building-blocks of discourse and argument, our words and concepts, are irremediably subjective. But in order even to engage in the argument, it is necessary to assume that our language and concepts are not totally fluid; we can acknowledge change only within certain parameters. For both the scientific and moral concepts that play a part in such discussions, a degree of convergence or constancy of meaning is needed. In other words, if reflection and enquiry are to be possible at all, we need an anchor-point for understanding beyond the egotistical limits of ourselves and own thinking.

Forms of Life

Until recently, a fairly naive scientism, ultimately derived from the Cartesian search for irrefutable foundations, would have been assumed to hold the answer. In philosophy, however, we have entered a new era in which a form of bounded, culturally-confined holism holds sway. As in nineteenth-century metaphysics, coherence is once again the test of truth, but it is a limited coherence, not the universal inter-relatedness of Parmenides' 'whole' or Bradley's 'Absolute'. It is not surprising that the currently favoured ethical parallel to this is a new Aristotelianism, based on the virtues, which locates morality in a tradition and way of life. For the only step available to contemporary holistic theorists which stops short of the ancient metaphysical solution—a single interlocking truth in which any partial truth has implicit within it every other—is the Wittgensteinian doctrine of forms of life, Quine's web of belief, Davidson's conceptual schemes or, as Putnam has put it (1986, 89), 'ideal coherence of our beliefs with each other and with our experiences as the experiences are themselves represented in our belief system'. We might include here, too, the Leibnizian notion of 'possible worlds' as developed in its modern form by, for example, David Lewis (1986).[1]

But this conception provides a false security. It is understandable that philosophy, confronted by the possibility of solipsistic shipwreck, should have sought safety on the raft of localized consensus known as 'forms of life'. But this is no substitute for dry land—reason, objectivity, truth, and a secure notion of the good. There is, of course, companionship in the relative security of the life raft, but as a solution it opens up a confusing diversity of possibilities, even for members of a single cultural or geographic community. The raft solution leads to the fragmentation of human reason; apart from divisions into whole areas of thought—the religious, the scientific, the moral, the aesthetic—there are separations based on persons: the raft of Marxist sociological analysis, for example, located truth within groups defined by class; today the favoured divisions may be race, colour, gender, sexual orientation or practice; but there are others—neo-Hobbesians—speaking the language of terrorism, nationalism and ethnic diversity—in Richard Rorty's phrase (1989, 51) 'an indefinite plurality of standpoints' in which 'truth is made rather than found'. All these divisions may be presented as ways, often mutually exclusive, of construing the human world, using 'languages' which are not ultimately intertranslatable. In contrast, the idea of convergence, belief in the possibility of a unified science and a common conception of truth may be dismissed, as it is by Rorty (1985, 10), as old-fashioned religion, based on the kind of 'motives which once led us to posit gods'. This leaves as the only alternative available to us, as human beings with liberal leanings, a 'lonely provincialism' in which we have freed ourselves psychologically from the need to pursue the humanistic ideal of a common intellectual tradition based on a common reason.

Behind this view, which allows for different or alternative 'true' pictures of the world, is the belief that observation is essentially theory-laden. Rorty attacks 'representationalism', arguing that ideas, words

[1] The relation between plural 'actual' worlds and relativism is discussed in Margolis (1991, ch. 6)

and language are not mirrors which copy the 'real' or 'objective' world but rather tools we use to cope with our environment. But it is worth repeating that words cannot *simply* be tools we use to cope with our environment. 'We', 'our' and 'environment' are all terms which smuggle back the realist ideas that are purportedly being banished and it is significant that Rorty finds it necessary to abolish the 'we'—the subject—in step with the abolition of the object. In contrast, Putnam's notion of 'objectivity for us' is, despite its relativistic overtones, wider than this, if 'us' is taken, as it may be, to comprise *all* human beings; for this suggests a notion of coherence that depends on the universals of human psychology and biology and the possibility of a broader human culture. Such a notion is more than a life-raft and, indeed, may be so close to dry land that, as human beings, we would be foolish to want more.

A fractured and fragmented view of philosophy, then, gives us a fractured and fragmented world; it offers truth in compartments: the 'truth' of Western science, the 'truth' of this religion or that, the purely relative validity of morality and, in an unavoidable progression, truth for my social class or my race, truth for my age-cohort or my sex. These are unfortunate consequences for the True and the Good, which have already many enemies in the real—the public—world, away from the debates of philosophers, for this view provides no weapons with which to defend them. It leaves the western tradition, stemming from Plato and Aristotle, with nothing to say to its less inhibited rivals or critics but 'This is *our* tradition . . . or at least the tradition of *some* of us . . . at least just *now*.' This is particularly so when another dimension of the contemporary analysis is added to the picture: a half philosophical, half empirical analysis of social and political power, sometimes called the sociology of knowledge.

Fractionalism and power

Once particularity has replaced universality, there is a need to account for the particular view that prevails in any one human group, however identified—whether by class, by ethnicity, by gender, or in some other way. It is natural that this should lead to an explanation in terms of power-relationships. For if the authority of reason or truth is unavailable as an explanation for the dominance of a view, explanation will inevitably be personalized. There will be a preoccupation with the *source* rather than the intrinsic strength of an argument.

Although modern versions of this view are associated with Marxism and in particular with the Marxist doctrine that ideology—thought, philosophy and opinion—derives from power-relationships created by hard socio-economic facts, it is less novel than its advocates sometimes appear to suppose. In practical terms, it is not essentially different from the view originally put forward by Thrasymachus as a challenge to Socrates in Book I of Plato's *Republic* and later, in Book II, given illustrative force in the story of Gyges' ring. Thrasymachus argued that law and morality are what the strongest factions in society choose to invent and enforce for what they perceive to be their own interest. In the story, Gyges acquires the magical power to pursue his own interest without fear of legal or judicial interference and punishment and it is assumed that he *will* therefore pursue his own interest without regard for any moral constraint.

The role of Socrates' adversaries is today played out by a variety of theorists of the social and physical sciences. In particular, Michel Foucault, in a series of analyses—indisputedly brilliant and penetrating—has revealed something of the ways in which human beings manipulate each other in law and punishment, in sexual relationships, in psychiatric medicine. They have done this, he suggests, by creating false categories of criminality, sexuality, or madness (Foucault, 1978, 1979). These are significant reflections but popular conclusions have gone beyond the subtle insights of the analyses to an uncritical acceptance of the tacit standpoint: that the question 'Whose view?' is the central one. This generates a practical cynicism in which 'What view?', i.e., the merits and demerits of the claim itself, gets no hearing, indeed is dismissed as a meaningless question. It is a process helped along by other popular thinkers, some of whom, such as Ivan Illich (1971, 1976) have conducted a generalized attack on the institutions of Western society: in particular, its schooling and health-care systems. This is not an accidental development, for relativism and an attendant cynicism, once intellectually established, have a tendency to invade every area of practical life: the family-structure, approaches to medicine and bio-medical research, the conduct of business and public affairs and, most of all, education.

Education

The sociology of knowledge arrived in Britain in direct application to education in the 1960s with the publication of a widely influential book by the educational sociologist, Michael Young (1971). Young argued that those in positions of power will attempt (a) to define what is to be taken as knowledge, (b) to determine the accessibility of that knowledge for different groups, and (c) to determine the relationships between knowledge areas and those who have access to them. He argued that it is possible to trace significant relationships between the pattern of dominant values in society and the distribution of power and rewards.

The implicit relativism in this view was not, however, new to educational theory, any more than the more general theory was new to political theory. That there was such a tradition even in ancient times is shown by the fact that Socrates is depicted as attacking it in the *Protagoras* and the *Meno* in the context of discussions on raising the young in the values and virtues respected by their parents. The *Meno*, too, contains a clear argument for the possibility of rational enquiry outside the moral sphere: the search for truth and avoidance of error which is open to all, independently of social group or status, using only the innate and universal capacity of reason. This is the point of Socrates' famous educational experiment, in which an uneducated slave succeeds, on the basis of questioning only, in deducing one of the most difficult and abstract of mathematical theorems. In the dialogue the experiment is presented as proving the doctrine of Anamnesis—that we remember these truths from a previous existence—but to regard it as only relevant to that doctrine would be like regarding the parable of the Good Samaritan as being entirely about behavioural standards amongst Samaritans and Pharisees in ancient Palestine.

In essence such passages confront the contemporary issue: is the kind of knowledge that it passed on in instruction the product of an impartial search for truth, or is it, as Protagoras suggested, no more than the intellectual equipment of the day, required only to help its recipient succeed in life, irrespective of the issue of truth and error? Two traditions in the philosophy of education, each disposed to respond differently to this question, battle for acceptance at the level of theory and, less self-consciously, at the level of practice. The first tradition, which in modern times may be traced from Rousseau via Dewey to A. S. Neill, ultimately finding its expression in the post-Plowden primary school, stresses the value of knowledge gained from *experience*, and hence promotes the development of practical skills. Its starting point is the learner and his or her needs. Because the approach is problem-centred, it is favourable to integrated studies in a classroom arranged as a well-equipped workroom. Its empiricist epistemological base is reflected in a democratic and egalitarian ethos and orientation.

The second tradition, while historically associated with rationalism and idealism, is not necessarily incompatible with empiricism. It does, however, see reason as providing access to abstract conceptual truth, and education both as a framework for conveying the accumulated knowledge of human civilization, and as a means of activating the latent rational insight of the learner. Thus the logical structure of knowledge takes priority in teaching strategies, dictating a phased presentation of subject-matter in which the learner proceeds by mastery of a necessary sequence of steps. Politically, because its end-product is specialized knowledge in different spheres, leading to a variety of outcomes and achievements, and because it assumes an initial inequality of knowledge between teacher and taught, it acknowledges at least the authority bestowed by that knowledge. Thus its ethos is meritocratic and competitive, ultimately supporting a diversified and role-differentiated society.[2]

What its advocates recommend should form the content of education in this second tradition is, to quote Matthew Arnold (1960, 70) 'the best that has been thought and known' or, as T. S. Eliot put it (1948, 27), 'that which makes life worth living'—that which, from some future perspective, would make it worthwhile for a civilization to have existed. Its scientific and practical content is whatever is the nearest approximation currently available to factual truth. The judgment of both the best and the true is, according to this view, indifferent to the question of *who* may have thought or said it. Hence it is antithetical to the views of such scientific irrationalists as Kuhn or Feyerabend, for whom scientific 'truth' is what currently influential scientists amongst us assert; and even more antithetical to the view that it, together with the judgment as to what is best in literature or art, or the interpretation of history, is a matter of who has emerged as top dog in the shifting power-struggles of contemporary society.

It is in the light of this that one should view current demands in British schools and, in a remarkable parallel, in some American universities, that the curriculum should be arranged on the basis of the authors or *sources* of ideas or materials, irrespective of their *character* or quality. These are explicitly aimed at abolishing the hegemony of what is sometimes called inexactly the 'European mind' or, more crudely but more precisely the white male bias in all areas of knowledge. This is part of a more general iconoclasm which rejects the privileged position of 'high' art and culture, together with the people or groups seen to be its authors and originators. From this point of view, the defence of Plato and Shakespeare, Beethoven and the Bible, is inextricably linked to a form of political conservatism that is rooted in yet older and more unacceptable traditions of imperialism.

These much-remarked developments are a logical consequence of the theory that the key question is always '*Whose* view?' rather than '*What* view?' or, as MacIntyre's title has it 'Whose justice? Which rationality?' (1988), and it is another Epimenidean irony that those who have provided the sophisticated philosophical under-pinning for this practical programme are themselves, almost without exception, white

---

[2] I have discussed these aspects of educational theory more fully in Cohen 1981, 1982.

and male. Meanwhile, this latter view pushes its way into the higher education system in Britain too, with rejection, not so much of a basic canon of texts suitable for study, but—perhaps more far-reachingly—of the traditional notion of a *subject* as something that is defined by a specific conceptual structure and distinctive methodology. In its place, to quote a recent contibutor to the debate (Winter, 1991), who manages to compress much of the associated jargon into a single paragraph, the new approach emphasizes: 'the learner's biographical resources . . . the roots of conceptualization in significant experience, the sense of relevance required by effective learning, and the shifting boundaries and linkages between current structures of knowledge'. Not surprisingly, this approach involves demands for new criteria for 'learning outcomes or competences' and inevitably only 'individualized performance criteria' will qualify as replacements for the inter-subjective public comparisons provided by a traditional examination system.

While these philosophical undercurrents have important implications for the content and organization of education in general, they are more significant still in relation to morality and moral education. While the second view is compatible with an approach to moral education based on prior commitment to an acknowledged and agreed range of values and principles, the first is very often associated with an explicit ideology of value-neutrality, expressed strategically in the limited goal of values clarification—helping people identify their *own* pre-existing values and attitudes. Thus children are offered a choice of competing frameworks for guidance—as though this were not a contradiction in terms—in a context of pluralism and practical relativism. Inconsistently, however, value-neutrality is typically abandoned where certain fashionable moral prejudices are concerned, as the retreat from confidence in individual judgment leads to collective moral decision-making on a non-rational basis—a lemming rush to conform to the moral stereotypes of the day.

Biomedicine

This rejection of normative rationality is similarly apparent in other fields, most notably, to take a second example, in biomedicine, where problems are posed both by new technologies—new reproductive techniques, for example, and new control over human genetic potential—and new diseases, in particular AIDS. Here, the repudiation of any substantial rational basis for ethical judgment leads to a scaling down of ethical alternatives to, on the one hand, a 'deontological' approach, frequently religiously-based, which asserts as moral intuitions such principles as the sanctity of life; and, on the other, teleological or utilitarian approaches which focus on *quality* of life—often a licence for any developments which produce a favourable balance of benefit over harm. For the onlooker, this may seem to represent an unpalatable choice between, on the one hand, adopting a range of essentially irrational reactions—horror, disgust, or satisfaction, as the case may be—and, on the other, an abdication of moral sensibility which leads to an ethical free-for-all.

In this debate, consequentialists may favour a case-study method of resolving specific ethical issues, not only for methodological reasons, but because it reflects the utilitarian view that all moral judgments are essentially individual and particular. This brings utilitarianism in medicine close to situational ethics, with its necessary rejection of universal moral constants. Is is not surprising, then, that this rejection should also embrace constants with legal and political overtones such as human rights, of which the most central is the right to life. The biomedical expression of this principle in the sanctity of life doctrine may be dismissed as being wholly dependent on out-dated or contentious religious belief. In the words of Singer and Kuhse (1985, 125): 'The principle of the sanctity of human life is a legacy of the days when religion was the accepted source of all ethical wisdom . . . Now that religion is no longer accepted as the source of moral authority in public life, however, the principle has been removed from the framework in which it developed. We are just discovering that without this framework it cannot stand up.'

In the case of these and other writers, dismissal of the principle is combined with rejection of two medically important distinctions: between ordinary and extraordinary means of preserving life, and between killing and letting die. Many theorists, including, for example, Jonathan Glover and R. M. Hare, proceed to argue for quality-of-life considerations to take priority, permitting, for example, the 'replacement', via selective abortion and infanticide, of defective and undesired offspring by others with better prospects for a happy life (see, for example, Glover, 1977, 109, 112–114). This requires some reconceptualization of the notion of a 'person', resulting in the conclusion (which, presumably fortuitously, happens to favour philosophers writing on the subject) that only 'continuing selves' have a right to life. Against this can be set what may initially seem to be no more than a vague uneasiness—a feeling that, whatever decisions are reached in these and other difficult cases, they should not be reached *easily*; that there is a need for what David Lamb (1988) has called a feeling of respect and a sense of what Mary Warnock called 'outrage' when this respect is ignored. In the case of embryo research, for example, while recommending a limited liberality of practice, she speaks, nevertheless, of 'barriers which should not be passed' and 'things which, regardless of consequences should not be done' (Warnock, 1987, 8).

The sense that special moral taboos may apply to some of the developments made possible by technological and medical advance, independently of purely cost-benefit considerations, is not itself, however, a concession to irrationalism. On the contrary, what is involved here once again are competing views, not of 'personhood', but of human nature: what humans are in essence, and how they may best flourish and find their fulfilment. An understanding of this, even in the prosaic ground-level sense of biological flourishing, requires the application of reason to the task of defining an ethical framework in which this flourishing is most likely to be achieved.

In sum, then, if, in education, the cult of unreason undermines the status of both morality and reason-based truths such as those of mathematics, in the biomedical field it cedes the ground, potentially more catastrophically, to utilitarianism of a crude cost-benefit kind. Education and medicine are not, however, the only contemporary practical areas of contention. A third battle over reason is being conducted in relation to feminism. This takes the form of an influential critique from the perspective of feminist philosophy.

The Feminist Critique

Feminists have argued that both reason and the notion of universal morality, are gender-based. Specifically, they see these as male inventions, created by means of the oppressive power-structures through which men in all societies and epochs have sought to control women— the patriarchal hypothesis. Once these excrescences are stripped away, they argue, the intellectual space they occupied is available for new insights, from a female perspective, on ethics, on epistemology, on logic, and on scientific method. In this enterprise, subscribers to this point of view at first believed they had found support in the tenets of postmodernism, particularly in its rejection of the Enlightenment conception of reason. One feminist writer (Nicholson, 1991, 8) has chronicled the development as follows:

> Feminists, like postmodernists, have sought to develop new paradigms of social criticism which do not rely on traditional philosophical underpinnings. They have criticised modern foundationalist epistemologies and moral and political theories, exposing the contingent, partial and historically situated character of what has passed in the mainstream for necessary, universal and ahistorical truths. They have called into question the dominant philosophical project of seeking objectivity in the guise of a 'God's eye view' which transcends any situation or perspective.

Inspiring this view were such writers as Rorty in America, and Lyotard in France with his demand for a war on the notion of totality—a symbol for the rejection of stories or narratives, like those of Hegel or Marx, that claim to encompass all of human history. Feminists at first embraced this thesis of particularity—that there is, as one writer summarizes it, only what is 'ad hoc, contextual, plural and limited' (Hartsock, 1991, 159). It is possible, however, to trace the origin and source of these views not only in philosophy, but also in politics. Responsibility for uncovering what she describes as 'the pretensions and illusions' of the ideals of epistemological objectivity, foundations, and neutral judgments is, according to Susan Bordo, really to be attributed to the liberation movements of the sixties and seventies, which emerged 'not only to make a claim to the legitimacy of marginalized cultures, unheard voices, suppressed narratives, but also to expose the perspectivity and partiality of the official accounts' (Bordo, 1991, 136–137).

Whoever is to be named as ultimately responsible, however, this has recently begun to be recognized as a false dawn, a false liberation. For feminists themselves began to take seriously the differences between women that this programme necessarily dictates, and they discovered that the category of 'woman' dissolves into a range of mutually incompatible categories: the white woman, the black woman, the Moslem woman, the middle-class or working-class woman; Jew, Catholic; rich, poor; first world or third world; old, young; fit or disabled; wife and mother, lesbian or single parent. Those who draw attention to these differences argue with some justice that the differences are more important, epistemologically and politically, than that which is held in common—after all, mere gender. In the words of another feminist writer: 'In the rationalist framework, *she* dissolves into *he* as gender differences are collapsed into the (masculine) figure of the Everyman . . . With postrationalism, *she* dissolves into a perplexing plurality of differences.' (Di Stefano, 1991, 77).

What these writers have noticed, then, is that if there is no universal man—no human person (in German, more usefully, *Mensch*, the human person, is distinguished from *Mann*, a male person)—then there can be no universal woman either, and the enterprise of feminism loses its point and purpose. The earlier feminist attack, then, was directed against 'modernism, humanism and rational discourse' and the writer quoted above succinctly sums up the ontology this precludes as: 'standards of normalcy, of judgment, of hierarchical distinctions which must be rooted within some organizing and legitimating ground or framework' (ibid., 76–77). But, as feminists have noticed, the alternative to these old Enlightenment assumptions is to locate oneself *politically,* i.e., within a particular group with its distinctive specific characterization. Some search for plural and complexly constructed identities which include, in particular, the axes of race, class, ethnicity, age and sexual orientation, and they express this idea politically by adopting a strategy of *alliances* or *coalitions* rather than *identification*. Hence the now familiar grouping of peace, environmentalism and feminism. Politically, the general term for this policy is the development of an 'oppositional consciousness', and it is combined with a message which is essentially destabilizing and revolutionary. Jane Flax, for example, writes (1991): 'Our lives and alliances belong with those who seek to further decenter the world . . . If we do our work well, reality will appear even more unstable, complex and disorderly than it does now.'

Some, then, are prepared to see 'woman' give place to 'women', with all the consequences that this entails. Originally, however, the feminist enterprise was to create a political location within the broad and much-encompassing category 'woman'. What is now increasingly recognized within feminst philosophy itself is that, far from superseding the much-criticized liberal-humanist ideal of a single rationally and morally significant group, human-kind, the category 'woman' is only one step away from it. For some, this is an unwelcome recognition, but others are willing to reconsider the philosophical premises which have led to politically fractionalizing conclusions. Nancy Hartsock, for example, proposes a new positive programme for feminism based, not only on a renewed confidence in the possibility of *knowledge*, as opposed to mere 'conversations', but also on recovering the *subject*, accepting once again the legitimacy of the attempt to become, as she puts it (1991, pp. 170–171), 'makers of history', its subjects as well as its objects. The enlargement of the subject is something that has appeal also beyond feminist frontiers. Writing in another context altogether, Michael Freeman remarks (1991, p. 10): 'There can . . . be no metaphysical limit to the scope of "we." The liberal is dedicated to enlarging that scope. The liberal is an ethnocentric who has been brought up to distrust ethno-centrism.' One might add that the liberal is also a man who has come to distrust his gender-locatedness, or a woman who has attempted to remain within *her* gender-locatedness, but who has found in the end no metaphysical barrier of gender to separate man from woman, woman from man.

This reference to liberalism provides a reminder that there is a certain coincidence between the enterprise of liberalism and the enterprise of philosophy itself. That is to say that, in a very similar way, being able to recognize philosophy as a unitary enterprise also depends upon being able to abstract from the particularities of human existence and to find significance in their commonality.

Conclusions

The brief for this paper included some autobiographical reference, and I regret that this has not featured here so far. However, I will end by supplying the deficiency to this extent. As a child, the two things that most filled me with resentment and indignation were unfairness of treatment and unreasonableness of argument. As a child, I was obliged to accept these, but I was attracted, when I came to hear of it, by the notion of philosophy as an enquiry conducted solely according to the reverse principles. I am still reluctant to let go the idea of philosophy as the pursuit of truth through the medium of reason, with the attendant moral virtues of honesty, openness, courage, impartiality and respect for persons that this entails. The impulse to philosophise is, as I have tried to argue here, the impulse to pursue these ideals of justice and reason without qualification. Questions such as 'Whose justice?' 'Whose criteria of rationality?' are questions of an entirely different order. They are questions which permit of empirical answers, and should therefore be left for empirical enquiry by the sociologists and psychoanalysts to whom they rightly belong.

Philosophy itself is defined less by its content than by its strategy, and with the rejection of the ideal of a common reason, it has nowhere to go. Its single core element is the use of argument. Many recent developments in philosophy, from Hegelian and Marxist dialectic to structuralism and postmodernism, are attacks on this single core element and therefore on philosophy itself.

It is necessary to retain the idea, therefore, if not of absolute truth, at least of getting *nearer* to the truth. This is to echo the Platonic view that it is only the possibility of conceiving of absolutes that makes sense of out notion of approximation (the *roughly* triangular or circular, the *more or less* beautiful or good). As Popper writes: 'Although I hold that more often than not we fail to find the truth, and do not even know when we have found it, I retain the classical idea of absolute or objective truth as a *regulative idea*; that is to say, as a standard of which we may fall short.'[3] The notion of error, then, also requires this background. As Theodor Adorno also says (1976, 21): 'the study of false consciousness, of socially necessary illusion, would be nonsense without the concept of true consciousness and objective truth.'

Positivism, which began with Comte locating knowledge in intersubjective observation—*le réel, la certitude, le précis*—has ended with Quine and others attacking the 'dogmas of empiricism'. But as Quentin Skinner (1985) has remarked, this attack on theory is itself a theory, the

---

[3] Cited by Margolis, 1991, 25.

'antitheorists' uniting to present a common view, the *Zeitgeist* of contemporary philosophy.[4]

But let us not be misled by the fashionable iconoclasm of our times into convincing ourselves that we have discovered something unknown to our philosophical predecessors. The debate about irrationalism is as old as the tradition of philosophy within which it is embedded. After all, the Pythagoreans apparently took the issue of irrationalism so seriously that they were reputed to have arranged a fatal accident at sea for a philosopher who had the temerity to reveal the irrationality they had encountered at the heart of mathematics.

Rather than recommend such violent measures for today's purveyors of irrationality, I should like to levy against them two charges of inconsistency. Of course, to charge those who reject reason with being unreasonable may itself seem unreasonable, and I would concede that in a sense accepting the sovereignty of reason is simply and necessarily a commitment, and not an arguable position. About reason itself, we must be fideists. Nevertheless, it is notable that the repudiation of reason has not prevented the appearance of a large number of substantial books and texts apparently consisting almost entirely of argument. To this extent, then irrationalists' actions belie their words. More substantially, however, their position is flawed by some unintended inconsistencies of a more old-fashioned sort.

The first of these is the problem already referred to, of the disappearing subject. There is, it seems, no position from which to survey the world, no place from which the correspondence or otherwise of our ideas with reality may be judged. And yet, the knowledge/power analysis associated with Foucault, or with feminism, or with the sociology of education, is entirely dependent on being able to locate a source of judgment, a determiner of knowledge. In other words, the power analysis itself depends upon the ability to locate, define and recognize a knowing subject. It is striking, too, that this recognition itself must tacitly be understood to take place from a secure vantage-point, and implies the existence of another subject or observer, at a higher level of judgment, who is the author and originator of the knowledge/power analysis itself.

Of course, the point of this analysis is to fractionalize, to suggest that there are only particular persons, located in particular times and places. But here a second inconsistency appears. For the ultimate object of attack here is the individual as construed by liberal philosophy and politics. This attack is, however, based on a very widespread misunder-

---

[4] Skinner describes Foucault, Wittgenstein, Feyerabend and Derrida as 'the grandest theorists of current practice throughout a wide range of the social disciplines' (1985, 21).

standing. For the individual of liberal theory is not a universal in the sense intended by its detractors—not a transparent, featureless entity—but, on the contrary, the ultimate particular, always set in contrast to the state, the political totality, the source of power. Not to be defined by membership of any group, this 'individual' is in the end a list of names—not an infinite or endless list, but one which could only be exhausted by enumerating all the human inhabitants, past and present, of the world. In other words, that to which opponents of liberalism most object is actually something they ought to accept as the logical terminus of their own point of view.

These quasi-metaphysical arguments are, perhaps, of purely theoretical interest. It is in its ethical and political consequences, however, that the contemporary debate has most significance and practical importance. Feyerabend makes the connection between metaphysics and morality clear when he writes that: (1975, p. 18) 'anarchism is not only possible, it is necessary . . . And Reason, at last, joins all those other abstract monsters such as Obligation, Duty, Morality, Truth, etc, which were once used to intimidate man and restrict his free and happy development.'

The judgment as to whether happiness is best served by the abolition of those abstractions is in the end a practical one. What I am certain, of, however, is that they cannot be abolished by philosophy itself. For philosophy to attempt this would be the paradox of Epimenides writ large. In other words, if what philosophers are currently saying is true, there is no need to listen to them. Only if what they say is false do they continue to be the guardians of a significant and important enquiry—an enquiry which is the common quest of a common human mind, based on a necessary prior commitment to truth and its attendant moral virtues.

Is Philosophy a 'Theory of Everything'?

G. M. K. HUNT

When Wittgenstein moved from Manchester to Cambridge he was following a path from the study of the natural sciences to the study of philosophy which was then not unusual, and has since become increasingly common. Russell had preceded him in that intellectual emigration and many more were to follow. Of the three philosophy departments I have been in, two were headed by natural scientists (and the third by an historian). Both my research supervisors in philosophy were natural scientists (as I was myself). Less surprising, but still significant, a considerable proportion of Presidents of the British Society for the Philosophy of Science were originally trained as natural scientists. Yet it is a subject still unrecognized by the Royal Society. The editors of both the *British Journal for the Philosophy of Science* and the journal *Analysis* were both originally natural scientists. Eminent scientists seem to feel impelled to discuss there own subjects in a wider context of philosophy. Bohr, Schrodinger, Kilmister, Hoyle, Hawking and Penrose, are but a few from a long list.

Of course their motives for moving into philosophy, sometimes out of science, are probably as many and varied as any human motives. But from their writings one feels that at least part of the rationale was to integrate their research into a wider whole—to seek a consonance between the apparently disparate parts of science and to produce a coherent, integrated view of human knowledge. This integrative aspect of philosophy is what I would like to examine here. Philosophy is, I think, the only likely integrator of all our knowledge because it is the only systematic study of both the knower and the known. Psychology singles out the knower for examination, and the rest of science, the objects of knowledge. Of course where the boundary between the two is drawn—at the edge of the cognitive faculties? the perceptual apparatus? the human body? the research group? the invisible college of science? the culture?—is a matter of continuing debate. But wherever and however it occurs it is inevitably a philosophical debate.

There are many other parts and divisions of philosophy. I shall not discuss them here. This is not to denigrate them, but simply to economize. I want to delineate and discuss one impulse to philosophise. It is the impulse to integrate all our knowledge into a comprehensive, consistent scheme, to produce *the* Theory of Everything.

To discuss a theory of everything is not, you will be relieved to know, to discuss everything. Nevertheless there are a number of different aspects of this topic I want to touch on. In discussing the relationship of philosophy to theories of everything I shall concentrate on the nearest and most likely candidate: the philosophy of science. I am not able to show that philosophy of science is typical of the rest of philosophy in respect of the issues I will raise. And different philosophers have seen the role and place of even philosophy of science quite differently. It is sufficient here to contrast the view which I am discussing with John Locke's *underlabourer* conception of the philosophical task: the task of analysis of scientific concepts and the making orderly the current scientific theories. Our view is the grand view of philosophy; to adapt Collingwood's terminology, philosophy is the master science.

Those who have heard John Barrow speak most eloquently on Theories of Everything, or perhaps read his excellent book, will know that theories of everything are not new. His examples show that they have been with us since the Greeks, and attempts to produce them have been one of the major guiding forces in nineteenth and twentieth century science. Their appearance, or assumed appearance, has guided, or in some cases misguided, policy making. I have in mind Professor G. H. Bryan's 1891 report to the British Association for the Advancement of Science (summarized in *Nature*, 1894), where he concluded that physics was virtually complete and that scarce educational resources should not be squandered on the training of any more physicists. The difference we notice today is that such policy conclusions are even less informed by the state of science but more by the state of the economy.

Philosophers too have produced such theories. May I mention W. V. O. Quine's small answer to the big question *what is there*. He said simply *Everything*. An answer which is as compendious as it is uninformative. It lacks—and this will be central to my paper—explanatory value.

The general plan of this paper is as follows. I will first look at the nature of a theory of everything. To do so I will examine the theories which philosophers of science have proposed about the nature of scientific theories. In doing so I will argue that the classical theories of scientific method are, at first sight, more suitable for this purpose than more modern theories of method. Nevertheless, I shall conclude that, as far as the analysis of theories of everything are concerned, these theories fail to find a place in theories of everything for that important function *explanation*.

Is Philosophy a 'Theory of Everything'?

To tackle the problem of the explanatory function of a theory of everything I shall first look at five distinct attempts to stop the infinite regress of explanations implicit in scientific theorizing. This regress is generated whenever it becomes possible to ask at each level of scientific explanation why the elements of the explanation are as they are and not otherwise. And the explanation of that fact in turn begs for a further physical explanation, and so on *ad infinitum*. But if each successive explanation in the ascending hierarchy stands in need itself of further explanation, then we have given no real explanation of the phenomena which our theories were produced to explain.

In discussing this destructive regress we shall come to the second main theme in my paper: the distinctive role philosophy could play in the resolution of the problem. I shall then succinctly, perhaps overly so, characterize the nature of this philosophical contribution by relating it to the Turing thesis—which is the fundamental principle of modern theories of computing. I shall show that this principle is false and that therefore this distinctive role of philosophy—or at least this branch of philosophy—is an illusion. That is, the view that philosophy is the master science, *the* theory of everything, is untenable.

I shall finish by producing a Grand Turing Thesis, which relegates both philosophy and computer science to being branches of applied science.

For the purposes of this paper I shall regard scientific theorizing as aiming to give us not only predictive power over the natural world but also an understanding of it. There is nothing radical in this bifurcation of aims. It is the centre-piece of the classical theories of explanation, and has become known as the symmetry thesis—if you can explain then you can predict and vice versa. And I shall interpret the explanation in a strong realist manner: to explain is to give a true description of higher level, or more general aspects of the world, from which we may infer descriptions of lower level, more particular events. It is worth noting that some influential philosophers, for example van Fraasen, are wholly opposed to this realist interpretation, while others, Cartwright and Hacking, would allow the realist more modest claims. Although I would have to change, and perhaps complicate my story to accommodate their views, I do not think it renders what I have to say irrelevant.

An explanation, then, is to be taken as a description of higher level, or more general features of the world. But how can mere descriptions of phenomena be explanatory? Often they are not. So-called *cross-section* theories which simply relate the values of one set of variables at a given time to another set are clearly not explanatory. For example, Boyle's Law, which relates the pressure of a given mass of gas to its volume is not intended as an explanation of the gas's behaviour—merely a codification of the same. To find an explanation of that behaviour we would need to find the underlying structure of the gas and the mechanisms involved in changes of state of this structure. Kinetic theory does this very nicely. This latter sort of theory might be called a process theory. It is often expressed using differential equations, and their solution gives a history of the evolution of the system. Boyle's Law comes out as a nice snapshot corollary.

But how can *any* description be explanatory without describing properties of some system which themselves stand in need of further explanation—and thus further description? We look to be involved in a regress which has no obvious stopping point. Philosophers have taken a variety of views about this regress of explanation. These views fall into two main classes: the classical and the modern.

Classical theories of science addressed the question of the nature of science by investigating traditional philosophical problems. These included the problem of what makes a (good) explanation as well as investigating both the structure of scientific theories and the relation of these theories to experimental evidence. An important element of this work was the development of a number of semantic theories of the significance of theoretical explanations. We shall return to this theme at the end of the section.

Although much progress was made in the detail of such studies they came under increasing criticism for their ahistorical assumptions and methods. Historians of science seemed more interested in questions related to scientific growth and change and saw the philosophers' preoccupation with formal, abstract relations between the elements of a theory as at best irrelevant, at worst misleading in so far as it ignored the dynamical aspects of the scientific enterprise. Practising scientists, as well as policy makers, largely concurred with this criticism.

So, more modern theories of scientific method, kick-started by the criticisms of Thomas Kuhn in his book *The Structure of Scientific Revolutions*, (1962), but foreshadowed in important ways by Popper and Reichenbach, concentrated on characterizing science by its method of growth. There are now many variations on this general theme, witness the work of Lakatos, Laudan, and many others. All have in common a concern with the growth of science, not only of its increasing truth-likeness (a neo-traditional problem about which there is much controversy) but with its increasing scope and content. A good theory is one which is poised for real growth. And a good explanation is that provided by a good theory. (Although recent work on explanation, for example Lipton's *Inference to the Best Explanation* (1991), has sought to reverse the order of this relationship.)

It is easy to see that any theory which claimed to be a (successful) theory of everything could not—by definition—found its claim to be scientific on a promise of further growth. This is ruled out in principle.

So to understand how such a theory might be a success, which is to say an explanatory success, we must return to classical—static—theories of the nature of science.

So apparently, inevitably, one is forced back to classical theories. One can identify six such classical views. Yet, I shall argue, they are all fatally flawed, and cannot be rescued by a philosophical kiss of life.

Of these six, the first two are semantic views of the nature of scientific, explanation. I have grouped them together under the title *semantic* because both address themselves to the sources of meaning, and explanatory potential, for the *theoretical* terms in a theory. By calling them theoretical we draw attention to their lack of direct empirical reference—electron or space-time point, for example. If a satisfactory theory of the reference of these terms—terms which bear the brunt of the explanatory function of theories—could be found then we might feel that the explanatory regress would be terminated. For then the explanation of the properties which these terms named could be explicated without begging the need of a yet higher level explanatory stage.

The first of these two semantic views is called the *implicit theory of meaning*. According to this view the meanings of the terms of the theory are those given both by their place in the theory and by the relation of the theory to experimental observation. This latter provides the initial meaning input. For example, mass in Newtonian theory is just that property which requires force to accelerate and acceleration is given meaning by measurement of displacements and times in the laboratory. Force is also implicitly defined—hence the name of the theory of meaning—in terms of mass and of displacement and time.

There are many difficulties with such a theory of meaning. I wish here to raise only the difficulty which arises when it is applied to a theory of everything. The theory has the appearance of vicious circularity. It is like explaining why opium sends you to sleep by referring to its dormative virtue, when dormative virtue really just means *inclined to put to sleep*. In the case of a theory as extensive as Newtonian Mechanics the circularity is less obvious. But nevertheless, we are saying no more than the explanatory elements of theory are just, and no more than, what they need to be to allow derivation of the phenomena. The theory is no more than a tautology, or platitude, in respect of its explanatory power.

But in a theory which is not about *everything*, there are usually related theories which have terms in common. For example force appears in physiology as a consequence of muscular action. So we can escape the implied circularity in Newtonian Mechanics by appealing outside the theory in question to give the required extra meaning and hence explanatory power to the subject theory. Clearly this escape route is not available to the proposer of a theory of everything.

A similar difficulty afflicts the second semantic view. This view is that theoretical terms derive some of their meaning via analogical relations with theories other than those in which they appear. The theories on which they draw are those with a similar structure to the theory at issue. So Bohr's atomic theory drew on similarities between it and the theory of the solar system to give significance and hence explanatory power to its theoretical terms. The motion of billiard balls, subject as they are to Newton's Laws gave significance to the particles of kinetic theory. The list is long and the details are complex. (See Mary Hesse's *Models and Analogies in Science* (1964) for a particularly clear discussion.)

We do not need to know the details to see, again, that a theory of everything cannot avail itself of other recognized theories with similar structure. For the other theories must share their subject matter with the theory of everything. So they are either identical which is no help at all, or subsets and thus not theories of everything. Or they are false and explain nothing. Either way they cannot provide a model for the theory in question and therefore cannot facilitate the hoped for explanatory power needed.

So the classical semantic views of the meaning of theoretical terms do not provide us with any means of escaping from an explanatory regress. Nor, we saw, can modern theories of science. We seem to be at an impasse. However there are some particular classical views about regress of explanations which address the issue directly. In the hope of salvation we now turn to these further four views.

The first view could be called the *linguistic* solution. It is espoused by Braithwaite in his 1953 book *Scientific Explanation*, but variants of this view can also be found in Popper and many other writers of the period. The view is curious, since Braithwaite, like other sensible people, does not believe that a study of language is a good starting point for a sound knowledge of the world. Rather, our language is more like a repository of dead theories. Nevertheless, Braithwaite is trying here to dissolve, rather than solve a problem. His suggestion is simple: We should regard the highest level laws in our theories as expressing physically necessary truths and thus, not being contingent, not in need of further explanation. Ultimate explanation is a pseudo problem.

To use Russell's phrase this view has all the virtue of *theft over honest work*. To be sure Braithwaite no doubt felt impelled to this view by good Humean reasons, but to allow such power of fiat over philosophical problems invites a lack of proper respect for the subject and its methods. His conclusion is, however, not unlike that of other philosophers who start from different premises. Brian Ellis in his 'The Nature and Origin of Newton's Laws of Motion' in Robert Colodny's *Beyond The Edge Of Certainty* (1965) provides a detailed, historically grounded, argument which seeks to end this vexing regress of explanation.

This second view of the fate of explanatory ultimates might be called *conventionalist*. The arguments are quite complex: an example will serve our needs. Consider a person looking through a window and seeing a stone thrown past, curving in a parabolic path. If the viewer held Aristotelian views the stone's behaviour would not need explanation, except to observe that the stone was naturally seeking its proper place. Only if the stone had not fallen would a causal explanation be sought: a forceful updraft of air, for example

A Newtonian would take a different view. The falling stone would be seen as deviating from a natural straight path because of the attraction of the earth's gravitational field. A stone moving in a straight line requires no explanation for its particular behaviour, only a deviation requires explanation, and this is provided by the gravitational force.

Contrast this with a General Relativistic view. Like the Aristotelian view, the parabolic path is in no need of explanation. It is really a straight line or geodesic in space-time, and represents the natural, unforced motion of the stone. It is any deviation from the geodesic, such as a straight path in 3-space which would be in need of explanation.

I wish to stress here that I am not concerned with the particular causal explanation of the motion *per se*. That level of explanation merely requires us to find the external origins of the perturbing forces. I *am* concerned here with the explanation of the nature of the stone and its habitat which shows why it reacts to perturbation (or lack therof) in the way it does. I am concerned with the theoretical rationale of the whole interacting system, not just an identification of the particular causes acting in a particular case.

These examples are not an argument. Ellis uses them to draw attention to the differing *conventions* about natural or forced motion implicit in physical theories. That we have *no* alternative to accept a fundamental *conventional* element in our explanation requires an analysis of the structure of our theories and this is what Ellis does in considering the foundations of Newtonian Mechanics. But if we had chosen to analyse a different theory would we get the same result?

We shall see that the answer is 'no!' In consequence we cannot claim that we have established a general philosophical truth about the existence and nature of the endpoint of regresses of explanation. We are moving toward my ultimate conclusion that attempts to stop the regress of explanation must be parasitic on scientific theories.

A third view from this group, and the penultimate of the sub-group of four direct attacks on the problem of explanatory regress, is that of Harré, given in his *The Principles of Scientific Thinking* (1970). In his

225

analysis of current scientific thought he reaches a conclusion very different from that of Ellis. The difference is so radical that I will call this view *ontological*. Harré observes that the regress of explanation occurs because we hypothesize entities which we endow with properties, usually to some metrical degree, specified numerically. Electrons, for example have a particular quantity of mass, charge and perhaps other properties and this explains much sub-atomic phenomena. But why do they have *just* this degree of *those* properties? And what *is* the electron that allows these properties to co-occur? For when we move the mass, lo!, we move the charge. Clearly we deserve an explanation of this aspect of micro-existence. But if we simply invoke leptons, bosons, photons, etc., propertied as they are, we invite the same criticism. It is not clear that even super-strings avoid this problem.

Harré notes that there is one (he thinks only one) entity which does not beg this explanatory question. It is a field. Perhaps an electromagnetic field. For a field is wholly described by its effect at a place. There is nothing extra that *has* the effect. As with Ellis's examples, the size and shape of the field in a particular case is caused by external agencies. But our concern is the fundamental physical relations through which these agencies produce their effects.

Nor is there more than one effect, so the coexistence of properties which puzzled us in the case of the electron is not a problem either. This is because, as Ellis also notes, forces are both a necessary and sufficient condition for their effects, and are thus definitionally related to them. So once we have the field we no longer need a further, higher level explanation of why fields act as they do. If Harré is right we would expect theories of everything to be based on fields. At the moment they are not, but that does not show him wrong, merely anticipatory. I will return to Harré's view later, for if he is right then the next, and last view I wish to discuss will fall, and with it the view of Philosophy I am assessing.

This regress of explanation I have been discussing has attracted the attention of not only the professional worriers, the philosophers of science, but also the amateur worriers, the practising scientists. One eminent example of the latter was the physicist John Archibald Wheeler, whose work in physics was crowned by the production of a theory of everything called 'Geometrodynamics.' (Wheeler, 1979)

The fourth and last view, I will discuss in the context of work by Wheeler and his commentator Deutsch. It might be called *epistemic* since it involves the search for a regress stopper which arises out of the nature of the knowledge seeking process of the enquirer.

Wheeler took the view that physical laws could not appear in a truly fundamental description of nature. His reasoning is familiar. If there were no fundamental explanation in our physical theories then parts of nature must remain inexplicable—a conclusion which is incompatible with the intellectual forces driving science. But if this fundamental description involved a physical law then we would have no explanation of why the law took the form it did, rather than some other. Hence there can be no ultimate physical law, a situation he characterized as *law without law*.

Wheeler looked at a number of possible solutions to this quandary— chaos, pure mathematics, invariance principles, the active role of measurement and consciousness—and rejected them for reasons any philosopher would recognize. According to Deutsch, commenting on Wheeler, although Wheeler unsuccessfully proposed solutions, he rightly rejected the view that the search was either pointless or fruitless. However Deutsch identified an epistemic principle which he claimed would solve Wheeler's problem without falling victim to the criticisms which Wheeler himself recognized. Deutsch believed that the epistemic principle that he unearthed could be known *a priori*, because it *must* be assumed in the process of physical enquiry. This might be thought to be an example of a transcendental argument in physics. We shall eventually conclude that it is not.

The principle he sought had a status not unlike that of the Anthropic Principle. We cannot deny such a principle while at the same time producing theories of the world. In this it is also not unlike Descartes' *Cogito ergo sum*.

The principle might read *every theory can be encoded in the states of realizable physical systems*. In other words our physical theories must not exclude our existing *and doing theoretical physics*.

But with both of these principles (the anthropic and the coding principle) there seems to be no loss in simply regarding them as further empirical restraints on our theories—no different from common experimental testing. After all, if one of the results derivable from a theory entailed the impossibility of humans producing the theory then that theory is clearly refuted. And this situation is no different logically from the refutation of a theory which predicted that the earth must be made of green cheese. Both theories simply fall foul of easily performed experimental tests.

But Deutsch's principle appeared to have, in addition, an *a priori* twist. It relies on a mathematical thesis: The Church-Turing thesis. So if the principle did end the regress of explanation without itself being a physical principle, then Deutsch would have succeded where Wheeler had failed. He would have produced a *law without law*. But because the principle is epistemic rather than physical, it looks as though he is playing the philosophical trump card which will give him the game.

Re-worded to make its reliance on the Church-Turing explicit, the principle is: *Every physical system can be perfectly simulated by a universal model computing machine operating by finite means*. The word simulated is, I think, doing no more than restricting the thesis to process theories to which I referred earlier. In due course we shall have to question the final *"by finite means"*.

But how could such a principle end the regress of explanation? It does so by restricting the number of empirically supported theories of everything to just one. That is, it attempts to show that the empirically successful theory of everything is unique, and in doing so it answers the question *why is the fundamental law(s) of physics as it is and not otherwise?* by production of a non-physical principle.

The principle does not replace the need for experimental testing of any theory of everything. That process, and the methodological, logical and philosophical problems which it raises are not answered, nor attempted to be answered. It merely addresses the query about the nature of the most theoretical part of an empirically satisfactory theory of everything.

How does the Church-Turing thesis restrict the choice of theoretical staring points of a theory of everything and give us the required uniqueness? Notice first that it is a thesis, not a theorem. It cannot be proved mathematically, but it could be disproved by a counter-example. The thesis sets limits to computational power. It surmises the nature of the most powerful computing machine, and shows that its power has limitations. Power, here, does not refer to practical matters—size and speed. It refers to ultimate capability.

So Deutsch hopes that the limits on computability set by the Church-Turing thesis will deliver a unique theory of everything which is empirically satisfactory. Deutsch does not show the relation between the thesis and his hoped-for uniqueness, for the very good reason that he had no extant, empirically satisfactory theory of everything to link it to. (Wheeler's Geomagnetodynamic offering is now seen as a theory of much, rather than a theory of everything, and even the much canvassed superstring theory of everything is far from being demonstrated as a theory of everything in physics, let alone taking on *everything*.) But if it is shown that the Church-Turing thesis is not the pure epistemic principle that Deutsch thought, then we will have shown that it cannot do the job he hoped.

To see how the thesis delivers the hoped-for constraint on theorizing we need to examine the arguments for the thesis. The argument takes the following form:

1. We identify an (ideal) physical mechanism (the computing hardware) with the requisite structure. The mechanism that Turing devised now bears his name. It consisted of a paper tape as long as required and

a moving read/write head which traversed the tape erasing and writing symbols.

2. We give a semantical interpretation to the states which allows the running of the mechanism to be regarded as a computation of a function. In a sense this is equivalent to writing the software which allows the machine to perform the calculation. In Turing's original machine the programme was a small set of conditional instructions which controlled the machine's writing, moving stepwise along the tape and its reaction to subsequent symbols. Turing spent considerable effort finding a very simple set of instructions which was still powerful enough to let the machine carry out mathematical calculation. On the other hand, the instruction set was simple and mechanical enough to persuade all concerned that no mathematical tricks were hidden up its sleeve. It was a dumb machine.

3. The semantics or programming language defines what we mean by a function. That is, what counts as the starting point and ending point of a programme or calculation.

4. We can now show that there is an enumerable number of distinct Turing machines, each of which computes a function.

5. We can also show that there is a non-denumerable number of functions.

6. Hence there are a non-denumerable number of uncomputable functions—there are infinitely more functions than there are Turing machines, so if a Turing machine is the best we can do there is an infinity of uncomputable functions.

The *thesis* is that there is no more powerful computational device than a Turing machine. Over the last fifty or so years various other devices—cascades of Turing machines, register machines or abacuses, recursive function theory, parallel computers, neural networks—have been invented and all are probably equivalent to the original. The thesis still stands (at least until near the end of this paper).

Functions seem one thing, theories another. Fortunately, Chaitan, a computer scientist interested in algorithmic information theory, has shown that all theories can be expressed as functions—that is programmed on a Turing machine. So the Turing thesis provides Deutsch and Wheeler with an apparently non-physical thesis which constrains the derivation of physical theory. In short, a non-trivial but non-physical primitive hypothesis. Just the trick for ending the regress of explanation!

But we should recall Harré's argument about the uniqueness of fields as the ultimate explanatory entity. If he is right, indeed if fields exist, then the Turing thesis may be wrong. For the mechanisms invoked by Turing, and his challengers were discrete. The functions they dealt with started only with integers. All other mathematical entities were constructed from these integer representations. More importantly, the proof relies on us not being able to finish a task which has enumerably infinite extent.

The natural numbers, 1, 2, 3, . . ., are enumerably infinite (by definition). Any computational task which can be put in a sequence with all the natural numbers cannot be completed since there is no last number; a number after which we can find none more.

The uncomputable functions are those which would require us to first finish an enumerably infinite sequence of calculations then do some more—a clear impossibility for a Turing machine. But the physics of fields are different. They are continuous entities. We seem to need the real numbers, not the integers to describe them. More importantly, to describe the influence of a field on, say, a conductor, we need an integral equation, for example the Biot-Savart law. So the interaction of fields on objects actually depends on an integral, a sum of a non-enumerable sequence of computations. So it looks as though the objective world, in contrast to our theories, actually works by completing calculations beyond the reach of a Turing machine. A similar point is made in Stannart 1990.

We therefore have here a physical mechanism which might be given a semantic interpretation to refute the Turing thesis. But there is a difficulty in providing such a semantical interpretation of the states of the system. Although such a system might possess a continuum of states, we could not discriminate any two states below some level of measurement accuracy. So we appear to be back to a finite number of discriminable states, and hence a standard Turing machine.

But such a restriction on the totality of results does not prohibit any particular result. There is still a non-enumerable number of functions we might have calculated, but just which is never perfectly clear. We are still able to perform a non-enumerable calculation in a finite time—whether this is useful is a different question, one which depends on the nature of the function being calculated. But by having the capacity to perform an infinite number of Turing style calculations in a finite time, we can solve the famous *halting problem* and hence show that the Turing thesis is false.

There are two consequences of this claim, both fatal to the Wheeler–Deutsch progranmme. The first is that we can no longer show that their epistemic/computation principle yields non-trivial results: there may be no uncomputable functions and if so the principle is idle.

Second, any principle such as this depends upon the truth of a physical thesis (in this case field theory) so it is not epistemic either.

The mechanisms available for interpretation in a Turing-like argument is part of *what is to explained, not part of the explanation*.

The relativization of the Turing thesis to that of physical theory I shall dub the *Grand Turing Thesis* since it may take us smoothly and in some style over the whole terrain of physics. Whether a field theoretic, or a superstring theoretic Grand Turing machine yields uncomputable functions I do not know. But this does not matter for the present argument. It is the relativization of the computer-theoretic result to the nature of the world, and hence the relativization of these epistemic arguments to the current physical theories which destroys the Deutsch–Wheeler programme.

I have tried to show that Philosophy, construed as a the master science, *the* theory of everything, is impossible. Likewise I appear to have relegated Computer Science, and perhaps Philosophy, to the outer reaches of applied physics. I therefore conclude by commending Locke's under-labourer conception of Philosophy: not least because in the present political climate it is likely to be better rewarded.

References

Adorno, T. W. 1976. 'Introduction', in *The Positivist Dispute in German Sociology*, D. Frisby (ed.) (London: Heinemann).

Aldrich, V. 1989. 'Photographing Facts', *American Philosophical Quarterly*, Vol. 26, No. 1.

Almond, B. 1990. *The Philosophical Quest*. (Harmondsworth: Penguin).

Apel, K.-O. 1979. 'Types of Social Science in the Light of Human Cognitive Interests', in *Philosophical Disputes in the Social Sciences*, S. C. Brown (ed.) (Brighton: Harvester).

Apel, K.-O. 1980. *Towards a Transformation of Philosophy*, trans. Adey and Frisby. (London: Routledge & Kegan Paul). Originally published in 1973 as *Transformation der Philosophie*. (Frankfurt am M.: Suhrkamp).

Arnold, M. 1960. *Culture and Anarchy*. (Cambridge University Press). (First edn. 1869).

Augustine, St. 1909. *The Confessions*. (London: Chatto & Windus).

Ayer, A. J. 1990. *The Meaning of Life*. (London: Wiedenfeld & Nicholson).

Bambrough, J. R. 1974. *Wisdom: Twelve Essays*. (Oxford: Blackwell).

Bar-Hillel, Y. 1969. 'Formal Logic and Natural Languages (A Symposium)', in *Foundations of Language*, Volume V.

Berkeley, G. 1950. *A New Theory of Vision* and other Select Philosophical Writings. Everyman's Library. (London: Dent).

Berkeley, G. 1962. *The Principles of Human Knowledge*. G. J. Warnock, (ed.) (London: Fontana).

Bitter, F. 1960. *Magnets, The Education of a Physicist*. (London: Heinemann).

Boolos, G. S. and Jeffrey, R. C. 1989. *Computability and Logic*. (Cambridge University Press).

Bordo, S. 1991. 'Feminism, Postmodernism and Gender Scepticism', in Nicholson 1991.

Braithwaite R. B. 1953. *Scientific Explanation*. (Cambridge University Press).

Bryan, G. H. 1894. Summary of a Report to the British Association for the Advancement of Science, *Nature*, 50.

Cacoullos, A. R. 1974. *Thomas Hill Green: Philosopher of Rights*. (New York: Twayne Publishers).

Carnap, R. 1959. 'The Elimination of Metaphysics through the Logical Analysis of Language', in *Logical Positivism*, A. J. Ayer (ed.) (New York: Free Press).

Cassirer, E. 1981. *Kant's Life and Thought*. (New Haven: Yale University Press).

Chaitin, G. J. 1987. *Algorithmic Information Theory*. (Cambridge University Press).

Chihara, L. and Fodor, J. 1965. 'Operationalism and Ordinary Language', *American Philosophical Quarterly*.

Clark, R. W. 1975. *The Life of Bertrand Russell*. (London: Cape & Wiedenfeld and Nicholson).

References

Cohen, B. 1981. *Education and the Individual*. (London: Allen & Unwin).

Cohen, B. 1982. *Means and Ends in Education*. (London: Allen & Unwin).

Collingwood, R. G. 1944. *An Autobiography*. (Harmondsworth: Penguin Books).

Copi, I. 1953. *Introduction to Logic*. (New York: Macmillan).

Dearden, R. F. 1968. *The Philosophy of Primary Education*. (London: Routledge & Kegan Paul).

Deutsch, D. 1965. 'In Wheeler's Notion of "Law Without Law" in Physics', *Foundations of Physics*, 16, 6.

Dewey, J. 1909. *How we Think*. D. C. Heath & Co.

Di Stefano, C. 1991. 'Dilemmas of Difference: Feminism, Modernity and Postmodernism', in Nicholson, 1991.

Eliot, T. S. 1933. *The Use of Poetry and the Use of Criticism*. (London: Faber).

Eliot, T. S. 1948. *Notes towards the Definition of Culture*. (London: Faber).

Ellis, B. D. 1965. 'The Origin and Status of Newton's Laws.' in *Beyond the Edge of Certainty*, R. G. Colodny (ed.) (New Jersey: Prentice Hall).

Feyerabend, P. K. 1975. *Against Method*. (London: New Left Books).

Findlay, J. N. 1973. 'My Encounters with Wittgenstein', *Philosophical Forum*.

Fisher, A. (ed.) 1988. *Critical Thinking: Proceedings of the First British Conference on Informal Logic and Critical Thinking*. (Norwich: University of East Anglia).

Flax, J. 1991. 'Postmodernism and Gender Relations in Feminist Theory' in Nicholson 1991.

Foucault, M. 1978. *The History of Sexuality: an Introduction*. (New York: Pantheon).

Foucault, M. 1979. *Discipline and Punish: the Birth of the Prison*, trans. A. Sheridan (New York: Vintage Books).

Freeman, M. 1991. 'Speaking about the Unspeakable: genocide and philosophy', *Journal of Applied Philosophy*, vol. 8, i.

Gilbert, M. 1989. 'Rationality and Salience'. *Philosophical Studies*, Vol. 57, pp. 61–77

Glover, J. 1977. *Causing Death and Saving Lives*. (Harmondsworth: Penguin).

Govier, T. 1987. *Problems in Argument Analysis and Evaluation*. (Dordrecht: Foris).

Goytisolo, J. 1991. In *The Times Literary Supplement*, 9 December.

Grice, H. P. and Strawson, P. F. 1956. 'In Defence of a Dogma', *Philosophical Review*, Vol. 65, pp. 141–158.

Grice, H. P. 1975. 'Logic and Conversation', in *Syntax and Semantics*, P. Cole and J. L. Morgan (eds) Vol. 3, *Speech Acts*. (New York: Academic Press).

Habermas, J. 1971. *Knowledge and Human Interests*. (Boston: Beacon). (Originally published in 1968 as *Erkenntnis und Interesse*. (Frankfurt am M.: Suhrkamp).

Hacker, P. M. S. 1972. *Insight and Illusion*. (Oxford: Oxford University Press).

Hamlyn, D. W. 1967. 'Logical and Psychological Aspects of Learning', in *The Concept of Education*, R. S. Peters (ed.) (London: Routledge & Kegan Paul).

Hamlyn, D. W. 1978. *Experience and the Growth of Understanding*. (London: Routledge & Kegan Paul).

Harré, H. R. 1970. *The Principles of Scientific Thinking*. (London: Macmillan).

Hartsock, N. 1991. 'Foucault on Power: a theory for women?', in Nicholson 1991.

Heidegger, M. 1962. *Being and Time*, trans. J. McQuarrie and E. Robinson, (Oxford: Blackwell

Heidegger, M. 1985. *History of the Concept of Time*. (Bloomington: Indiana University Press).

Heller, E. 1988. *The Importance of Nietzsche*. (Chicago: Chicago University Press).

Hesse, M. B. 1964. *Models and Analogies in Science*. (Indiana: University of Notre Dame Press).

Hobbes, T. 1651. *Leviathan*. (London: Fontana, 1962).

Housman, A. E. 1945. *The Selected Poems of A. E. Housman*. (New York: Armed Services Edition).

Hume, D. 1739. *A Treatise of Human Nature*. (London: J. M. Dent, 1911).

Hume, D. 1748a. *An Enquiry Concerning Human Understanding*, L. Selby-Bigge (ed.) (Oxford: Oxford University Press, 1902).

Hume, D. 1748b. 'Of the Original Contract' in *Moral and Political Essays*. Reprinted in E. Barker (ed.) Social Contract. (London: Oxford University Press, 1947).

Husserl, E. 1970. *The Paris Lectures*. (The Hague: Martinus Nijhoff).

Illich, I. 1971. *De-schooling Society*. (London: Calder & Boyars).

Illich, I. 1976. *Limits to Medicine*. (London: Calder & Boyars).

Inhelder, B. and Piaget, J. 1958. *The Growth of Logical Thinking from Childhood to Adolescence*. (London: Routledge & Kegan Paul).

Johnson, R. H. and Blair, J. A. 1985. 'Informal Logic: the Past Five Years 1978–1983', *American Philosophical Quarterly*, Vol. 22, No. 3, pp. 181–196.

Johnson-Laird, P. N. 1983. *Mental Models*. (Cambridge University Press).

Kahane, H. 1971. *Logic and Contemporary Rhetoric: The Use of Reason in Everyday Life*. (Belmont, California: Wadsworth).

Kenny, A. 1982. 'Wittgenstein on the Nature of Philosophy' in McGuinness (1982)

Kitchener, R. F. 1986. *Piaget's Theory of Knowledge: Genetic Epistemology and Scientific Reason*. (New York: Yale University Press).

Kitchener, R. F. 1990. 'Do Children Think Philosophically?', *Metaphilosophy*, Vol. 21, No. 4.

Kuhn, T.S. 1962. *The Structure of Scientific Revolutions*. (Chicago: Phoenix Books).

Lakatos, I. 1970. 'The Methodology of Scientific Research Programmes', in *Criticism and the Growth of Knowledge*, I. Lakatos and A. Musgrave (eds.) (Cambridge University Press).

References

Lamb, D. 1988. *Down the Slippery Slope: Arguing in Applied Ethics.* (London: Croom Helm).

Lawrence, D. H. 1960. *The Ladybird.* (London: Penguin).

Levy, P. 1979. *Moore: G. E. Moore and the Cambridge Apostles.* (Oxford: Oxford University Press).

Lewis, D. 1969. *Convention: A Philosophical Study.* (Cambridge, Mass.: Harvard University Press).

Lewis, D. 1986. *On the Plurality of Worlds.* (Oxford: Blackwell).

Lipman, M. 1974. *Harry Stottlemeier's Discovery.* (New Jersey: IAPC).

Lipman, M. 1989. 'The Institute for the Advancement of Philosophy for Children—looking backwards and looking forward', *Cogito*, Vol. 3, No. 12.

Lipman, M., Shary, A. M. and Oscanyan, F. S. 1977. *Philosophy in the Classroom.* (New Jersey: IAPC).

Lipton, P. 1991. *Inference to the Best Explanation.* (London: Routledge).

Locke, J. 1979. *An Essay Concerning Human Understanding*, P. H. Nidditch (ed.) (Oxford: Oxford University Press).

MacIntyre, A. 1981. *After Virtue.* (London: Duckworth).

MacIntyre, A. 1988. *Whose Justice? Which Rationality?* (London: Duckworth).

McGuinness, B. (ed.) 1982. *Wittgenstein and his Times.* (Oxford: Blackwell).

McGuire, W. and Hull, R. F. C. 1980. *C. G. Jung Speaking: Interviews and Encounters.* (London: Pan Books).

McTaggart, J. 1988. *The Nature of Existence*, Vol II. (Cambridge University Press).

Malcolm, N. 1986. *Nothing is Hidden: Wittgenstein's criticism of his early work.* (Oxford: Blackwell).

Margolis, J. 1991. *The Truth about Relativism.* (Oxford: Blackwell).

Matthews, G. 1980. *Philosophy and the Young Child.* (Cambridge, Mass.: Harvard University Press).

Mill, J. S. 1873. *Autobiography.* The World's Classics Edition. (Oxford: Oxford University Press, 1924).

Monk, R. 1990. *Ludwig Wittgenstein: The Duty of Genius.* (London: Jonathan Cape).

Moore, G. E. 1903. *Principia Ethica.* (Cambridge University Press).

Nagel, T. 1986. *The View from Nowhere.* (Oxford: Oxford University Press).

Nicholson, L. (ed.) 1991. *Feminism and Postmodernism.* (London: Routledge).

Ortega y Gasset, J. 1963. *Man and People.* (New York: Norton).

Ortega y Gasset, J. 1964. *What is Philosophy.* (New York: Norton).

Passmore, J. R. 1957. *A Hundred Years of Philosophy.* (Harmondsworth: Penguin).

Pears, D. 1988. *The False Prison.* (Oxford: Oxford University Press).

Popper, K. 1976. *Unended Quest.* (London: Fontana).

Pitcher, G. (ed.) 1968. *Wittgenstein.* (London: Macmillan).

Putnam, H. 1981. *Reason, Truth and History.* (Cambridge University Press).

Quine, W. V. 1951. 'Two Dogmas of Empiricism', *Philosophical Review*, Jan. Reprinted in Quine 1953.

Quine, W. V. 1952. *Methods of Logic.* (London: Routledge).

Quine, W. V. 1953. *From a Logical Point of View*. (New York: Harper and Row).

Radford, C. 1989. *The Examined Life*. (Aldershot: Gower).

Read, H. 1943. *Education through Art*. (London: Faber and Faber).

Redpath, J. 1990. *Ludwig Wittgenstein*. (London: Duckworth).

Richards, I. A. 1950. *Coleridge on Imagination*. (London: Routledge).

Richards, I. A. 1953. *Practical Criticism*. (London: Routledge).

Robinson, W. 1988. 'Philosophy for Children', in Fisher, 1988.

Rorty, R. 1980. *Philosophy and the Mirror of Nature*. (Oxford: Blackwell).

Rorty, R. 1985. 'Solidarity or Objectivity?' in *Post-Analytic Philosophy*, J. Rajchman and C. West (eds.) (New York: Columbia).

Rorty, R. 1989. *Contingency, Irony and Solidarity*. (Cambridge University Press).

Russell, B. 1948. *A History of Western Philosophy*. (London: Allen and Unwin).

Russell, B. 1953. *Mysticism and Logic*. And other Essays. (London: Penguin Books).

Russell, B. 1959. *My Philosophical Development*. (London: Allen and Unwin).

Russell, B. 1963. 'My Mental Development', in *The Philosophy of Bertrand Russell*, P. A. Schilpp (ed.), Vol. I. (New York: Harper and Row). Originally published in 1944 in the Library of Living Philosophers series.

Russell, B. 1983. *Collected Papers of Bertrand Russell* Blackwell, K. *et al.* (eds) (London: Allen & Unwin).

Ryle, G. 1949. *The Concept of Mind*. (London: Hutchinson.

Ryle, G. 1954. *Dilemmas*. (Cambridge University Press).

Ryle, G. 1953. *Formal and Informal Logic*. (Cambridge University Press).

Ryle, G. 1966. *Plato's Progress*. (Cambridge University Press).

Salmon, W. C. 1990. *Four Decades of Scientific Explanation*. (Minneapolis: University of Minnesota Press).

Sartre, J.-P. 1943. *L'Etre et le Néant*. (Paris: Gallimard).

Singer, P. and Kuhse, H. 1985. *Should the Baby Live?* (Oxford: Oxford University Press).

Skinner Q. 1985. *The Return of Grand Theory in the Human Sciences*. (Cambridge University Press).

Smith, A. 1759. *Theory of Moral Sentiments*. (Oxford: Oxford University Press, 1976).

Smith, A. J. 1992. *Metaphysical Wit*. (Cambridge University Press).

Stannart, M. 1990. 'X-Machines and the Halting Problem: Building a Super Turing Machine', in *Formal Aspects of Computing*, Vol. 2, No. 4

Sugden, R. 1991. 'Rational Choice: A Survey of Contributions to Economics and Philosophy'. *Economic Review*, vol. 101, pp. 751–785.

Tolstoy, L. 1854. *Boyhood* in *Childhood, Boyhood, Youth*. Penguin Classics. 1964, (Harmondsworth: Penguin, 1964).

Updike, J. 1986. *Self-Consciousness: Memoirs*. (London: Penguin).

von Wright, G. H. 1982 'Wittgenstein in Relation to his Times', in *Wittgenstein*. (Oxford: Blackwell).

References

Warnock, M. 1987. 'Do Human Cells have Rights?', *Bioethics*, 1, 1987, pp. 1–14.

Weil, S. 1951. *Waiting on God*, trans. E. Cranford (London: Fontana).

Wheeler. J. A. 1979. *Relativity, Quanta and Cosmology*, F. de Finis (ed.) (New York: Harcourt Brace Jovanovich).

Wiggins, D. 1991. 'Moral Cognitivism, Moral Relativism and Motivating Moral Beliefs', Aristotelian Society, *Proceedings,* Vol. LXXXXI, pp. 61–85.

Wilson, Edmund, 1971. *Axel's Castle*. (London: Fontana-Collins).

Winter, R. 1991. 'Looking out on a Bolder Landscape', *Times Higher Education Supplement*, 18 October.

Wisdom, J. 1953. *Philosophy, Metaphysics and Psycho-Analysis*. (Oxford: Blackwell).

Wittgenstein, L. 1949. *Tractatus Logico-Philosophicus*. (Oxford: Blackwell).

Wittgenstein, L. 1953. *Philosophical Investigations*, trans. G. E. M. Anscombe. (Oxford: Blackwell).

Wittgenstein, L. 1956. *Remarks on the Foundations of Mathematics*, G. H. von Wright, R. Rhees and G. E. M. Anscombe (eds), trans. G. E. M. Anscombe, (Oxford: Blackwell).

Wittgenstein, L. 1958. *The Blue and Brown Books*. (Oxford: Blackwell).

Wittgenstein, L. 1965. 'A Lecture on Ethics', *Philosophical Review*, January

Wittgenstein, L. 1966. *Lectures and Conversations on Aesthetics and Religion*, C. Barrett (ed.) (Oxford: Blackwell).

Wittgenstein, L. 1967. *Zettel*. (Oxford: Blackwell).

Wittgenstein, L. 1969. *Notebooks, 1914–1916*. G. H. von Wright and G. E. M. Anscombe (eds) trans. G. E. M. Anscombe (Oxford: Blackwell).

Wittgenstein, L. 1975a. *Lectures on the Foundations of Mathematics*, C. Diamond (ed.) (Chicago: Chicago University Press).

Wittgenstein, L. 1975b. *Philosophical Grammar*. R. Rees (ed.), trans. A. Kenny (Oxford: Blackwell).

Yalden-Thomas, D. C. 1974. 'The Virginia Lectures', in Bambrough 1974.

Young, M. (ed.) 1971. *Knowledge and Control: New Directives for the Sociology of Education*. (London: Collier Macmillan).

Notes on Contributors

Brenda Almond is Professor of Moral and Social Philosophy at the University of Hull. She is one of the founders of the Society for Applied Philosophy, which she now chairs while being Joint Editor of its *Journal*. She is a contributor to Philosophy and her latest book is *The Philosophical Quest* (Penguin, 1990).

Stuart Brown is Professor of Philosophy at the Open University. Editor of the Royal Institute volume *Objectivity and Cultural Divergence* and editor of or contributor to many others, he is the author of books on Leibniz and on the philosophy of religion and of papers on late seventeenth-century philosophy.

Frank Cioffi is Professor of Philosophy at the University of Essex and has contributed articles to *Philosophy* and to Vols. 4 and 16 in this series. His many articles on Wittgenstein and on Freud include 'Wittgenstein on Freud's "abominable mess"' in Vol. 28.

Ilham Dilman is Professor of Philosophy at University College, Swansea. The latest of his many books is *Phaedo: Philosophy and the Philosophical Life* (Macmillan, 1992). He has contributed many articles to *Philosophy* and its supplements over the last 20 years.

Alec Fisher of the University of East Anglia is the author of *The Logic of Real Arguments* (Cambridge University Press, 1988). He is to be Assistant Director of the Centre for Critical Thinking and Moral Critique in California in 1992–93.

Martin Hollis is Professor of Philosophy at the University of East Anglia. He contributed to the Royal Institute volumes *Philosophy and Medical Welfare* and *Philosophy and Practice*, and among his books is *Invitation to Philosophy* (Blackwell, 1985).

G. M. K. Hunt, Senior Lecturer in Philosophy at the University of Warwick, is the Editor of the *British Journal for the Philosophy of Science*. He edited the Institute's supplement *Philosophy and Politics* (1989).

Bryan Magee is a Visiting Fellow of Wolfson College, Oxford, and Honorary Senior Research Fellow in the History of Ideas at King's College, London. Formerly a Member of Parliament for 9 years, he is the Opera critic of the *Independent on Sunday*. His books include *Popper* (1973) and *Schopenhauer* (1983). His *Men of Ideas* (1978) and *The Great Philosophers* (1987) were based on his two series of televised discussion programmes.

Mary Midgley was formerly Senior Lecturer in Philosophy at the University of Newcastle on Tyne. Her first book was *Beast and Man* (Cornell Press, 1978) and her latest is *Science as Salvation* (Routledge, 1992).

Notes on Contributors

Anthony Palmer is Professor of Philosophy at the University of Southampton. He has contributed articles to *Philosophy* and to previous volumes in this series. His *Concept and Object: the Unity of the Proposition in Logic and Psychology* was published by Routledge in 1988.

Colin Radford is Professor of Philosophy at the University of Kent. His *The Examined Life* was published in 1989.

Frederic Raphael is a leading novelist and the author of biographies, screenplays, and translations of the complete plays of Aeschylus. That of the *Oresteia* trilogy was televised as *The Serpent Son* in 1979.

Michael Tanner, Fellow of Corpus Christi College, Cambridge is the author of a number of papers on Nietzsche, including a contribution to Vol. 20 of this series; and on aesthetics, especially the aesthetics of music.

John White is Reader in Education at the University of London Institute of Education. His most recent book is *Education and the Good Life* (Cogan Page, 1990).